Praise for *Killer Presentations with Your iPad*

"You will throw out the overabuse of bullet point 'traditional' slides and, instead, dive into the powerful 'four gears' (Creativity, Technology, Strategy, and Psychology) so vital to making ultracompelling 'Killer Presentations' that will radically transform how you interact and engage your audience with an iPad—or any tablet."

> —ROSE NEWTON, Assistant Professor of Communication Design,
> Texas State University

"*Killer Presentations with Your iPad* is the ultimate book, especially for those companies that strive to be learning organizations and that want to be far ahead of the pack by giving strategic presentations that make a significant difference."

> —NEIL DOUGLAS AND TERRY WYKOWSKI, authors of
> *Beyond Reductionism* and *From Belief to Knowledge*

"*Killer Presentations with Your iPad* is a must-read. I found it interesting, insightful, and enjoyable to read. Shaped with creativity at the very core of the book, it should be kept by your desk and used as a constant guide for giving extraordinary presentations that deliver spectacular results."

> —STEVE COKER, Course Director, Senior Leader
> Education Division, Joint Special Operations University,
> United States Special Operations Command

"It's not just about creating stunning visuals and applying the latest technology—it's about the ultimate winning strategy. *Killer Presentations with Your iPad* will not just 'supercharge' and inspire you—it will show you how to be the ultimate rock-star presentation performer and WIN BIG!"

> —RAD BIELICKI, Creative Director at Zen Machine Inc.

"This superb book uses sound psychological principles to create stunning and effective presentations that will inspire you and your audience to strive for something 'beyond the 'moredinary'' and into the extraordinary!"

> —MICHAEL DEVOLEY, MA, Professor of Psychology,
> Lone Star College–Montgomery

"Wow... is this ever needed in the communications world... it's abou[t] one tackled it head on and with such insight!"

> —PHILIP MORABITO, CEO, Pierpont Communications, Inc.

Killer Presentations

WITH YOUR iPad

HOW TO ENGAGE YOUR AUDIENCE AND WIN MORE BUSINESS WITH THE WORLD'S GREATEST GADGET

Ray Anthony and Bob LeVitus
with Barbara Boyd

McGraw Hill Education

New York   Chicago   San Francisco   Athens   London   Madrid
Mexico City   Milan   New Delhi   Singapore   Sydney   Toronto

1 2 3 4 5 6 7 8 9 0   FGR/FGR   1 9 8 7 6 5 4 3

ISBN 978-0-07-181662-5
MHID 0-07-181662-3

e-ISBN 978-0-07-181663-2
e-MHID 0-07-181663-1

Library of Congress Cataloging-in-Publication Data
Anthony, Ray.
   Killer presentations with your iPad: how to engage your audience and win more business with the world's greatest gadget / Ray Anthony and Bob LeVitus
      pages cm
   ISBN 978-0-07-181662-5 (pbk.) — ISBN 0-07-181662-3 (pbk.) 1. Business presentations.
2. iPad (Computer)—Handbooks, manuals, etc. I. LeVitus, Bob. II. Title.
   HF5718.22.A557 2014
   658.4′520285—dc23
                                                                2013023690

McGraw-Hill Education books are available at special quantity discounts to use as premiums and sales promotions or for use in corporate training programs. To contact a representative, please visit the Contact Us pages at www.mhprofessional.com.

CONTENTS

This book is very different and very valuable. Don't be fooled by the title. It is not "about" the iPad—since I use a Nexus 7. This book is about reimagining, reinventing, and remaking your presentations even if you are using napkins and a pen in a coffee shop or drawing your ideas in dirt around a campfire. This is a must-have book even for people who simply want to kick butt and change the world.

Ray and Bob's presentation model is called P-XL²—Presentation Excellence Squared. It focuses on combining creativity, psychology, strategy, and technology in ways that not only cater to left-brain intellect, but also stir up and ignite right-brain emotions and feelings. In short, it's a model for transforming any presentation or speech into an enchanting experience.

Read this book and it will help you create an inferno of possibilities and opportunities that propel you ahead at warp speed. By applying the uber-imaginative ideas and techniques in it, you will not only enchant others into action, but find that giving Killer Presentations is immensely more satisfying, pleasurable, and worthwhile for you. The results you get will amaze and astound you.

GUY KAWASAKI
Advisor to Motorola
and former chief evangelist of Apple

v

From Ray Anthony

Special thanks to my genius friend Charlie Lindahl, who did extensive, superb research for the Resources section along with contributing lots of great feedback and insights. Barbara Boyd is the ultimate professional, who helped us out with her writing contributions and iPad app reviews. Barbara is the author of several books about the iPad and Pinterest marketing. She was a delight to work with. Donna Mosher, my excellent editor, wonderfully helped to get my chapters tight and sparkling. Thank you so much, Donna, for your expertise and experience that made the real difference. Much appreciation goes to my two graphic designer friends, Allison Ashton and Leonard Broussard, who did illustrations for the book. Both of you are creative illustrators to the max. Thanks to Professor Michael Devoley of Lonestar College, who gave me great advice and feedback on the psychology of communication. The fine people who posed for my photos include Peter Han, Christie Cannon, Serena Duncan, and Lori Van Deilen. Your modeling added much to the book. Final thanks go to Casie Vogel of McGraw-Hill, who was a delight to work with, and Carole Jelen of Waterside Products, our most competent, "get-results" literary agent. And I thank Almighty God for giving me a rich life filled with overflowing opportunities and wonderful people!

From Bob LeVitus

Thanks to Ray Anthony for asking me to become a part of his vision. You're the man! Thanks also to Charlie Lindahl for his excellent research and numerous helpful suggestions. And thanks to Barbara Boyd for stepping in at the eleventh hour and doing magnificent work. I'd be remiss if I didn't also offer profuse thanks to our editor, Casie Vogel, for her ideas, for her enthusiasm, and, most of all, for her patience with yours truly when deadlines loomed. I'd also like to thank everyone else at McGraw-Hill who had a hand in the book you now hold in your hand. I may not know you by name, but I appreciate the hard work you put into this project. Thank you all. And finally, thanks to my superagent, Carole "Swifty" Jelen, of Waterside Productions. She's been my literary agent for my whole career (almost 25 years and still going strong), and she is the best in the biz, bar none. I don't say it often enough, Carole, but you freakin' rock!

Owner's Manual

Important Safety and Operating Instructions

⚠ **WARNING.** When using an innovative, vanguard book such as this one, certain precautions should be considered prior to implementing the exclusive information, ideas, tips, and techniques within. Please observe to the following:

- This is not a how-to book, but a how-to-magnificently-*succeed* book.
- Read through this whole book thoroughly to get maximum benefits from it.
- Using creative presentation ideas such as those in the following pages can become an addictive activity.
- Anecdotal evidence shows that using the concepts and techniques in this book has resulted in a drastic reduction in audience inattention, yawning, e-mail checking, restless leg syndrome, eye rolling, throat clearing, and seat squirming during presentations.
- Sudden withdrawal ("presentation detox") from using boring, text-laden PowerPoint slides can result in bouts of euphoria, freedom of expression, and elation as you transition to our new P-XL² Model™ that focuses on combining creativity, technology, strategy, and psychology for extraordinary results.
- Ethics must be considered. Giving extreme Killer Presentations can decimate competition from rival presenters, salespeople, or others vying for the same goal. It is not warranted to pulverize your competitors by using the intense *shock and ah!* power in this book.

- Whether you are an aspiring motivational speaker or an established professional one, be warned that applying the material in this book will cause standing ovations to increase, giving you goose bumps, flushing and redness of the face, and warming of the heart.
- The producers of this product are not responsible for any potential adverse side effects as a result of its use, including a swelled head, shameless bragging, or impulse buying as a result of sudden career advancements, gains in making money, escalations in prestige, popularity, or power brought about by this book.

Congratulations and Thanks for Buying This Book!

We hope you enjoyed our opening tongue-in-cheek introduction. But in all seriousness, we believe that this book will certainly give you powerful, new, and vital ways to reimagine and reinvent your presentations so that they produce all kinds of benefits for you and your company. The very fact that we call this section the "Owner's Manual," instead of the traditional "Introduction," should give you a first-peek preview of how different this book is.

Important:

1. We wrote this book with the assumption that you have a working knowledge of how to use your iPad already. We will not cover the basics, but at times we may give some refresher tips to ensure your facility using your iPad in a presentation.
2. If you want to quickly get up to operating speed using your iPad with specific presentation apps along with useful tips, go to Chapters 5, 6, and 7 first and then read the rest of the chapters in order from Chapter 1.

This Is a Hybrid Book About Four Key "Wares"

While our book focuses on the digital power of various impressive technologies, grabbing that huge sale, giving a winning pitch to investors, or launching into an impressive elevator pitch is as much about masterful presentation skills as it is about a great gadget like the iPad, along with its abundantly cool apps. However, when you combine the creativity-amplifying magic of an iPad with our P-XL² Model and add in the new material and innovative techniques offered in the following chapters, you will learn how to impress your audiences as never before and achieve results you thought were beyond your grasp. A top-notch golf club or expensive camera does not a skilled golfer or photographer make, but they can give that critical, winning edge to those who already possess superior technique and skills. That's why we chose to offer you the newest and most innovative strategies to win *big* with the help of your iPad in the presentation game.

Killer Presentations with Your iPad: How to Engage Your Audience and Win More Business with the World's Greatest Gadget is all about how to give a stunning and riveting presentation using your iPad. Throughout the book, you will experience four primary "wares":

- *Knowledge-ware.* A great mix of traditional and new information about general presentation topics that will be invaluable in giving you a competitive edge
- *Hard-ware.* Key iPad features, tips, and functionality along with cool presentation accessories
- *Soft-ware.* New and established apps that give communication power to any type of presentation or speech
- *Idea-ware.* Over 100 ideas and examples of imaginative concepts, approaches, and strategies that will transform your presentations, catapulting them out of the PowerPoint text dark ages into the exhilarating, visual, digital twenty-first century

At its essential core, *Killer Presentations* is a category-defining work focused on powerful, *innovative* communication that can have a profound effect on you and your audience. Get ready to explore new vistas of presentation possibilities!

What Makes *Killer Presentations* Such a Different and Vital Book for You?

In most books, the introduction chapter goes through a summary description of every chapter. We're not going to bore you by doing that. You can read the Table of Contents. Instead, we will tell you what makes this book unique and exceptional to help you become a Killer Presenter.

Focused on the iPad

You will learn about all the most important strategies for using your iPad to give a stunning presentation: apps, tools, tips, techniques, and ideas *just* for the iPad. No guessing involved. We'll make it easy on you!

Compelling Photos and Screenshots

While we strive to describe things simply and accurately, we have included dozens of interesting photos throughout the book to show you precisely what the idea, tactic, or product is about. When it comes to the iPad and key apps, we give you enough screenshots to understand the technique and become competent with it.

Comprehensive Resources Section

In the back of the book we've provided a resources section. It includes information about stock photos, videos, animations, audio and video special effects, props, costumes, displays, iPad apps, supporting equipment and accessories, audio and video equipment, and many more valuable products and services.

Cool Presentation Props

There are all types of props that can strengthen and enliven your key points, messages, and strategies. You will see photos, examples, and even stunning architectural models that will give you tons of great ideas. We discuss one of the hottest technologies going—3-D printers. We show you pictures of what they can do and how they can make a huge difference when showing prototypes and custom-made props during your talk.

Winning Strategies

How can you win any game or challenge if you don't know exactly what it takes to be on top? We describe the components of presentation success; the 30 traits, competencies, and skills for the ultimate (presenter's) score card; and the 10 characteristics that define a Killer Presentation. You will have no doubt what it takes to win consistently with great results.

Compelling Introductions and Conclusions

Killer Presentations includes a special chapter solely dedicated to explaining how to build, structure, and give introductions and conclusions to your presentation that are essential to establishing your credibility and professionalism. You will get over two dozen powerfully scripted examples of how to grab your group's attention and hold it tightly. At the end of this chapter, you will see unique and highly imaginative handouts that serve as executive summaries of your presentation. This can give you an enormous competitive edge over those who have traditional (mediocre) endings to their presentation.

Choose from a Continuum of Mild-to-Wild Ideas

Goethe, the famous German writer and philosopher of the eighteenth century, said, "Daring ideas are like chessmen moving forward; they may be beaten, but they may start a winning game." He also said, "Boldness has genius, power, and magic in it." *Killer Presentations* takes bold and daring creative communication to new levels that will give you the edge in winning, but only if you choose to dial up more innovation in your business, technical, or sales presentations. There are those who think that imitating an art form is good. We believe, though, that innovating is the true "art nouveau" of presentations today. With the raw power of the iPad, along with other technology and apps available today, it is so much easier to add those brilliant, imaginative elements that make your speech or presentation outsparkle, outwit, and outmatch all others.

You have likely heard Einstein's quotation, "Imagination is more important than knowledge." You will learn how to powerfully meld knowledge and imagination together to form the "mortar of communication." Just as there are various tools to use in your presentation, so there are ideas. They add flavor to your talk. Everyone has experienced presentations that could definitely use more spice and flavor!

In Figure I.1, the Mi-Wi Idea Gauge shows the mild-to-wild continuum of creative ideas for you to think about and choose based upon your presentation situation. When it comes to giving a Killer Presentation, there is no right or wrong answer about whether to select mild creativity—to essentially present mostly inside the box—or to go bodacious and adventurous to present way outside the box. You can throttle back on the creativity power curve and still have a professionally conventional presentation with enough of the right stuff to get the job done... or you can light up the afterburners of your imagination to accelerate with a kick in the pants far ahead of other competitive presentations, if need be.

Killer Presentations will show you how to be the "master of creative communication disruption" by changing the rules for presentations—or making new ones for yourself. Once you get used to leaving imitation behind, going from inspiration to innovation, and experience the liberating results, you will never go back to the dark ages of ordinary presenting.

It's been said that 80 percent of a big idea is figuring out how to deliver it. In this book you will see powerful examples of how it can and should be done. John Cage, an American composer and music theorist, said, "I can't understand why people are afraid of new ideas. I'm frightened of old

FIGURE I.1
Mild-to-Wild
Idea Gauge

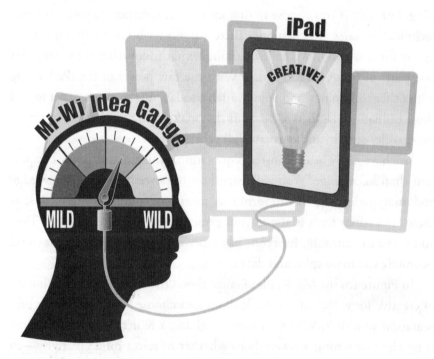

ones." In a world of lightning-quick changes and fierce competitors where you can be suddenly left in the dust, old ideas can be awfully dangerous. In the lists below, you will see the words that generally describe the ranges of mild-to-wild ideas for presentations, and Tables I-1 and I-2 give the pros and cons associated with moving along the Mi-Wi Idea Gauge.

We begin with these mild descriptors, which almost surely you are familiar with:

Descriptors for Mild Ideas

acceptable	plain
predictable	normal
conventional	tried and true
traditional	moderate
unchanged	benign
established	proven
average	routine
cautious	usual
ordinary	ordinary
incremental	tame

Table I-1 shows the pros and cons of using mild ideas.

Table I-1 Pros and Cons of Mild Ideas

PROS OF MILD IDEAS	CONS OF MILD IDEAS
▶ They are relatively safe	▶ They are dull and uninspiring
▶ Typically these ideas are less risky with any audience	▶ Such ideas usually yield mediocre reactions from your group
▶ You don't stand out in an obvious way	▶ You don't stand out in an obvious way
▶ They are understood by and acceptable to most people	▶ They are unable to achieve impressive, stellar results for you
▶ "Low-hanging fruit" of ideas requires less thinking effort on your part	▶ Your competitors can easily trump your presentation with better ideas

So, when should you use mild ideas in your presentation? *Use* mild ideas when you:

- Are presenting to very conservative or older groups
- Would rather not take any risk at all at possibly diminishing your credibility or professionalism
- Feel you do not need to be more creative to easily reach your presentation objectives

And now for the wild ideas:

Descriptors of Wild Ideas

breakthrough	exceptional
visionary	bold
unconventional	authentic
radical	unorthodox
unusual	exotic
clever	astonishing
dazzling	profound
unlikely	remarkable
unprecedented	daring
avant-garde	advanced

Table I-2 identifies the pros and cons of using wild ideas. *Use* wild ideas in your presentation when:

- Your group will likely appreciate and need your creative communication approach
- You face heavy competition from other presentations and you have little to lose
- Your objective is to radically change the attitudes, beliefs, or values of the group to whom you are talking
- Your presentation's focus is to primarily entertain or amuse
- You really want to stand *far out* from and *far above* the crowd
- You want maximum impact from your presentation or speech and are willing to take chances

Table I-2 Pros and Cons of Wild Ideas

PROS OF WILD IDEAS	CONS OF WILD IDEAS
▶ They can be exciting, stimulating, fascinating, spectacular, and ingenious ▶ They make you stand out positively from and above the crowd ▶ They impressively show your breathtaking originality ▶ They can deliver extraordinary, over-the-top results ▶ They are a powerful way to overcome a competitor's mild ideas	▶ The wilder ones can fall flat and damage your credibility with certain groups ▶ They may come across as outlandish, wacky, or too clever ▶ The wilder the idea, the more risky it is since it has not be tried and proved ▶ Wild ideas can require lots of brainstorming and fine-tuning to be effective

Your Exciting Transformation from Presenter to K-I-L-L-E-R Presenter

After reading *Killer Presentations* and effectively applying the ideas, techniques, tips, and information within, you will see an *ah!some* difference in your presentations because you will:

1. Quickly choose and use the best presentation apps with your iPad to make your talks interesting, compelling, entertaining, and, most of all, successful.

2. Learn about special iPad operating tips, accessories, and cool ways to make your iPad the "greatest gadget," driving your presentations to new realms of excellence.

3. Get accustomed to being more creative in how you communicate and also better appreciate how boosting your imagination can help in other ways in your job.

4. Engage and interact with your audiences (in person and through your iPad and theirs) in a dialogue that will boost their participation and cooperation.

5. Start thinking more like a "street psychologist" who has to deal with various personalities and their needs, wants, concerns, and priorities

regarding your presentation. This will help you to better influence their decisions and actions.

6. Become more of a "communication strategist" (not just focus on content). That will enable you to outthink and outpresent your competitors.

7. When needed, become a "performer," not just an accomplished "presenter," and do it in the most professional way. You will actually enjoy doing presentations more because this book will give you more confidence. You will see how becoming a Killer Presenter can make a big difference in your career, your life, and your community.

Alexander the Great of Macedon (356–323 BC) was one of the world's foremost leaders, military commanders, and conquerors. He said he did not fear an army of lions led by a sheep; he feared an army of sheep led by a lion. We can't promise that you will be a roaring, conquering lion in the meeting room, on stage, or in the boardroom after reading this book, but it will certainly greatly increase your odds of that happening. American writer E. B. White said, "Always be on the lookout for the presence of wonder." We hope you discover that sense of wonder and embark on an exciting journey to transcendent communication through our book!

CHAPTER 1

The Big Picture: The World Has Changed. Have You Changed Your Presentations?

In 1970, Alvin Toffler wrote *Future Shock,* an international bestselling book that chronicles the impact of "too much change in too short a period of time." Toffler declared that society would be undergoing an enormous structural transformation—a revolution from an industrial society to a "superindustrial society" with unfathomable technological change. In the same year, Intel announced a DRAM memory chip storing more than 1,000 bits of data, IBM Selectric typewriters filled offices, and minicomputers were just starting to take off. Toffler called that "radical change." At the time, it was considered so.

Can you imagine how "change" back in 1970 would appear to us today when we *really* can't keep up with the lightning-quick onslaught of amazing innovations in science, medicine, aviation, engineering, and digital products that seem to come out overnight? Everything is spinning faster, more furiously, and often unpredictably in worldwide politics, society, the environment, and the global economy. People's sense of "future shock" almost 45 years ago now seems shockingly tame. You have heard the alarm about impending change all too often. What does it have to do with presentations?

If You Don't Change, You Will Be Changed—and You May Not Like It!

With the introduction of the iPad, new presentation apps designed especially for it, and our innovative P-XL² Model, it's time to change or be changed.

The way your company gives important presentations can directly and indirectly affect its longevity and growth. Let's compare the list of Fortune 500 companies in the "future shock year" of 1970 with the 2012 list as a telling reference point. Only 78 companies appear in both lists. That means about 16 percent of the Fortune 500 companies in 1970 were still on the list 42 years later. Almost 84 percent of the companies were gone—they either went bankrupt, merged, became private, or fell from the list of companies ranked by gross revenue. That's a lot of churning and creative destruction—it's likely safe to say that new companies in new industries will replace many of today's Fortune 500 companies over the next 42 years.

Look at the computer industry in the 1970s. While Apple, founded in 1976, is still a dominant force, you probably don't remember or never heard of a group of big mainframe computer competitors known as the "BUNCH"—Burroughs, Univac, NCR, Control Data, and Honeywell. Only NCR is still around, and it was radically restructured. Then, there were successful minicomputer firms like Digital Equipment Corporation, Data General, Wang, Datapoint, and others. Recall them? They all went belly up. They didn't change when change was desperately needed. They shunned "planned abandonment" and clung tightly to yesterday's successes rather than seeing they were no longer relevant in a changing world. The signs were there, but many chose to ignore them and hoped they would go away.

IBM, which is now over 100 years old, has been through numerous upsets and some near-death experiences in the industry. The company not only survived, but thrived, because it adapted, innovated, and moved quickly to take advantage of new trends and new directions. Who made the list of most admired companies in the world by *Fortune* magazine in 2013 and why? Apple was number one. It, above all others, embraces and religiously practices planned obsolescence. Apple and other companies, such as Google, Intel, Boeing, and John Deere (which made the most admired list), master changes that others dread or ignore. These companies know a competitor can pop up suddenly with a potentially disruptive technology, product, or process and threaten their market share. They have to keep their lead and never be complacent.

The most admired companies and those that have longevity on the Fortune 500 list are continually reinventing themselves to own the future. Some in those companies gave stirring Killer Presentations—critical presentations at a critical time—that helped to bring about necessary change and innovation. Those Killer Presentations were so compelling and convincing that senior management bought into them, often in spite of initial reservations, doubts, or hesitancy to change course. Those presentations were the spark that made the difference between moving ahead as industry rock stars or falling back into oblivion. Just as companies need to change, so do presentations that are stuck in a time warp around the black hole called PowerPoint.

What Is Your Business, and What Is *Killer Presentations* About?

Peter F. Drucker, who wrote 39 books, is considered one of the greatest management gurus and business thinkers of all time. He said the two essential functions that business needs to focus on are innovation and marketing—innovation in products, services, business models, processes, management techniques, and overall operations. And who would disagree about the critical nature of marketing in a world where clever spin doctors can weave gold from straw?

One of Drucker's most important books is *The Age of Discontinuity*, which presents innovation and entrepreneurship as vital disciplines an organization must wholly embrace. Discontinuities are those unanticipated events that can suddenly shift and upset the landscape in an industry or for a company, requiring an immediate response either to mitigate loss or to capture opportunity. His books and advice were early warning systems, cautioning us to be the change and not suffer the change that is unrelenting and often unforgiving for those sitting on the sidelines. We know of companies that lost huge deals because their competitors outpresented them with innovative Killer Presentations, while they continued to use presentation models that were becoming increasingly obsolete.

Peter Drucker believed that the first responsibility of managers was to ask themselves a simple question: "What is your business?" He believed that only the customer could accurately answer that question from different perspectives. For example, a person might say her company is in the financial software business, while her customer might say that the company was in the business of helping the customer to simplify and better understand financial variables to make better, faster, and safer investment decisions.

Okay, what does all this have to do with our book? This question begets two more. First, what is this book about? You will find that *Killer Presentations* is all about how to create innovative presentations—how to move far beyond the dull, predictable PowerPoint presentations that are giving you mediocre or disappointing results. Innovation is at the heart of this book. Second, what is the business of this book, as Drucker might ask? You the reader (as customer) might tell us it is ultimately about:

- Closing more and bigger deals and gaining an increasing competitive lead
- Having your company buy into a new marketing program and strategy
- Convincing your management to adopt a new course of action
- Getting your executives to shine in the public eye as a result of their "Killer" speeches
- Persuading your management to develop exciting new products and services
- Showing how to get a greater return on investments in new ventures and projects
- Communicating a potential engineering solution that will solve a major problem
- Enlightening your customers about your company's new, improved value proposition
- Selling your team on creating new training programs to improve operations
- Communicating an exciting new vision for your organization that will galvanize and energize employees, customers, and other stakeholders

Following the advice in this book will transform your presentations into a powerful *strategic tool* to improve your business operations, affect your financials, and give your company that much-needed competitive boost. The goal of just "giving more effective presentations" will become a thing of the past. Killer Presentations will bring about much needed change and progress in your organization . . . and in your career.

State of Presentations and How You Can Take Smart Advantage of It

If Killer Presentations can bring about numerous benefits for your organization, the converse is true: bad presentations will lose deals, cause missed opportunities, and otherwise negatively affect the chances of success in any number of organizational ventures and projects.

Besides being a waste of time for most people, bad presentations are costly, notes Dave Paradi, coauthor of *Guide to PowerPoint*. He says that, according to Microsoft, about 30 million PowerPoint presentations (of all types) are given every day. Assuming conservatively that there are four people per presentation, that each presentation takes on average a half hour, and that the time wasted in a poor presentation is one-quarter of the presentation time, Paradi calculates that bad presentations waste 15 million person-hours per day. Based on an average (conservative) salary of $35,000 per year for those attending the meeting, the cost of that wasted time is a staggering $252 million each day. And that does not include costly opportunities lost in other ways.

Ray Anthony's company conducted a comprehensive 25-question research survey with over 200 executives from 14 companies in which he asked mostly C-level individuals to rate presentations given to them.[1] Keep in mind that presentations given to important decision makers are likely to be better prepared and delivered than those lower-priority talks done on an everyday basis. The question asked in the survey was, "Looking back on presentations that you were a member of, how would you

---

[1] Summary Report. "A Winning Executive Presentation." A report involving the analysis of data received from responses to the executive survey, which covered the important area of giving an effective presentation to senior executives.

rate the overall quality of those presentations?" Here were the responses from the survey:

8 percent   Excellent
21 percent   Good
38 percent   Acceptable
23 percent   Mediocre
10 percent   Poor

Only 30 percent rated typical presentations given to them as excellent or good! Acceptable, mediocre, and certainly poor presentations (the other 70 percent) would not likely impress executives enough to encourage them to approve a project or commit to something important. When it came to rating the quality (design, type, other) of visual aids used by most people giving presentations to the executives, here were their answers:

- 0 percent   Excellent quality
- 42 percent   Good quality
- 53 percent   Moderate quality
- 5 percent   Poor quality

In this case, executives said that about 6 out of 10 presentations essentially had mediocre visuals that could adversely affect their understanding of the content and their decision making.

Ray Anthony's former company, Genesis Training Solutions, surveyed almost 500 salespeople and sales managers in 29 organizations from 9 industries on creativity in selling.[2] Some key findings indicated that:

- 92 percent either agreed or strongly agreed that using creativity in selling is critical in today's market.
- 95 percent wanted to be more creative in their jobs.
- When asked, "How much creative potential do you use on the job?" the average answer for all respondents was 60 percent. Only 5 percent of people admitted they were using their full creative power at work.

---

2 Creativity... in Selling? Research findings on personal creativity assessment and management and organizational indicators of sales innovation. Genesis Training Solutions.

■ When asked which of 23 sales activities would improve with increased creativity, "Delivering Sales Presentations" was ranked first, with "Creating Competitive Sales Strategies" as second in importance.

The survey confirmed the overwhelming importance and competitive advantage of being more creative in selling and presenting from the perspective of sales professionals and their managers.

Do You Want to Grab a Huge Opportunity?

If a select percentage of presentations can be that important, and if most are bad, you may be wondering why more people don't deliver more Killer Presentations. One reason is that everyone is overworked these days, whether in Europe, America, China, Japan, or elsewhere. People are simply doing more and working longer hours; they find little extra time to devote to what they might perceive as a lower-priority task. Yet it really does not take a lot more time to put together a better talk and learn several key techniques and skills that will make you shine in front of a group.

Second, if everyone else is giving relatively shoddy PowerPoint presentations, why bother if managers don't seem to care? How many companies are pushing staff to improve their presentations? Third, many professionals (especially executives) don't believe they need presentation or speech training or coaching. Finally, most people don't appear to see anything really wrong about the way they give presentations, especially if they have not yet experienced consistently negative consequences. However, when people can experience the real difference a Killer Presentation can make, they wonder why they haven't jumped on board that bandwagon sooner.

Here's the huge opportunity to be grabbed: if most presentations are poorly done and you have to give important (sales, marketing, technical, or executive-level) presentations, you have a perfect chance to shine above other presenters, including your competition. Delivering an especially impressive Killer Presentation or speech will quickly elevate your professional image and status, perhaps putting you in front of people who could be influential to your career. With competition so (internationally) iFrenetic and iFerocious, giving superb presentations will assure you a leading edge in many outcomes. In that case, you and your iPad might stand for "I Produce Awesome Deliverables!"

How Presentations Have Changed over Time

Business presentations have come a long way over the last century. Visual aids came into widespread use in the 1920s and 1930s with the introduction of filmstrips and large charts, often called poster boards. The 1950s saw the frequent use of 35-mm slides in the ubiquitous Kodak carousel projector, overhead transparencies displayed through an overhead projector, and flip charts. Some training events and some rare presentations showed 16-mm film from a projector.

Now fast-forward to May 22, 1990, and the official launch of Microsoft PowerPoint as part of the Microsoft Office Suite. Instead of waiting days or weeks to get your 35-mm slides back, you could now create everything on your computer and use it immediately. You could print out your slides as handouts and make changes right up to the moment you got up to present. And you had all those fancy animations, transitions, sounds, and abilities to do much graphic or otherwise distracting damage to your presentation. In 2003 Apple introduced its Keynote software as an alternative to PowerPoint.

As powerful as PowerPoint and Keynote were, perhaps 95 percent of users still designed and presented as if the programs were simply digital replacements for 35-mm slides. Of course, there were new and impressive capabilities, but most of us shunned good design techniques and filled the slides with machine gun bullets, paragraphs of small text, crowded tables, and incredibly busy charts that could only be read with an electron microscope. The misuse of PowerPoint (and even Keynote) continues to this day, as you know. It's not that PowerPoint is the sole problem itself—it's how it is used and abused. Unfortunately, its many options led people to think that you should have some exploding or other fancy transition after each slide. And because they are available, why not mix a couple dozen different animations on slides that take up precious time and do nothing but add visual noise to clutter up one's presentation?

"The future has a way of arriving unannounced," said journalist and commentator George Will. And so it was on April 3, 2010, Apple ushered in a new era in giving presentations with the iPad, followed by the mini on December 2, 2012. New apps like iPresent were especially designed for the innovative new capabilities of the iPad. Now, instead of giving one-sided, sequential presentations with dated software apps, you could deliver more interactive presentations—the start of a revolution in presentations.

But just as laptops using PowerPoint and Keynote were a technological advancement over 35-mm slides, replacing your laptop with an iPad without changing your presentation style is merely another technical evolution. The iPad begs for a whole new model, a paradigm shift, in presenting (like the P-XL^2 Model we developed and describe in the book) and for new presentation apps. Only then will the exclusive features, abilities, and power of the iPad bring about more than evolution. They offer the possibility for a revolution. *Viva la revolución!*

Use Killer Presentations as a Vital Strategic Asset and Tool

Killer Presentations that are creative, compelling, and strategically designed will give your company a decided advantage over your competitors and contribute toward your steady growth and long-term prosperity. Improving presentations internally will work wonders in your organization, association, government agency, military branch, or university. Companies that integrate presentations as part of a grand strategy can expect boosted business opportunities and the more efficient use of resources as a result. Whether justified or not, your presentations to audiences often appear as an impressionistic microcosm and reflection of your organization's branding and professionalism. Important presentations made by your organization's leaders are "executive visibility amplifiers" that can operate in both directions— helping or hurting one's image, career, and reputation. Killer Presentations will help people in your company grab the big deals you thought were out of reach. Your marketing professionals will promote your company and its products and services with renewed vigor. And your R&D, manufacturing, and product design teams will be able to give sharply focused internal presentations that help your higher-ups make favorable decisions.

Finally, by engineering and applying your presentations as vital strategic tools in your organization, your presentations will help improve overall productivity, efficiency, quality, effectiveness, and innovation in your operations, thus boosting revenues and profits. Here are some recommendations for developing and using Killer Presentation as strategic assets and tools in your organization:

- Identify high-priority presentations that will have a major impact on your organization and apply the information, ideas, and techniques in this book to transform them into Killer Presentations. This includes your company story, high-profile C-level (CEO, COO, CFO) presentations, boardroom presentations, and major sales and marketing presentations.
- Create organizational standards for presentations that define and describe excellence in communication and then monitor those standards for compliance. These are guidelines and core competencies you can take from several chapters in our book.
- Create a valuable centralized company "presentation resource library" of videos, animations, photos, audio files, illustrations, and graphics for people to use in their custom presentations. Direct them to outside resources such as those listed at the back of the book.
- Showcase superb Killer Presentations that have been creatively designed and successfully delivered by the best presenters in your organization. Consider building an ongoing archive of the finest presentations in your company as exemplary models from which your employees can get good ideas.
- If possible, evaluate the presentations of your competitors and identify specific ways to outshine them in every respect.
- Every six months or less, do a review of what new software, apps, iPad accessories, resources, and technology are available to enhance your company's presentations. Have a continuous presentation improvement process in place.
- Provide your staff with excellent presentation training, coaching, and mentoring.
- Consider having quarterly Killer Presentation contests where you let anyone volunteer to give a five-minute presentation on any company-related topic. These contests can be delivered live, or entries can be videotaped and sent in. Winners get prizes, and their entries serve as

model presentations for others to emulate and to further improve. Think about incentives and rewards that will encourage great presentations.

When questioned about his colonial policies, an English statesman and diplomat, the Marquis of Salisbury, replied, "Gentlemen, get larger maps." If your organization will incorporate Killer Presentation models, ideas, and characteristics as a strategic tool and asset to be exploited throughout your corporate culture, you will have "larger maps" to explore and be positioned to conquer new territories of business opportunities and possibilities. You will have polished professionals who do more than just "give out" information—they will "get through" to others, and that will make all the difference in the world.

Why the iPad? Why Now? And Some New Killer Technologies for It!

Welcome to a new world of presentation and visualization possibilities using that marvelous gadget called the iPad. People are wondering "Does the iPad replace a laptop when it comes to giving presentations? What's really a better device to use for presentations?" That's like asking, "What is better for transporting stuff—a truck or a big SUV?" The answer to those types of questions is, "It depends upon what you want to do." While your iPad has new and exciting capabilities that your laptop doesn't, your laptop has some clear advantages too when it comes to using it for certain select types of presentations.

In this part of the chapter we will look at some important comparisons between both types of devices. We will describe how presentation formats will change and should change. And you will discover exciting new developments in virtual and augmented reality among other future innovations in how we will communicate, understand, and "see things" in ways never before imagined. Throughout our book, we highlight the wondrous things *only* an iPad can do when it comes to giving that Killer Presentation. Make no mistake about it, though; your iPad is not a replacement for your laptop. It was not meant to be. Your iPad is a different and highly flexible communication tool for a unique set of uses.

A question we sometimes get asked is, "Why didn't Steve Jobs use an iPad when he gave his presentations at MacWorld, for example?" The answer is that his presentations were straightforward, sequential (slide after slide), one-way talks that did not require interaction with the audience and that did not need to randomly access information to answer suddenly posed questions. So it was easier and better to use a laptop and hold a small, remote RF mouse that had only three buttons: slide forward, reverse, and screen blackout.

Your iPad Is a "Natural" Communication Device

Now let's say you are sitting in an airline club in the morning having a relaxing cup of coffee, waiting for your flight to take off in two hours. You are using your iPad to check the news, read your e-mails, and perhaps catch glimpses of a morning TV show. You strike up a conversation with a friendly person next to you, and as an astute sales professional, you rather quickly discover that she may be a potential prospect for your company's products.

As the conversation slowly shifts into a subtle sales mode, you ask if she would like to see a two-minute video of your product line. You adjust your iPad case into a better viewing angle for her on the counter next to your coffee and start your video. No taking out your laptop, setting it up, playing with a mouse or touchpad—just a simple, informal, comfortable, and *natural* transition into a business conversation using your iPad. Notice the difference? Because people see the iPad in a different light, the ability to give an unexpected, on-the-spot informal presentation is a very valuable asset uniquely suited to it.

When you hear the term *elevator pitch*, you likely envision a brief, encapsulated summary (30 seconds to about 2 minutes) designed to compellingly present an idea or product or service in an accidental meeting (like in an elevator). What better tool to use than an iPad where you can say, "May I show you something in less than a minute that I think you'll be quite interested in?" You can't do that easily and gracefully with a laptop in an elevator or elsewhere. But you can communicate a concise value proposition fluidly and *naturally* with your iPad.

Motivational speakers can walk into their audiences with an iPad and interactively summon information as they engage people's questions or comments. And the iPad is perfect for imaginative *virtual reality* and *augmented reality* applications. Overall, your iPad is ideal for spontaneous communication. But when it comes to very structured presentations (with limited audience interaction) that may require showing advanced 3-D or engineering application software, your laptop may still be your best bet to get the job done. Let's take a look at how both devices stack up in several categories.

Differences Between a Laptop Computer and an iPad

In considering the differences between the two, we identified the pros and cons of each. Table 1.1 shows the pros and cons of a laptop—whether it is a Retina display MacBook Pro or other high-end laptop—as it compares with

Table 1.1 Pros and Cons of a Laptop

PROS OF A LAPTOP	CONS OF A LAPTOP
▶ Faster processor	▶ Heavy to carry, bulky
▶ Greater RAM (working memory) storage	▶ No touch screen
▶ Larger screen size (about the same resolution as that of an iPad)	▶ Lower battery life
▶ Greater connectivity with more devices (i.e., Firewire, HDMI, Ethernet, Thunderbolt)	▶ Much less convenient to give on-the-spot presentations
▶ Better audio speakers	▶ Less suitable for taking notes, diagramming, mind mapping
▶ High-level multitasking	▶ Impossible to walk with and difficult to operate while presenting
▶ Superior graphic processing for rendering, gaming, video	▶ Does not have many of the cool, useful apps that the iPad has
▶ Very high storage capacity (especially with external disk drives)	
▶ Able to run complex software	
▶ Run Windows and PC applications (using Apple Boot Camp Software or Parallels Desktop for Mac)	
▶ Upgradable and customizable hardware	
▶ More versatile portable workstation	

Table 1.2 Pros and Cons of an iPad

PROS OF AN IPAD	CONS OF AN IPAD
▶ Much lighter, easier to handle during presentations	▶ Content loading through iTunes
▶ Less likely to malfunction or break down	▶ No optical drive, direct USB port, or SD/Micro SD slot
▶ Terrific portability and ease of use	▶ No upgrades in software or hardware features
▶ Can be used more creatively in presentations	▶ No Adobe Flash feature
▶ More flexible and useful in daily activities	▶ Data backup inconvenient and slow
▶ Full flash memory for speed	
▶ Immediate startup	
▶ Better for informal, impromptu one-on-one presentations	
▶ Access to app store with over 500,000+ apps	
▶ Better camera and flexibility in using it	
▶ Longer battery life	
▶ Better for interactive (nonsequential) presentations	
▶ Typically less expensive apps	
▶ 4G LTE connectivity	
▶ "Cool factor" when used competently	
▶ Great videoconferencing with FaceTime	
▶ Touch screen and finger gestures	
▶ Can be used as a creative prop during presentations	
▶ Connectivity with other iPads and iPhones	
▶ Better at doing virtual walkthroughs and augmented reality	
▶ GPS and accelerometers, allowing impressive capabilities	

an iPad. Keep those in mind when you look at the pros and cons of an iPad shown in Table 1.2. While specifications and capabilities of both devices will change over time, you can see the general comparative differences.

Bear in mind that compared with laptops, iPads are relatively new to the presentation scene, and we predict that the hardware, software, accessories, and add-ons will dramatically improve in capabilities, making the iPad even more flexible, powerful, and valuable to use in presentations.

Engaging Them with Your iPad

The one overriding advantage of your iPad is its ability to better *engage* your audiences (compared with using a laptop with PowerPoint) by applying a new format of flexible and responsive presenting—whether it is with one person or a thousand. After all, that's part of our book's title, *Killer Presentations with Your iPad: How to Engage Your Audience and Win More Business with the World's Greatest Gadget.*

In the recent excellent business book *American Turnaround: Reinventing AT&T and GM and the Way We Do Business in the USA,* author Ed Whitacre, the former CEO of those two companies, talked about the antithesis of engagement in presentations that he attended as the top boss. He told how meetings at GM almost always had PowerPoint presentations using a large number of detailed slides and charts, accompanied by a thick booklet.

He made no qualms about his distaste for that method of restrictive, inflexible, and inefficient communicating, "I consider PowerPoints to be a waste of time and money, for the most part, and I had neither of those to spare during this period (with GM). If someone came in to see me and started in with those slides, I'd say, 'wait, stop,' and make them shut it down and talk to me. I don't need all those charts. I just need to know the end conclusion or larger point—tell me that, and then let's talk about it. But tell me—don't point with some laser from the other end of the room and click, click, click through fifty slides . . . ."[3]

---

3 Ed Whitacre, *American Turnaround: Reinventing AT&T and GM and the Way We Do Business in the USA,* New York: Business Plus, 2013, p. 210.

Before board meetings at General Motors, Whitacre would pull senior managers aside and actually coach them on presentations. He slowly weaned them off using long, complicated PowerPoint presentations overflowing with numbers and charts and wordy explanations and instead recommended a streamlined format for their presentations. He said, "I told them to prepare short—ten minutes max—presentations that covered need-to-know information only: how many cars we sold by type, what the average price was, how much money we made—those things that directly related to GM's business and the bottom line."[4] Whitacre related how pleased board members were with the new presentations that enabled them to ask questions and become more engaged as opposed to sitting through a daylong meeting, which was happily pared down to a few hours using the new, brief presentation formats.

Your iPad Can Be the Engine to Run a "Nonpresentation Presentation"

Let's take a look at how an iPad with a different format of presenting might impress someone like Ed Whitacre if a senior executive, for example, came in to discuss his new truck engineering and design plans for the future to get the top guy's feedback and approval. First, our executive would know what he wanted from Mr. Whitacre (his goal), how he planned to achieve it (his strategy), and, most importantly, what Whitacre expected of him. In advance of the meeting, he would select high-priority areas of content such as sales projections, competitive analysis, photos of prototypes, and anything else he needed for his basic dialogue (not one-sided presentation) with the boss. He would start off with a concise, effective summary of his key points and ask Whitacre if they were the main areas he was interested in and what else he would like to know.

The head of truck engineering would *not* start showing slides. He would cover his key information by discussing it conversationally as he engaged Mr. Whitacre. When needed, he would access his iPad and look down at additional data to provide that information. His aim would be to show the CEO that he knows his engineering business inside and out and does

---

4 Ibid., p. 212.

not need to depend upon lots of slides. However, while he was interacting with Whitacre and maintaining eye contact with him, he would be *casually and naturally* using his iPad—at timely points in his discussion—to focus attention on photos of the future truck prototypes along with key engineering and financial data relating to production costs and profit structures—no sequential slide after slide, but only visuals and data randomly accessed and shown *as needed* from a special iPad presentation app like iPresent (described in detail in Chapter 5).

But this smart executive had one more card up his presentation sleeve: by doing his homework ahead of time, he found out the likely types of questions Whitacre would ask, especially about competition. So, using his iPad, he was able to quickly and easily navigate to other automotive and industry websites to answer the CEO's questions and *show* him competitive designs and responses from those industry experts regarding how GM was viewed by focus groups after the unveiling of new-concept truck designs.

The engaging, interactive "presentation" in this what-if example was more of a natural give-and-take *structured conversation* with readily available important data, photos, and other information (both planned and in reserve if needed) that were easily accessed from the executive's iPad and projected onto a 60-inch TV in the meeting room. The executive in charge of the truck division had a prepared but fluid presentation that focused not on slides, but on the exact information and visuals needed and wanted by Whitacre—*when* he asked for it. That's the way to engage someone and still provide great information with your iPad!

The world is constantly changing—it is changing as you read this. Creating innovative presentations and designing them as strategic assets in your organization will give you a significant winning competitive edge.

CHAPTER 2

Let's Face It—*You Are* the Winning Message!

You have likely heard the saying in the sports world that winning is a game of inches (or seconds). The difference between a home run and a double or a triple, for example, is a baseball that has passed over the fence by maybe just an inch. It could be the decisive run that spells victory in a World Series. Likewise, in today's fiercely competitive business world, just a slight difference—in this case, in how you design and deliver a presentation— can be the determining factor in whether you and your team win or lose a gigantic deal you have been working on for months. It pays handsomely to understand how the communication game is played and what the rules and scoring system are so you can play by them, improvise, and even change the rules in your favor to score and win.

If you know what performance indicators, characteristics, and components will make you and your presentation stand out and above others, then you have the advantage. You own the high ground of fighting for your winning game. Even a slight edge may be all that is necessary to tilt an audience in your favor. But this chapter and the next two are about giving you a large edge—a *wow* advantage—for a whizbang, game-changing Killer Presentation.

In this chapter, you will get to fully appreciate that, along with your content, *you* are the message (not just the messenger). Your credibility, your presentation style, and the way you interact with the audience are paramount in winning. You will know exactly what traits and behaviors describe not only a Killer Presenter with an iPad, but a leader with command presence who will impress, inspire, and galvanize an audience into action. Playing the best presentation game involves knowing the typical errors most people make. We include 15 things to avoid, so you can overcome them before they cause a loss. And who wouldn't want to learn how Steve Jobs owned the stage and how acting and storytelling can turn you from a presenter into a performer, even in the boardroom. Let's get started!

Projecting a Command Presence Leadership Aura

Many types of presentations involve not just providing information, but recommending implementation of a program, major change, or innovation of some kind. If you are proposing being in charge of making change happen, the audience of decision makers and recommenders wants to ensure that you and your team have the strong leadership qualities to make it a success, especially if it is a complex and costly endeavor. Whether bold or otherwise, a plan, strategy, or idea is only as good as its execution. An audience needs to feel that sense of leadership ability from the presenter.

Men and women who display strong leadership characteristics in front of executives or other important audiences quickly move up their career ladder, earn more money, and make a meaningful difference in the work and personal lives of others. Ask those who have risen quickly in their organization, and most will tell you that the image they projected was a key factor. It is one thing to come across as a professional during one's presentation—it's another to come across as a consummate professional who is a dynamic "get-it-done" leader. Consider the following ways to help you become that kind of leader.

Mastery of Your Topic. Clarence B. Randall, former chairman of Inland Steel Company and a special assistant to the president of the United States (during Eisenhower's administration), aptly said, "The leader must know, must know that he knows, and must be able to make it abundantly clear to those around him that he knows." Whom would you trust more—a person who had to read from his 48 slides or a person who used no notes or other presentation aids but effectively communicated an impressive in-depth knowledge of his topic and proposed an impressive plan?

Numerous executives have told us that they wish more people would come into a presentation without slides (or only a few) and just update them on their department or division by clearly and concisely communicating key information. One chief operating officer from a major southern California energy company told us, "My directors should know their operating and financial numbers cold without referring to those damn slides and be able to have a well-structured, but informal conversation with me instead of tediously clicking through slide-by-slide or constantly referring to detailed notes to inform me." When you see a presenter who is not glued to a lectern or projection screen but able to (seemingly extemporaneously) articulate key information in an organized, fluent way, you get the strong sense that this is a person in total command of her topic.

Throughout several chapters of Ray Anthony's book *Talking to the Top: Executive's Guide to Career-Making Presentations*,[1] he lists the results of a comprehensive survey he did with over 200 C-level and senior executives from major corporations regarding their opinion of presentations given to them. Here are the top four areas deemed "very important" that senior executives wanted from people presenting to them and the percentage that listed it as top priority:

- Knowledge of topic, 98 percent
- Ability to be concise, yet thorough and accurate, 79 percent
- Enthusiastic and energetic, 72 percent
- Fluent and clear in communication, 71 percent

According to Anthony's research findings, the one thing that would overwhelmingly impress executives—more than anything else—about presenters was their having "an absolute mastery of their topic." That is essential to building a leadership image on the platform!

Decisiveness and Crispness in Answering. You won't find a strong leader hesitating, vacillating, or "overanswering" when it comes to a question. For example, if an executive asks a presenter if she is confident that her proposed project should be implemented and why, the command presence presenter would reply something like, "This project absolutely should be capitalized upon for three primary reasons: One, if we don't, our competitors will—

---

1 Ray Anthony, *Talking to the Top: Executive's Guide to Career-Making Presentations*, New York: Prentice Hall, 1995, p. 153.

very soon. Two, we can accomplish it better than anyone else. And three, the attractive financial returns on investment are perfectly attainable." Notice how concise, positive, and self-assured that type of response is.

Positive and Confident Attitude. History tells us that General George S. Patton, Jr., had "an unequaled sense of what was possible on the battlefield," and he proved it. It was the ultimate "can-do and will-do" belief and behavior. Napoleon said, "A leader is a dealer in hope." Audiences want to know that the task or goal (which has risks, challenges, and obstacles of varying types and degrees associated with it) being proposed by the presenter will be accomplished in a successful way. The saying "A frightened captain makes a frightened crew" applies to how an audience reacts if a presenter seems tentative, nervous, or otherwise not completely confident in the outcome he or she is advocating. Being calmly optimistic and definitively positive in tone and word reassures people that their decision to support the presenter is a good one.

Dynamic Voice and Gestures. A dynamic person is one full of stamina and new ideas. Leaders are high-energy, constructive, and forward-thinking people. Can you picture a successful leader being constantly tired or acting withdrawn and pessimistic? Several techniques can help make a presenter more dynamic. Strong voice volume along with well-timed, deliberate pauses and eye contact with the audience is important. Purposeful gestures are also highly effective. One gesture in which the person's arms are spread far from the body in an arclike way from the waist up is what experts call a "power gesture" because it enlarges the presenter's personal physical area. Another unique and strong gesture is one where the arm temporarily freezes in a certain position rather than continuing to move. For example, if a presenter talks about a "beckoning vision [of the corporation, for example] over the horizon," she points her arm and hand outward and holds that pose (for maybe 7 to 15 seconds) as if solidly pointing toward the distance as she talks about it. That stationary (energy-implied) gesture—as she continues—is highly effective in a somewhat exaggerated, attention-getting way.

Purposeful Body Movement. For many presenters, there are often two opposite forms of body movement that negatively affect their image. The first is standing rigidly either behind a lectern or without a lectern, not moving around the front or sides of the room or stage. That makes a presenter seem inanimate and devoid of energy. The other kind of movement occurs when a presenter is constantly rocking back and forth on his feet or moving side to side (like little dance steps) in nervous fashion.

A unique technique we recommend for those wanting to project confident command is what we call a "bolt-and-move" body movement. This is where a speaker moves in a purposeful direction toward the audience and stops with feet planted firmly on the ground—as if they were bolted to the floor. After a while she may move again to another part of the room or stage and again "bolt" her feet to the floor. This is effective movement with energy, yet without shuffling or shifting.

Bold, Big-Picture Thinker and Strategist. Leaders focus on future change, innovation, and big-picture visions of exciting possibilities. They demonstrate that their daring ideas, proposed solutions, or innovations are congruent and aligned with the overall strategic goals and mission of their organization. By creating and communicating a well-thought-out, aggressive plan and strategy for success, along with demonstrating the will and drive to achieve impressive results, you will clearly display important leadership characteristics.

Avoid 15 Potentially Deadly Mistakes Most Presenters Make

Everyone occasionally makes mistakes when giving presentations, even Killer Presenters. But it's the type and extent of the mistakes that determine the negative impact they will have. These 15 mistakes will adversely affect the way your audience pays attention to, understands, and accepts the information or ideas you are discussing. Part of creating and giving a Killer Presentation is not entirely what you do—it's also what you *don't* do—and you need to know both to get it right. Here are the common no-nos to avoid.

Mistake 1. Not Knowing How to Use Your iPad Competently

It doesn't take much to be a laptop wizard. You load your PowerPoint or Keynote presentation, put it in play mode, and advance the slides by keyboard, mouse, or remote control. But your iPad is different, and it operates differently. You no longer push your mouse or click your presentation remote; you are a "finger maestro" who is using your iPad as a creative instrument of powerful interactive communication. You need to know what apps can help you, how to use them, and how to work your iPad seamlessly, competently, and smoothly to do some (as Steve Jobs would say) "amazing things."

Mistake 2. Keeping It Boring and Dull

The three biggest things that make a presentation dull are (1) a monotone, lifeless presenter, (2) uninteresting content that is of no apparent benefit to the audience, and (3) terrible visuals, each one full of text. People have a lot on their plates and a lot on their minds as they enter a meeting room for a presentation. So unless a presenter applies the ideas and techniques we give in this book, he or she can expect to have attendees who are physically in the room but are mentally and emotionally elsewhere for a while. If you are aiming to get superior results, you can't do it with a dull and monotonous presentation or speech.

Mistake 3. Including Too Much Detail

You don't have to "data-dump" people to get them to fully understand what you are discussing. Decision makers need relevant *summary* bits of data and information to see the value of making a decision, not to be fully educated on every small aspect of your topic. Decide how much "absolutely necessary" information is required and then include the rest in more comprehensive handouts or online sites for those who want more. Unless you are giving a technical, scientific, or engineering-based presentation where lots of specific data are wanted, keep it simple and clear with just enough "important stuff."

Mistake 4. Running Overtime

It is *never* a good idea to talk longer than your scheduled time. If your presentation goes past your allotted limit, you will not only lose your audience, but annoy or even alienate them. Always strive to end earlier (5 or 10 minutes) than the time you are given, especially if it is before lunch or toward the end of the day. A smart tactic some speakers use is to actually ask for at least 25 percent more time for their presentation than they think they will need, because most presentations usually take longer than we expect or plan. That will impress and please your group. Those who want to hear more will seek you out afterward.

Mistake 5. Causing "Death by Bullets"... Oh, the Mental Pain and Suffering!

"Death-by-bullets" PowerPoint-type visuals are a daily occurrence that are way too common in meetings, mainly because speakers use them as detailed notes so they don't have to prepare to become more familiar with the content. It's much easier to pack copious amounts of small-size text and complicated diagrams on a slide, instead of trying to create elegantly simple, cleanly designed slides that will visually convey messages, main points, and priority information immensely better than what you can say with text.

What's even worse is that presenters read each bullet point (or entire paragraphs) word for word. People can read about 7 to 10 times faster than you can speak. Keep your well-designed text, graphics, illustrations, and other visuals "lean and clean" with just the key points that further your goals.

Mistake 6. Winging It (Worse Yet, Faking It)

We are always amazed at and puzzled by people who apparently brag that they "speak off the cuff" and don't need to prepare or rehearse their speeches or presentations, even important ones. It seems that they are not aware that they come across in an unflattering way by rambling, going off on tangents, and not being crisp, clear, and focused. Don't fool yourself. Even if you've given a presentation a number of times before, always prepare and look for ways of making it even more concise, understandable, and convincing for each unique audience.

Mistake 7. Taking Chances with Unknowns

Imagine coming into a meeting room "cold" and having to quickly give your speech or presentation with a projector and screen in the wrong position for your liking. What if you have not used a certain presentation-related piece of equipment that you are given and you are confused about how to operate it? Your audience will see how unprepared you are. Your presentation could be in serious jeopardy.

Highly paid professional speakers always check out the room they will be speaking in long before they get up on stage. Most arrive at least four hours early or even a day before to familiarize themselves with the stage, the seating setup, and anything else relating to their performance. They test out the microphone and PA system. (Most professionals actually bring their own wireless systems and presentation remotes and controls to ensure predictable excellent operation.)

Mistake 8. Having Poor Eye Contact

If you want to evaporate rapport with your audience, bury your head in your iPad or your notes, or turn your back on the group and stare at the projection screen as you talk about your visuals. Or instead, you can engage your audience by making direct eye contact with various people around the room. Learn how to use your iPad in such a way that most of your eye contact is with the group and you only periodically need to glance down to operate your iPad in an inconspicuous way. Effective eye contact shows your poise and confidence while building trust with the group. It demonstrates that you are interested in and focused on the people in your audience, not yourself or your iPad or anything else. Looking at people also will enable you to gauge their reactions (e.g., are they receptive, confused, bored, restless?) so you can dynamically adjust your presentation, if needed.

Mistake 9. Making Excuses and Apologizing

Speakers often make the mistake of alerting the audience to their speaking inexperience, lack of full preparation, nervousness, or the fact that something was missing in their presentation. Many think that this is an act of humility or that the audience will sympathize with them. Chances are the group was not even aware of a speaker's perceived deficiencies or lack of confidence until he or she "sent up a verbal flare that lit up the sky." These apologies or excuses only serve to hurt a speaker's credibility and make an audience feel uncomfortable and distracted. If you feel that you messed up, chances are people might not know. Don't tell them—let them discover it all by themselves!

Mistake 10. Giving a Canned Pitch

How often do you give a "slide presentation" instead of a "presentation using slides"? There is a huge difference between those two options. It may be much easier and faster to take a shortcut by picking out certain slides from a standard slide deck to give an off-the-shelf presentation. But customizing content, visuals, and presentation style to each unique audience is always the preferred thing to do.

With major presentations, it is essential to find out as much as you can about the pain points, priority needs, and information desires of the people you will be talking to so you can tailor and precisely target your presentation to their preferences. In that way, you'll make a "can" pitch instead of a "canned" one.

Mistake 11. Not Communicating Benefits and Value to the Audience

Unfortunately, many presenters fail to communicate how their audience members can use, apply, and directly gain advantage from the information or ideas they are hearing. It is extremely important to repeatedly (in different ways) articulate how people will specifically benefit and gain value from what you are discussing or proposing. Using a combination of directly mentioning the benefits and subtly implying them to those in the audience will maintain the interest of the audience members and better engage them in the presentation.

Mistake 12. Showing Low-to-No Energy, Passion, or Conviction

If people have to sit and listen to monotone and dispirited speakers, they will quickly tune out, turn off, and either daydream, doodle, or work their iPhone. You don't have to be a motivational speaker to rivet a group's attention. Even a moderate level of emotion, energy, and passion will go a long way in having people feel that you are committed to and excited about what you are discussing. You can't raise the level of energy and excitement of any audience above that of your own. So use a quickened speech rate, a boosted voice volume, variations of tone, and more purposeful and energetic body language. Passion promotes success. It promotes profit.

Mistake 13. Making It All About "Me, We, Us, Our"

Presenters from sales and marketing groups who talk about their products, services, or company make the common mistake (we estimate about 95 percent of people do this!) of spending their time and attention on what we call the "*narcissistic focus*"—NARFO. With NARFO, presenters say, "*Our* company does . . . ," "*Our* engineers do . . . ," "*Our* products excel in . . . ," "*We* believe that . . . ," and "*Our* philosophy is . . ."

Instead, strive to put verbiage more on "them." For example, change your focus by saying something like, "*You* will find that our products will boost *your* productivity by speeding up ABC's [their company name] operations in the following three ways: . . . ," or "*You* told us that *you* wanted to work with a company that provided superb service to *your* field offices." Make it all about them—what they want, they need, they prefer—and cure yourself of the NARFO complex.

Mistake 14. Neglecting to Reduce Visual Distractions and Confusion

When a presenter puts up a slide or visual on the screen and leaves it up after she is finished talking about it, the bright image is distracting and interferes with people focusing on the speaker. As soon as you are finished referencing a part of a slide, make a point of either hiding the content or transitioning to an all-black slide. Now the bright light goes away, and the audience's attention refocuses on you, away from the visual.

If you use PowerPoint or Keynote on a laptop, depress the "B" key to instantly blacken the screen or bring the image back. Keynote on the iPad has no such option. Until the feature is added, just use an all-black slide in the appropriate place.

Another major distraction occurs when a presenter stands in front of a projection screen, partially blocking the view for some people in the audience. If an important part of the visual is overshadowed, that could affect the outcome of your presentation. Besides, it's annoying to have someone stand or constantly move in front of a viewing device. Stand in a position where everyone can see your visuals at all times.

Finally, a mistake presenters make is to put up a visual and talk about different parts on it without directing the audience members' attention to what *specific* part of the graphic, photo, or illustration they should be focusing on. They are trying to understand and see what the speaker is referring to on the visual. As a result, they could be intent on finding the pertinent place on the slide and not be paying attention to what the presenter is saying. Consider highlighting and emphasizing specific parts of a visual by underlining, using different colors, or drawing a temporary circle or box around an area to bring focus to that part.

Mistake 15. Not Engaging and Involving the Audience

Who wants to listen to a nonstop "presentation filibuster"? If you want to rivet people's attention, look for ways to interact with them. You can do that in a number of ways, including using your iPad to connect with their devices—before, during, and after your presentation. Encourage their opinions and elicit feedback from people in your group to open up productive discussions. Ask rhetorical or real questions to get them to think and respond to you. Effective eye contact around the room is an indirect way of interacting with people. There is something "psychologically reciprocal" about how when you look at someone, it begs them to look back. That engages them.

By being extremely vigilant to avoid these common 15 mistakes, you will find that your presentations and speeches will begin to shine compared with those of others, thus awarding you the stellar results you hoped for and worked toward.

Describing the Ultimate Killer Presenter: Master of Wow Experiences

Chess master. Master mechanic. Martial arts master. Master's tournament. The word *master* in those examples denotes an expert—someone of great and exemplary skill—a consummate professional who delivers the absolute highest level of performance. A Killer Presenter is a truly transcendent master speaker who creates a moving and memorable experience for an audience. Table 2.1 lists 30 characteristics of a Killer Presenter. After you look at the descriptors, ask yourself how many people you have seen in your career who have ever approached this level of ability and seeming perfection. Many high-earning professional speakers and corporate trainers are, indeed, masters of the platform and classroom. Don't be intimidated, though, by the "ultimate scorecard" and feel that these daunting performance characteristics are out of reach for you. They are not. We have known numerous people who have risen relatively swiftly from stage-frightened, speaking-shy novices to presentation maestros after disciplined work on the skills and traits that are described.

Use the performance indicators in the table to help you gauge your upward progress. The more of these you develop, the stronger your performances will be. Even if you achieve 50 percent of these characteristics, you will likely be 100 percent ahead of the average presenter! Make it a habit to review these 30 traits, competencies, and skills and score yourself on how you did with each one. That frequent self-evaluation will quickly build your skills into "Killer" ones that will make a big difference in your presentations within a short period of time.

Table 2.1 "Ultimate Scorecard" for Giving a Killer Presentation: 30 Traits, Competencies, and Skills

1. Is expert in the use of the iPad, apps, and latest technology for presentations
2. Develops superbly designed visuals (clear, attractive, and simple), animations, and video and knows how to direct audience focus to key areas on the visuals for understanding, context, and message emphasis
3. Displays extensive knowledge of the topic and can effectively discuss any aspect without detailed slides
4. Shows marvelous use of purposeful creativity and showmanship to add pizzazz
5. Uses great, colorful, descriptive, and psychologically impacting language for effect
6. Uses creativity to make presentation interesting, fascinating, and compelling
7. Makes a captivating positive first impression and sterling lasting impression
8. Is a "grand strategist" who uses best approaches to reach every presentation goal
9. Uses powerful verbal and visual metaphors and analogies
10. Has competent working knowledge about audiovisual equipment used in presentations
11. Uses voice and body language to add interest and meaning to the spoken word
12. Focuses relentlessly on addressing the highest-priority needs and wants of the group
13. Develops quick, strong rapport with audience, earning trust and respect

14. Radiates a supremely confident, in-charge command presence leadership aura
15. Is supremely polished, poised, and powerful in the ability to be persuasive
16. Strongly stimulates, motivates, inspires, and moves an audience to commitment and action
17. Makes compelling appeals to both left-brain logic and right-brain emotion
18. Is an excellent facilitator as well as presenter who knows when to be each
19. Takes complex, difficult-to-understand topics and elegantly simplifies them
20. Skillfully performs and subtly entertains, not just informs
21. Does not become ruffled by hostile audience members—"cool and pleasant under fire"
22. Handles touchy or sensitive issues diplomatically and tactfully
23. Uses appropriate humor and wit and knows just how to play with audiences
24. Is a masterful storyteller who will hold an audience spellbound with tales
25. Makes main presentation points and key messages stand out vividly
26. Speaks in a natural, sincere, and conversational way
27. Carefully observes and listens to audience members to detect subtle clues about how they are reacting and feeling during the presentation and adjusts content and style accordingly
28. Gives audience a realistic view of a topic with pros and cons, benefits and risks, to put forth a recommendation in an accurate and clear perspective for the group
29. Comes across as a riveting, dynamic, and charismatic public speaker
30. Taps into and activates an audience's collective desires, hopes, and dreams

What Can You Learn from the Dude Who Did the iPad?

Steve Jobs was a showman and salesman par excellence, considered by many to be an iconic Killer Presenter. He surely fit most (if not all) of the traits and skills described in Table 2.1, didn't he? Carmine Gallo, a communications expert, wrote a remarkable book about Jobs, *The Presentation Secrets of Steve Jobs: How to Be Insanely Great in Front of Any Audience*;[2] we highly recommend reading it.

---

2 Carmine Gallo, *The Presentation Secrets of Steve Jobs. How to Be Insanely Great in Front of Any Audience,* New York: McGraw Hill, 2010.

Learning about how Steve Jobs presented will give you more valuable insights and perspectives on how to ace the presentation game. First of all, he is one of the rare CEOs of a major corporation that took on the role of "chief presenting officer" and evangelist for his products. Other big shots would lock themselves in the executive suite and delegate that perceived lower-priority task to others. Not Steve. He proudly and purposely used his finely honed presentation skills to be the ultimate spokesman for Apple.

He didn't just present—he generated buzz, pizzazz, and an electrically charged atmosphere. When he first got on stage and the applause died down, he often teased his audience into a ramped-up state of anticipation and longing for the next revolutionary Apple product. "There is something in the air!" for example, he said, egging on his eager onlookers at one of his major events. As Gallo said in his book, "A Steve Jobs presentation is intended to create an experience—'a reality distortion field'—that leaves his audience awed, inspired, and wildly excited."[3] And his fans loved it! Granted, the keynotes we saw were a large-audience, on-stage performance that most of us seldom would do. While different rules and skills typically apply to those types of keynotes and product demonstrations, many of Steve Jobs's techniques will help you even if you are presenting to one person in the elevator.

Jobs was clearly charismatic, but in a more subdued way, as opposed to what people may envision as someone being energetic (in an exaggerated way), purposely exuberant, or perhaps flamboyant. Look at the way he was dressed. He didn't try to call attention to himself, but you knew that his charisma was there. It was like a powerful car engine under the hood that you could hear idling, restrained, but ready to unleash some serious whiplash. A big part of his charisma was evidenced by his outward passion and enthusiasm for the products.

His communication style was direct, simple, and (like his products and services) elegant in its execution and persuasion quality. He let his personality come through with absolutely no hint of chest thumping, shouting, or showboating. Jobs gave few media interviews in his lifetime, especially on TV, because he was essentially shy and private in that regard. Yet he

---

3 Ibid., xii.

overcame any stage fright he had in public and sharpened his presentation skills to a razor's edge over many years to reach that impressive master presenter status.

One of the things he did so well is what we advocate in our book—he had a natural, relaxed style of presenting that made people feel comfortable, as if he were talking just to them. A genuine feel of a good conversation. That's it... but it was more than enough. He made giving a presentation look easy. He wasn't "trying" to present. It seemed so natural and effortless. Part of that secret was his discipline to prepare, practice, and rehearse—aloud—for hours before his keynotes so that his carefully chosen (for impact) words would perfectly synchronize with his visuals, making his points and messages drill into your psyche.

He made sure that his transitions, his introductions of other speakers, the videos he showed, and the demonstrations he gave were silky smooth. And when things would sometimes go "bump on the stage," with a product not fully cooperating or a glitch in getting to a website, for example, Jobs kept his cool, made no big deal out of it, and calmly recovered to the extent that almost no one noticed, whereas other less poised and hot-headed presenters would lose their composure and bring undue attention to the problem.

Do you remember what the box containing your iPad looked like when you bought it? It was all white with a photo of an iPad lying flat on top. On the two sides of the box were matching silver Apple logos and the word *iPad* (in black) on the other two sides. That's it! Typical Apple simple elegance in design. Well, so were Jobs's visuals. Did you ever see him use an elaborate keynote software template? His background slides were white—no headers, no footers, no fancy designs or colors to distract. White background gave him lots of white space, so that his photos (usually just one per slide) or minimal text (usually several words in black font) would have high contrast and would "pop" against all that blank white space. Most templates waste "prime real estate" on a slide.

Why use a busy, graphically sophisticated template with $10,000 worth of artwork and $1 worth of communication value? Jobs didn't. It was Leonardo da Vinci who said, "Simplicity is the ultimate sophistication." Jobs often referenced that quote and worked and lived by it. We are not saying never to use a template for your slides. If called for, just use one that has a simple, elegant design for the specific purpose you intend and leave all the extraneous footer fluff out.

You certainly can have a Killer Presentation without slides filled with bullets. Jobs was never a "visual shooter." People who know what they are talking about do *not* need bullet-ridden PowerPoints. Presenters like Jobs, and then Tim Cook and others who took over the reins of Apple, aim to have slides with well-designed graphics, illustrations, diagrams, photos, and animations that visually communicate ideas, messages, and key information immensely better than stark numbers, text, or even the well-spoken word by itself. Unfortunately, few presenters add meaningful video to their presentations as Jobs did (about his products and TV advertisements). In your Keynote app, you can import full-screen, high-resolution video easily and quickly. Good-quality video (with excellent audio) can add wonders to your messages and help distinguish your presentations from all others.

A couple of caveats about his presentations and style. First, don't try to copy Steve Jobs's presentation style of delivery or anyone else's. That was his. You have your own special speaking style that reflects your unique personality. Second, the type of presentation scenario Jobs gave is different from the ones most of us will encounter. So understand that some of the things he did would not apply to presentations you give in everyday life to small groups or even larger ones. He was Steve Jobs of Apple—both a powerful and immensely respected "brand." He had enormous credibility and respect. He would not have had to start from zero to persuade people as we usually do.

We don't have his world-famous brand or image or his adoring fan club. He had a much easier job than we would when trying to convince the public. We face skeptical audiences, disinterested buyers, and strong competitors. Nevertheless, we can learn from his techniques, strategies, and ideas he so effectively used over his lifetime. Tim Cook and others at recent Apple new-product keynotes have effectively used Jobs's presentation methods and even many of his signature superlatives. In that respect, Steve still lives on.

Go Ahead—*Act Up* in Your Presentation!

"It's not enough for an actor to be honest. It's the actor's job to make the kind of choices that motivate exciting results," said Ivana Chubbuck, who runs a popular acting school in Los Angeles. Acting in your presentations can deliver some exciting results as well. Maybe you have a bit of the acting bug to begin with. Or perhaps you haven't yet thought of the idea of exhibiting some inherent thespian talents. But know that a little theatrics, humor, curiosity, or suspense-evoking drama could spice up your speaking delivery skills and ways of entertaining your audience. If you are shy or experience moderate-to-severe stage fright or just want to put some pizzazz in your talks or videos, take an acting class and learn some great techniques along with a good dose of confidence.

When asked how an actor can be president, Ronald Reagan replied, "How can a president not be an actor." We agree and believe the same applies to successful leaders, public speakers, and sales and business presenters. You will find that a lot of professional and motivational speakers have invested their time to effectively learn and apply acting skills. Reagan did not likely mean that the free world's most powerful leader should be someone he wasn't or that the president should fake it by playing the starring role on the world's stage. He meant that leaders should use acting techniques to project and use their best voice in speeches and to develop confident, dynamic, and poised body language that displays that important command presence leadership aura to any audience. Ronald Reagan projected charisma and a warm but forceful personality, likely forged and tempered by his confidence-building acting experiences.

It was another statesman, Sam Rayburn, former speaker of the U.S. House of Representatives, who said, "The real actor has a direct line to the collective heart." Logic impresses, but emotions move people to action. Learning a few key acting skills, or using your inborn talents, will enable you to show emotions—even subtly—in ways that will directly affect and move people. While presentation trainers and coaches generally agree that getting some good acting lessons can help people develop a more refined and poised stage presence and boost charisma, some others are divided on whether acting techniques can help or hurt people as they strive to become better public speakers.

Famed movie star Michael Caine said, "If you catch someone 'acting,' that actor is doing something wrong." Beginning actors often believe that it is necessary to continually speak, make gestures, or change facial expressions to help the audience interpret the script. But the savvy actors and public speakers use the art of the subtle, the slow, the not moving or making a sound to richly enhance the performance.

Bad acting, for example, shows a person reeling around the room when playing a character who is drunk, when in real life, the intoxicated person makes a strong effort to appear sober. Likewise, if presenters are trying to "act," they will come across as being unnatural, contrived, or perhaps stiff and mechanical. In that case, the audience might see such a presenter as being disingenuous, and that could damage the trust that person is attempting to develop with the group. Audiences like real people who are genuine with no put-ons, pretensions, or artificiality. You don't have to be an aspiring Meryl Streep or a Daniel Day-Lewis to use some relatively modest acting methods to leverage how your communication and behavior should be directed to what you are trying to accomplish.

An iPad as Acting Companion

Here's an example of how an aspiring Killer Presenter can use acting and creativity in a most unusual and impactful way. Let's say a woman is a semi-professional, part-time speaker who talks mostly to women's professional associations about being a better leader on the job and in the community. She wants to develop a following and a reputation as an engaging, imaginative presenter. At Las Vegas several weeks before her next presentation, she saw a female ventriloquist and wished she could do that. While she was out running one day—*pop!*—the idea came to her out of nowhere in an instant: instead of being a ventriloquist with a dummy, how about a spin-off idea from that? She thought of doing a skit.

The speaker had a life-size, front-facing enlarged photo of her made from her beltline up. She went to a sign store (one that makes big displays for trade shows) and had the people there attach her photo to a rigid piece of plastic that was then cut around her upper body and face to create a contour shape depicting her real body. She asked them to also cut out an oval area in the middle of her face and attach brackets in the back that would hold a full-size iPad; a hidden stand enabled the plastic silhouette to stand up straight. In addition, she had a speaker installed on the back (connected to that iPad) with inconspicuous holes cut through the plastic to let the sound out. She recorded a number of video clips of herself talking from a script that she wrote. Once edited, the videos just showed her head—life-size— filling the iPad screen. She stored all the videos on her iPad as part of an engaging skit where she would be "talking to herself" (her "plastic self") in front of her audiences.

She titled her new talk, "I Talked to Myself and I Believed Me This Time!" At her next women's business association luncheon where she was the featured speaker, she set up this life-size (from the waist up) photo-on-plastic replica such that when positioned on a table it was as tall as she was and looked exactly like her, right down to wearing the same outfit she wore. After being introduced, she said, "How many of us give ourselves frequent negative self-talk each day? We tell ourselves, 'I'm not smart enough, thin enough, attractive enough, educated enough.'" Almost all hands reluctantly went up in the audience. She continued, "This was me two years ago," as she faced her clone. Holding her mini iPad, she activated the first video clip on the embedded iPad that had her video face speaking to her. She was acting out a dialogue with her other self!

Three times during her 30-minute speech, she played out (in her talking-to-herself skits) how she transformed from negative self-talk to almost total positive affirmations. She varied her voice tone and pitch (both natural and recorded on video), facial expressions, hand gestures, and body language (expressing changing emotions during the dialogues) to make her rendition of self-talk come alive to the audience. She had rehearsed this for hours until the back-and-forth between her and her "iPad self" was smooth, realistic, and wonderfully enlightening and entertaining. Without a single acting lesson, her natural talents were sufficient to rivet her audiences throughout.

An Ancient Art—Powered by Your iPad— Is Even More Vital in Today's Presentations

Abe Lincoln and Ronald Reagan were superb practitioners of it. Professional speakers do it with seasoned aplomb. Steven Spielberg is among the best at it. Agents of change apply it as a powerful tool. It's been around since the dawn of humanity. It's great storytelling! And using acting techniques (whether natural or learned) will make stories sparkle and spring to life and cause people to ponder, to laugh, to cry, or to reevaluate something. Storytelling is a passport to the heart and soul and is one of the most neglected forms of communication in business presentations today. People will forget most dry facts, statistics, and other information, but not an imagination-sparking, burst-your-belly-laughing, or tug-at-your-heartstrings story that can sear into peoples' memories, sometimes forever. Stories can change lives.

Unfortunately, storytelling is often counterintuitive and dismissed as frivolous by many "buttoned-down" business executives, especially those coming from engineering and technical backgrounds where science rules the day. Yet even in the most conservative cultures in business and government organizations—which are overdosed with sterile facts and figures—stories serve as purposeful narratives to achieve important outcomes. Just about everyone loves a good story that can teach, entertain, and build bridges to new ideas and relationships. Now with the power of the iPad, storytelling will move into a new, more visual dimension and streamlined process.

If you are a salesperson, you can develop 30- to 60-second "success stories" about how your products or services help your customers achieve the results they want. You can also prepare satisfied customers to tell their own stories (in videos that you get produced) about how working with your company has enabled them to achieve various stellar results. Maybe you are an entrepreneur or innovator pitching to investors. In addition to providing them with the "hard-core data" that they require, you might tell them several interesting short stories about how your new product, service, business, or invention came to be and what an impressive impact it had— and will continue to have—on others. And instead of giving the traditional (yawn-inducing) PowerPoint presentation about your company with all the boring stuff that tells little about the uniqueness, personality, and soul of your company, weave an interesting story that sets your company and its employees apart from the other look-alikes in your industry.

A Business Story with Heart and Soul

While we changed the scenario somewhat, the following example is based upon a real presentation that occurred with a senior executive from an American car company who told his story (along with photos) to the company's board of directors, in addition to hundreds of product design people who worked for him. Success stories have a setting, a situation, and a solution, which this story does. The person telling this example story, Brad X, is an innovative executive of a large manufacturer, whose company, like thousands of others, felt the need to shift some factories overseas. The storyteller has several goals regarding his tale:

1. To engage the emotions of the group by showing the human side of events that impacted so many lives (that we care about) in so many ways
2. To tell a personal story involving himself that the audience can empathize with
3. To have the people in the audience see and hear for themselves what happened and what *can* happen now
4. To challenge the influential people in the audience to create a happy ending to now "their" story

Brad invited 48 people—technologists, business executives, state and federal agency leaders, potential investors, and the top management of a leading innovation center—to hear his presentation, whose title and theme was "renewal." At the beginning of the presentation, he walked to the lectern carrying what looked like a rich leather-bound book. He began, "Today I want to tell you a story from my book," and he raised his leather book, with gold-leaf lettering on the cover spelling out the title "Renewal," for all to see.

His audience did not realize that this handmade, vintage-looking, leather book (called the BookBook from http://www.twelvesouth.com) was a case that creatively hid his iPad. He placed the book on the lectern, opened it up, and said, "I want to tell you a story playing out in many cities across the country that is representative of what happened in my community." He explained, "This is my hometown growing up," as he showed photos from his iPad of his high school, the ball fields he played in, and the movie theater he and his friends frequented. He followed with more photos of an ice cream parlor, variety stores, and quaint restaurants with the smiling people who worked there. "These were the wonderful family-owned businesses I cherish and remember. It was a wonderful place to grow up. Families were friendly, happy, and helped each other. Life was good."

Brad continued, "Here are some photographs of our local manufacturing companies that made quality products and employed thousands of people who supported their families with a decent living." As he looked down at his iPad, people still thought he was reading (he was using his notes on the iPad as memory joggers). They wondered how he could articulate all the details and how the photos popped up on the projection screen. Next, he showed photos of a bustling railroad depot with forklift trucks, shipping containers, and loading docks, with hordes of workers. "Look at the activity back then!" he passionately exclaimed.

Now his voice and facial expression grew more solemn. "But something happened there over the last 20 years," he said. "Factories started to close down or go overseas. The railroad and trucking companies lost business as a result. The trickle-down effect hit small businesses in my town. People who owned their restaurants for generations had no choice but to close." While Brad continued his story of woe, he showed photos of shuttered factories deteriorating, rail yards in rusty disrepair, foreclosure signs on homes, and "Going Out of Business" signs on store windows. "Somehow we took our eye off the ball. In the last 20 years in the USA, we had over 46,000 factories either close or shift to other countries, and the effect has been devastating to people who lost their dream, their retirement, their sense of security," he said with a genuine sadness in his voice.

"I went back recently and talked to those still living in what some are calling a semi-ghost town. Here's what they said." From his iPad, Brad showed four 1-minute video clips of interviews with various people who have suffered the ravages of an economic reversal. The disappointment, pain, and sorrow in people on the video were palpable. "This is playing out all over our country and in Europe and elsewhere. My company was reluctantly forced to move a large percentage of production overseas. But we want to bring manufacturing back here and do it more profitably and better than we have ever done. I'm here to tell you that we can do something about it! We can have a major *renewal*," as he picked up his iPad BookBook case and pointed to the gold-leaf title on the cover.

"My company has partnered with several prestigious government research laboratories, along with two computer companies that have developed the fastest supercomputers. And in partnership with three of the nation's top engineering universities, we have developed a new model, a new process, and a new technology of manufacturing that will bring back prosperity, full employment, and the middle-class quality of living that millions have lost. We have discovered the 'Renewal Formula!' Now I want to tell you how—together with your help—we can transform these rusted factories—starting here, but spreading all over the country—into the most modern, thriving engines of economic fortunes ever experienced."

From his "iPad story book," he then showed five short videos of passionate testimonials from the country's leading researchers, financial analysts, and manufacturing experts about the efficacy and validity of his proposed renewal of manufacturing.

He then shifted into laying out his strategic implementation plan, including virtual reality walk-throughs of the proposed new factories and 3-D animations of the newly developed integrated technologies. He wrapped up with hard-core forecasts of estimated returns on investment, payback, and other financial investment considerations. His summary was crisp, his call to action was direct, and his ending was dramatic and memorable. He told his audience, "My theme and message are about vital renewal of our manufacturing base." From his iPad, he activated an animation that showed the word *renewal* in a large font; as the audience watched, the word *new* within the larger word *renewal* moved upward and the letters came together to create the word *real*. He ended, "This opportunity is both new and real, and together we can make it happen!"

As with all impacting stories, Brad used a psychological shift of perspective that changed the direction of the story from good to sad to "even better than before" to draw the audience emotionally into his story before he communicated his impressive plan leading to a probable happy ending that elicited the support and commitment of those at his presentation.

This chapter is about *you* becoming the winning message by showing your leadership, by avoiding the common mistakes most presenters make, by using a little acting to spark up your talks, and by becoming more of a storyteller instead of a bullet talker. Do those things and your Killer Presentations will *win big*!

CHAPTER 3

What Makes a Killer Presentation?

How many of the hundreds or thousands of presentations that you have attended throughout your business career were absolutely outstanding? The few that were exceptional you indeed remembered and marveled at. You might have forgotten most of the details, but you did not forget how you felt—mesmerized, mentally stimulated, and perhaps emotionally moved. They provided a deeply rewarding experience that excited you, maybe opened you up to fresh new ideas, somehow lifted your spirits, or even imparted a deep renewed optimism.

Average presentations leave your mind wandering while you check the time and messages on your iPhone. The bad ones are simply insufferable. No one should have to sit through a time-wasting, energy-robbing presentation when everyone can learn to make a much better presentation. The right words spoken just right by the right speaker have immense, spellbinding power. Great leaders, richly paid professional speakers, successful executives, top salespeople, and others who made a difference in their industry and the world surely know that.

In this chapter you will learn what a Killer Presentation is—how it is described and how audiences typically react to it. If you want to develop business presentations and speeches that are light-years ahead of others, you have to *reimagine* and then *reinvent* them. We will give you ideas and valuable examples to do just that with your iPad. Finally, you will be able to significantly improve by leveraging the vital Ideal 10 characteristics that will help you gain that "unfair advantage"!

There are all kinds of presentations and speeches. Some inform; others persuade. There are those that entreat, convince, and galvanize. Still others entertain, amuse, instill, and inspire. They can amaze, shock, and create *ah!* reactions. A Killer Presentation, though, is in a class by itself, as you will discover.

How Can You Tell If You or Someone Else Has Performed a Killer Presentation?

A Killer Presentation makes a formidable, positive impact! And your iPad, used effectively, is an "impact generator and amplifier"—that means *excellent, exceptional, outstanding.* A Killer Presentation is a transcendent one—surpassing others—being supremely superb by exceeding ordinary standards and expectations. It's a masterful performance! The best presentations and speeches open the eyes, minds, and hearts of people in attendance. A Killer Presentation can "disrupt"—reverse or otherwise radically change the thinking, attitudes, assumptions, and beliefs of people about a certain topic. It has the power to get people to do things they might not have done or even thought possible. Depending upon the type of Killer Performance experienced by people, you might describe it with a range of adjectives, such as those listed here:

Various Descriptors of a Killer Presentation

admirable	eye-opening	mesmerizing
awesome	fascinating	mind-warping
captivating	galvanizing	motivating
compelling	gripping	moving
convincing	impressive	riveting
dazzling	insightful	rousing
engrossing	inspiring	stirring
enjoyable	interesting	surprising
entertaining	irresistible	undeniable
exciting	life-changing	unforgettable

While describing a Killer Presentation or speech in various glowing terms is helpful, the surest way to know if you have given a sterling performance is in how an audience reacts, during the presentation and afterward. It's all about *impact*—how that information, your vocal delivery, and visuals affected people intellectually and emotionally, described in the following ways:

- People listened and watched with rapt attention and searing interest.
- You didn't see people fidgeting, looking at their watches, or working their iPhones or iPads.
- People sat straight up and leaned forward at times.
- They had direct, constant eye contact with you and the screen displaying visuals.
- The audience asked lots of questions throughout and perhaps after your presentation ended.
- Decision makers and influential people in the group openly shared supportive comments, such as "That's right on target" or "We need to do that!" or "I like that!"
- You saw heads nodding (sometimes vigorously) in agreement with many of your points.
- Facial expressions showed enthusiastic endorsement or had that indescribable look that says, "Wow!"
- People smiled, laughed, interacted, and engaged with you and among themselves.
- Many came up to you afterward to engage in a discussion or congratulate you on a great job.

Bottom-line reactions: If it was a Killer *Speech* (like a motivational talk or political speech), the audience erupted in a sustained standing ovation. If it was a Killer *Business Presentation*, the audience members immediately wanted to support, fully commit to, and take decisive action upon what you were asking them to do. If it was a Killer *Sales Presentation*, they made their unanimous decision right then and there to buy.

Reimagining and Reinventing Your Presentations

Let's venture into the unexplored frontiers of the mind to look at some examples of how to reimagine, reinvent, and remake the art of the Killer Presentation. And let's temporarily put aside conventionality and assumed practicality to look into new and exciting ways to get information and ideas across in a more interesting, innovative, and impactful way. Here are three examples to show you what we mean:

Example 1. What if you created a business presentation as a board game (like Monopoly) using iPads to deliver information or sell something? Moves might be made on a real, large game board (with attractive game pieces), depending upon the action created on each player's iPad. Every time people make a positive move, they get important pieces of information or a clue to get closer to winning the game—which has specific benefits associated with it: maybe winning prizes, incentives to buy, or something else.

Example 2. Say you wanted to build a presentation for technical training, teaching the operation of advanced machine tools as a (custom-built) game. Points would be accumulated every time a player did something right on the simulation of a machine tool shown on the iPad. What if you considered using some devices like iCades, which are miniaturized portable arcade cabinets (with a physical joystick and buttons) using an iPad as the arcade display panel.

Example 3. Suppose you have to make a sales presentation that involves advanced technology-based products or services, and your audience consists mostly of engineering and technical people who typically love solving problems or finding answers to tough questions. In this scenario, you develop a Jeopardy-type game where product information and your sales proposal are both hidden behind the electronic cards on a 60-inch TV. Participants answer using their own or presenter-supplied iPads (with some clues). Perhaps the winner gets a check to present to his or her charity, regardless of whether a sale is made.

Continuing the push for ingenious communication, imagine where key information is given:

- As a 30-minute newscast delivered by two anchors sitting at a desk using their iPads to show information on a large-screen TV or rear-projection screen.

- In the form of several "really cool" magic tricks done by a professional magician (possibly using an iPad as his prop) as part of your presentation team. Maybe a video is shown of the magician (if a live performance is not possible).
- With a ventriloquist and her dummy who, after giving a brief presentation, also answer (prepared and rehearsed) content-related questions and amusingly interact with and play off the audience. Going a creative step further, suppose the dummy was holding an iPad and the ventriloquist was moving the dummy's hand as if operating the iPad (but another person on the presentation team was really doing it from the sidelines).
- Through people performing a humorous live skit where they act out a story regarding the presentation topic.
- By children (who are actually accomplished, articulate actors).

If you are looking for something a little more traditional, picture your critical, high-stakes sales presentation being mostly delivered in a more conventional presentation format (but still using some Killer techniques). It then ends with a five-minute videotaped "news documentary" that tells a compelling success story dated six months in the future as if the prospects in the audience had authorized the sale. The news story would unfold a convincing, realistic, and attractive picture of how the organization and each major stakeholder had specifically benefited from buying. What a potentially powerful way to end one's presentation!

Who Wants to Risk It and Change?

Some of these more unusual ways of reimagining and reinventing a presentation can be valuable—yes, even quite practical—and extremely beneficial, depending upon the type of people in your group, their organizational culture, and the situation or event involved. Highly creative presentations are ideal for many types of:

- Trade shows
- Association presentations
- TED Talks

- Motivational or entertainment-type speeches
- Videotaped presentations shown on a website or YouTube and Vimeo
- Training workshops
- Multilevel marketing events
- Award shows
- Public seminars
- TV appearances
- Product demonstrations

Where do you draw the line when it comes to leaning toward "wild and crazy" with your presentation? You would not do these radical, highly unconventional presentations for a board of directors you know to be conservative, for an executive-level presentation, or at meetings where the risk of being different is not warranted, nor advisable. You would not take the chance to possibly diminish your professional credibility and alienate people who prefer a standard-type, traditional, no-nonsense presentation. Remember, the favorite ice cream flavor for most people is vanilla.

Even if you are giving presentations to the most buttoned-down group, you still can use many of the creative techniques in your iPad-based presentation that we cover in this book, but definitely hold off on the megaton imaginative techniques—or the bacon-flavored rocky road ice cream (there is such a thing!) ideas. Standing out and doing things differently means taking risks. If you are unsure of whether adding some super high-octane fuel to your presentation is a good idea, then start out making it incrementally more imaginative. Gamble with something that you can afford to lose or that you stand a slim chance of winning.

If you never take risks, you will never distinguish yourself from the faceless crowd that plays it safe to not lose, instead of playing to win (big) with that knockout performance. But keep in mind, there are those special innovative and strongly entrepreneurial companies with groups of counterculture senior leaders who would embrace and appreciate your reinvented presentations. Obviously, knowing your audience and their sensitivities and preferences, their organizational culture, and their acceptance and tolerance for uniqueness is key to determining how imaginative you should be.

Following are two detailed examples of how you can safely create innovative presentations and reap impressive results.

Scenario 1. A Company Story as a Short Film

Whether it is a three-minute, five-minute, or slightly longer overview of one's company prepared for potential customers, suppliers, investors, or others, just about all such presentations are straitlaced, predictable, and, well, *boring*! Just the plain, dull facts about the company's history, all the products and services, the financial data over time, and the different departments in the company. Included in many is the standard management structure organization chart with a bunch of boxes and names, with maybe a few photos thrown in of some of the bigwigs, a snapshot of the company's headquarters, and a stiffly posed photo of the board of directors. These PowerPoint presentations essentially give dry information in the vain hope of somehow showing off the company or organization. But most bland ones fall short and fall down.

What would a Killer Presentation of a company history look like? The following example is a composite of several real company stories that illustrate a century-old U.S.-headquartered company that is a manufacturer of specialty textiles, fabrics, and chemicals. The employees pride themselves on being innovative, with a legacy of doing good and nurturing a culture of integrity, environmental responsibility, and a rewarding, fun workplace in which to enjoy a longstanding, enriching career.

The goal of the film-style presentation is to tell a story in a typical week of several employees, customers, and others who interact with the company. The film opens with an actor portraying the founder who established the ethical values and creative, caring culture that is sustained and embraced to this day. The timeline quickly shifts to other actors playing the company leaders who succeeded him and who held fast to the founder's principles, even when the company's future was threatened, especially after the U.S. textile industry could not compete with foreign, low-cost operations. The message is "This company knows how to survive and thrive through great leadership, dedicated people, and innovation that together create profitable, high-value niche textile products." With a bit of drama and suspense, the film shows how the company's numerous PhD researchers experiment, struggle, and ultimately achieve remarkable success by developing impressive breakthroughs in chemical compounds, technology, and manufacturing processes that help to keep the company on a fast track in its fiercely competitive industry.

The story explores the lives of people using the company's unique products and captures the emotional impact—the difference the products make in their lives. Rather than having a predictable sequential story flow, the movie is broken up by clips showing how employees interact with one another in extraordinarily productive ways while actually having fun. Cameras follow managers and executives around, showing how their brand of "servant leadership" fosters a more collaborative, less hierarchical organization and promotes an efficient culture that produces quicker and superior results among teams of talented, dedicated people.

While seeing beautiful cinematography of the exquisite worldwide campuses, world-class research and education facilities, and futuristic-looking manufacturing operations along with the personal side of the company, viewers would clearly get the impression that this was not just an excellent company but a truly exceptional one with a responsible, caring, and altruistic corporate soul. In spite of telling a "soft story," the video cleverly, subtly, and indirectly embeds hard information about key financial data and other information viewers would want to know.

The company story is designed, written, and scripted in a collaborative development between employees, customers, suppliers, and leaders in the communities where the company has facilities. They use iPads with programs like FaceTime and Skype and note-taking, drawing, and brainstorming apps along with sample photos and rough videos to efficiently storyboard their ideas. Now compare that type of presentation about a company next to a series of PowerPoint slides filled with text, sterile facts and figures, and a bunch of posed people and photos of buildings!

So how does one develop a more interesting and hard-hitting presentation about your company? Start by looking for answers to these types of unusual questions:

- What really makes us different and special—from the perspective of our employees, customers, the communities we work in, our suppliers, and others?

- What is the "soul" of our company? How does our culture deeply reflect that?
- How do our people self-actualize on the job to the benefit of customers and other company stakeholders?
- How do we describe our leadership philosophy around here? What have been the positive results?
- What do customers say we do best by a long lead—so much better than anyone else?
- What fascinating and relevant bits of trivia do we have about our founder and our people, products, customers, and organization?
- What distinctive business model do we leverage to give us advantages and short- and long-term outstanding performance?
- What are our most impressive financial metrics and trends, and how do we measure success beyond those admirable financials?
- How did our company get where it is today?
- What interesting information about our programs to enhance productivity, effectiveness, efficiency, quality, and innovation throughout our company would impress people in our presentations?
- What are the two or three biggest mistakes this company has made but has corrected and learned from in ways that actually made this company better and stronger?
- What philosophy and values do we not just declare but really work by?
- What future vision is our company implementing to make a real difference in our industry?

Scenario 2. Entire Interactive Presentation from One Visual

One of the nation's largest energy producers, traders, and distributors developed an innovative new customer approach to buying gas, electricity, and energy-related services that reduced risk, improved price certainty, and gave customers better control over buying energy. The problem was that this new approach was a major departure from the way customers were used to dealing with energy issues. There was a high probability that it would confuse the customer and jeopardize sales if not communicated just right. Typically, most salespeople in the company used a printed, bound booklet of 35 to 40

PowerPoint slides. They would sit with a customer, who flipped through the booklet in a sequential manner as the salesperson went through each slide.

Around "8 B.I.P."—8 years before iPad—the energy company contracted with Ray Anthony's company to achieve several challenging objectives: dramatically simplify how the concept and new solution was communicated; make it easier, faster, and more effective for the salespeople to present the information; and make the presentation truly interactive, where a prospect could follow the presentation and ask questions rather than having to follow a bunch of printed slides, one after the other.

Together with the client, Ray's company developed an attractive laminated and framed visual (about 16 by 24 inches) with self-explanatory illustrations, graphics, and minimal but critical text, all carefully designed to replace the 32 slides that were initially used. Three blank pieces of magnetic cardboard lightly adhered to a metal frame to cover the entire visual. This enabled the sales rep to selectively remove an individual cardboard covering (as needed), showing a portion of the chart instead of immediately revealing all eight graphic illustrations that might have (visually) overwhelmed the prospect had they been shown all at once. The color-coded visual categorized the information on it, enabling the salesperson to comfortably and confidently address the vital points without delivering a one-sided pitch.

The visual was engineered in such a way that, should the prospect want information out of sequence, the salesperson could simply move to a different area on the large visual and address just about any aspect related to the prospect's requirements, concerns, and wants. The design prompted the salesperson to talk about the visual and its information (as a form of memory jogger) in a more natural and random way, as opposed to having to go through 32 individual slides sequentially.

This "reinvention" of the presentation was a major hit with salespeople and prospects, resulting in high sales closing rates. Think about designing your own interactive "one visual tells all."

The "Ideal 10"

If your presentations are not just unique, but superior in many characteristics, you will snag the immediate attention and tightly hold on to the often-fleeting interest of audiences. Before we explore our four-part game-changing model of a breakthrough presentation system in the next chapter, let's first understand the characteristics of a superb presentation or speech on which this innovative model will focus. We call these characteristics the "Ideal 10." Every time you plan an important presentation, you should check it for how well it incorporates these 10 vital characteristics.

It is an exceedingly rare speech or presentation that can attain all these criteria together. But if one does so, then that performance is often described by people who experience it as electrifying, mesmerizing, and dazzling. Though most general business presentations don't need all these 10 characteristics, it helps to add as many of them as possible to your most important presentations and speeches.

Ideal 1. Enlightening

It's important to provide thorough and accurate information to people at your presentation. However, "enlightening" them whenever possible goes beyond doing an effective job of educating or informing your audience about your topic. It is about giving people valuable *added* perspectives and rich, new dimensions surrounding your topic that they would not have been aware of. It provides a deeper, more meaningful insight and appreciation into the true nature and importance of your topic. It is about "illuminating"—shedding light upon—making clearer and freeing people from unproductive or obsolete beliefs and ideas. When it comes to advocating change about something, presenters often have to awaken people to the deeper importance of real, critical issues. Here are just a few ways to enlighten people about your topic:

- Ask yourself what unusual facts, statistics, stories, metaphors, or examples surrounding your topic would be most interesting, illuminating, and especially relevant to your audience. Presenters can do this by asking a rhetorical question such as, "Did you know that…?"
- Determine what would expand your audience's deeper understanding and appreciation of your topic beyond the general information that most people know. What could you tell people, for example, about

your products and technology, your company, and its leadership or history that might get people to wonder and say, "Wow, I didn't realize that. How fascinating!"

Ideal 2. Concise

Suppose your boss told you to condense your usual 30-minute presentation about one of your key products into a 10-minute talk. What if she wanted you to also make a product presentation into a two-minute video to be put on the company website? Can it be done effectively? Yes, because a vast majority of presentations have "information fat" within them that can be cut out or pared down. But it requires making smart choices about what priorities to focus upon, along with a concerted effort to communicate in more efficient and lean ways.

Writers know it is much harder to write short articles or newspaper columns than it is to write a book. That's because you have to have a frugality of words and spare sentence structure while striving to have an extravagance of meaning. The same applies to giving presentations. The ancient Roman orator and philosopher Cicero aptly said, "Brevity is the best recommendation of speech, whether in a senator or an orator." Picture being able to condense your information, ideas, and key messages into "efficient packets" or "sound bites," as you often hear on TV news programs. You only cover those key topics with the select information needed by the people in your audience to enable them to understand and be able to make informed decisions afterward. This is critical because the *more* you say or display, the *less* people remember. To keep your presentation concise:

- Separate your content into three categories: *critical* information your listeners need, *important* information to help their understanding, and *desirable* information they might want if you had sufficient time. Present your information in priority-descending order.
- Think about how photos, videos, animations, graphics, illustrations, and charts would more efficiently and effectively communicate your information and messages than spoken words or text.

- First structure your presentations as a brief "elevator talk" or executive summary of several minutes and then build your information further upon these lean structures.

When it comes to your sales or marketing presentations, adopt the philosophy that the fewer the words (and the fewer the slides), the greater the profit.

Ideal 3. Complete

Even though a Killer Presentation should be as concise as needed to reach its goals, it has to be complete in that you, as presenter, must ensure that you tell your audience *all* that is needed for you to achieve your intended objectives. There should be no empty spaces or ambiguous gaps in your content that might cause audience members to be confused, poorly advised, or misled in their conclusions. But "complete" is a relative characteristic, because what is considered complete for one type of presentation might be incomplete for another. TV news stories (such as told on the evening news for NBC, CBS, and ABC) use short, one-minute-video sound-bite stories to summarize information versus a documentary that provides much more information in 30 to 60 minutes. Both are "complete" for the purpose they are serving and the context in which they are developed. Here are a few questions to ask yourself to ensure your presentation is complete:

- Based upon what I know about my audience's needs, wants, preferences, and priorities, what categories and level of detail of information are truly necessary?
- Looking at my presentation, what might possibly confuse people, unintentionally mislead them, create skepticism, or cause them to ask excessive questions regarding the points I am communicating?
- What should ideally be put in a handout or other references (e.g., websites) rather than in the presentation?
- Does my ending summary effectively encapsulate all my vital points?

"Complete" also means having a balance of content types, not an excess of one type of information, whether text or statistics or audiovisual in nature. Carefully select a powerful mix of content such as those in the following list:

Types of Presentation Content

analogies	contrasts	forecasts	projections
anecdotes	definitions	graphs	quotations
animations	demonstrations	humor	research studies
assumptions	descriptions	illustrations	statistics
audio files	diagrams	interviews	stories
cartoons	examples	metaphors	testimonials
case studies	exhibits	models	test reports
charts	explanations	news articles	white papers
comparisons	facts	photos	videos

Ideal 4. Motivational

Any time your presentation is designed to persuade, influence, or get the members of your audience to act upon your requests or recommendations, you have to give them enough compelling *motives* for doing what you are asking. Perhaps it's galvanizing someone to change in some manner or take a new course of action. Motivating others is about letting people know they can and should do something, even in spite of possible difficulties or challenges. Motivating people involves your appealing to or affecting their specific emotional hot buttons (e.g., pride, fear, joy, altruism, justice, personal reward, satisfaction). Even motivating people to just apply the information you provided to their jobs can be important, as opposed to a passive communication of information with no seeming purpose in mind. Here are a few ways to motivate people:

- Use convincing testimonials, inspiring success stories, and other forms of evidence and proof to give weight to your points and messages.
- Determine the specific emotions you want to activate to arouse your audience's interest and desire to think and act in a way you recommend. Build an emotional connection and trust with your group.
- Communicate exactly how it is possible for people to achieve what you advocate.

- Show passion, enthusiasm, and excitement for your topic. Focus on an optimistic "can-do" attitude that your group can accomplish what you are recommending.

Ideal 5. Compelling

When a presenter gives a compelling presentation, she is providing urgent, undeniable, and extraordinarily convincing reasons—in an irresistible and appealing way—to make a decision about something. This aspect of a presentation is forceful (from both an intellectual and emotional standpoint) and demands attention from an audience. It can be overpowering in its ability to convince people to do something right away. While the term *captivating* generally reflects a speaker's impressive presentation delivery techniques, *compelling* often refers to the information, messages, or ideas that are so strong as to be unable to be easily refuted. To make your presentation more compelling:

- Use strongly convincing evidence and forms of proof to back up your claims.
- If selling a product that performs some operation, give a realistic demonstration of its most impressive features and capabilities.
- Apply a rich mixture of "persuasively combustible" facts, statistics, examples, photos, testimonials, videos, diagrams, and other persuasive pieces of content to dramatically illustrate (from numerous perspectives) and solidly establish the validity and urgency of your points.

Ideal 6. Entertaining

Famous former *Tonight Show* host and comedian Johnny Carson said something profound when he observed: "People will pay more to be entertained than educated." In our speaking experiences, we found this to be absolutely true. So why not, of course, aim for both—inform and entertain—within your Killer Presentation? Few business presentations need to be outwardly and directly entertaining, but adding some "spice, punch, and pizzazz" to your presentation, even in subtle and discreet ways, will reawaken an audience's attention that has been eroded by such boring presentations that people have resorted to self-induced out-of-body experiences to escape the tedium.

No, we're not suggesting your doing a stand-up comedy act, impersonations, or a song and dance, but rather your adding professional, tasteful, and appropriate elements of showmanship, just like Steve Jobs did at his new-product presentation keynotes. Businesspeople would warmly welcome a presenter using some clever ways to amuse or fascinate them and otherwise have them enjoy the presentation. To provide an interesting "experience" for them, here are a few tips:

- Use fascinating stories and anecdotes to make your points "pop" and come alive. Show amusing videos or movie excerpts that are meaningful and relevant to your objectives.
- Show imaginative cartoon illustrations with relevant captions that support your main messages and bring forth a chuckle.
- Try using purposeful props in your presentation to spotlight your concepts.
- Use stunning video and graphics, illustrations, and photos to add more variety and attention to your facts, statistics, and other information about your topic.
- If appropriate, play with people in your audience by bantering with them, asking questions, eliciting feedback from them, or engaging them in some way that interests them.

Ideal 7. Captivating

There are some speakers who are so charismatic, dynamic, and charming, who possess a magnetic stage presence, that they will lockset an audience's interest throughout every moment of the presentation. Although the term *captivating* generally refers more to a speaker's impressive qualities, the use of video, multimedia, or fascinating information—conveyed in an imaginative way—helps an audience to be eagerly fixated on your talk. To make your presentation more captivating, try these ideas:

- Make sure your speech or presentation is sufficiently fast paced, never rushing it, but keeping a tempo that moves things along at a good clip.

- Use your voice and body as an instrument of communication. Vary your volume, inflection, and speech rate to make it interesting. Apply well-timed pauses for emphasis and oral punctuation. Let your body movement and hand gestures synchronize with your words to add visual attraction to your delivery.
- Display enthusiasm, energy, and passion for your topic so that those feelings can't help but rub off on people.
- Wow them with words—use highly colorful language (including descriptive examples and insightful analogies that verbally paint a vivid picture of what you are describing, explaining, advocating, or countering, for example.
- Tell a stirring story (perhaps with a strong human interest slant) that perfectly ties your critical information together into a riveting tale.
- Brainstorm creative ways to pump up the interest level of your group with unusual approaches such as having magic tricks or other engaging theatrical effects.

Ideal 8. Clear

When every person in your audience can accurately understand, digest, and interpret your information, then your presentation is crystal clear to them. Your content and intentions will leave no doubt, confusion, or ambiguity about what you are communicating or asking for—your messages are transparent and obvious to your group. However, with many presentations, there are unintended misunderstandings that prevent a presenter from achieving his goals. The reasons can be vague, or abstract language, badly designed visuals, a poorly organized, disjointed flow of information, a speaker's body language and facial expressions that contradict his spoken word, and specific terminology and acronyms (e.g., technical, medical, scientific) that are not correctly understood.

Any time you can involve several senses of people in your group, the better they can understand exactly what you are saying. A Houston-based energy equipment consulting firm uses a multisensory (auditory, visual, and tactile), multimedia presentation approach for maximum clarity to teach skills critical for those who inspect and repair offshore rigs and equipment.

Instead of typical PowerPoint presentations that demonstrated the assembly and repair of oil-well components, this company developed innovations to make the learning process of complex components much easier and clearer for the students. Its training room contains a huge 20-foot Cyviz high-resolution projection screen featuring a superwide display of 2-D and 3-D images that significantly improve students' understanding.

While realistic 3-D images of cross-sections of equipment are valuable, the energy company went one significant step further to ensure the clearest understanding of the complex equipment that people were learning about. Using expensive 3-D printers, it created dozens of intricately detailed, color-coded models of components that trainees could physically hold, take apart, view from any perspective, and then reassemble. Making your presentation absolutely clear is a vital prerequisite of getting your group to agree with your ideas or recommendations and then to act upon them.

Ideal 9. Memorable

What do you recall about the last few presentations you attended? Did anything really stand out or hit you? If you're like most people, probably not much. How many of *your* presentations or speeches are worth remembering? If you have impacted an audience by using engrossing content and multimedia and props, or perhaps providing people with some "touching" experience, your audience will likely have a profound recollection of such a riveting event.

Top motivational speakers are known to tell powerful, heartfelt stories that people remember vividly (and perhaps were deeply affected or changed by) even decades later. It is often true that people will forget the name of the dynamic speaker, but not how he or she made them *feel*. One of the most charismatic, surprising, and memorable business presentations in any movie occurred at the climactic moments toward the end of the terrific movie *Executive Suite*. That scene epitomized how a brilliantly executed Killer Presentation will suddenly upset, stir, and sway a determined group to a surprising turnaround. Don't miss this movie! Several things that make a presentation or speech memorable are:

- A powerful, unusual, and mesmerizing story

- A dazzling display of diverse creativity and fascinating information used throughout the presentation that make it so different from and better than others
- A gripping introduction and powerful conclusion

Ideal 10. Inspiring

There are a few visionary corporate, organization, and government leaders who can consistently deliver emotionally moving speeches that give hope to and uplift the spirits of those in the crowd. While a consummate presenter can stir a group to action by building a convincing, airtight business case, *inspiring* an audience involves tapping deeply into people's emotions and making them feel optimistic, special, or good about something—or capable of achieving something of extraordinary and significant worth and meaning to others.

Considered by most experts to be the finest inspirational masterpieces of American rhetoric is Martin Luther King Jr.'s brilliantly written speech "I Have a Dream," given on August 28, 1963. Using piercingly emotional words, appeals to higher human values and principles, powerful metaphors and themes running throughout, and perfectly timed repetition of the phrase "I have a dream" was part of the electrifying oratory that held the crowd of 250,000 civil rights supporters in Washington, D.C., spellbound. Dr. King's superb ebbs and peaks of vocal mastery and his buildup to the crescendo ending ("Free at last! Free at last! Thank God Almighty, we are free at last!") forever elevated him to an exalted place among the greatest public speakers of all time. Go online and read the full text of Dr. King's speech. While you are there, Google "50 Top Inspiring Movie Speeches" to hear clips from each one. You will see what made them exhilarating and galvanizing. To better inspire others, consider these tips:

- Tell moving stories about seemingly "ordinary people" who have beaten the odds and achieved remarkable feats through discipline, hard work, and dedication.
- Challenge those in your audience to tackle a worthwhile cause or project and to excel at it.

- Be vulnerable and forthright about your own struggles, setbacks, and mistakes, but also your hard-won victories. Share generously from your own experiences.
- Communicate a sense of strong optimism while appealing to people's higher, noble principles.

When you learn to reimagine and remake your presentations, you will see a new world of opportunities coming your way. Gary Hamel, an American management expert and author, said, "Revolutionaries recognize that competition is no longer between products or services; it is between competing business concepts—when its most effective business concept innovation leaves competitors in a gut-wrenching quandary." The following chapters will give you even more great ideas and information to become the ultimate Killer "Revolutionary" Presenter.

CHAPTER 4

The P-XL² Model:
Gearing Up the Power of Your iPad

Launched in 2010, the iPad was brought out by a beaming Steve Jobs, who introduced it to the world as a truly "magical and revolutionary device." Innovators quickly came out with imaginative apps in just about every industry and application. But those doing presentations were using the iPad merely as a lightweight replacement for their laptops, still mostly giving "boredom-by-bullets" slide presentations because they did not know how to best use this thunderous tablet to create and deliver presentations worthy of its fantastic features and capabilities. That's tantamount to driving your ferocious Ferrari slowly around a crowded parking lot. That's not what Ferraris are built for. Likewise, your "digital Ferrari" iPad needs an open road to open up full throttle! This chapter is about helping you to do just that. You will be introduced to our exclusive P-XL² Model, where P-XL² stands for "presentation excellence squared." Our P-XL² Model is engineered to mate with the power of the iPad so you can truly reimagine and reinvent your presentations into Killer ones.

Conventional presentations yield conventional results. It's as simple as that. Being part of the crowd of PowerPoint plodders is a recipe for stark mediocrity. Remarkably successful people, those who stand out and above the faceless crowd, habitually do what other people won't do or can't do. Albert Einstein profoundly said, "I must be willing to give up what I am in order to become what I will be." Rule-breaking innovators and nonconforming visionaries venture where others don't go because there's practically no competition out there on the unbeaten paths. So there's a much greater chance for spectacular success. Killer Presenters go the extra mile to presentation *excel*-lence. It's harder work that's smarter work—but effort that pays off mighty *big*!

Your iPad deserves and demands an equally dynamic new presentation model to enable you to give presentations that far exceed the bounds of ordinary. Otherwise, simply substituting your iPad for a laptop while using a stuffy, traditional style of presenting is like putting a Ferrari engine in an old beat-up Chevy and expecting it to handle like a supercar. You need a Ferrari transmission, chassis, and suspension to get the most out of that roaring, sophisticated engine. So your iPad begs for our special methodology to match it and let it redline.

Figure 4.1 depicts the powerful P-XL^2 Model as a transmission (connected to the iPad "engine") with four gears—*technology, strategy, creativity,* and *psychology*—with each being able to mesh with the others in various combinations depending upon your presentation. For example, some of your (perhaps more conservative business) presentations will require lots of strategy, some technology and psychology, but less creativity, while others (such as motivational or entertainment-focused speeches) might need an abundance of technology and creativity with less psychology and strategy.

FIGURE 4.1
P-XL^2 Model depicted as an iPad "engine" connected to a "transmission" with the four gears of technology, strategy, creativity, and psychology.
(Copyright Ray Anthony)

This model or system is about engaging, shifting gears, and synchronizing the four model components as needed to achieve the 10 ideal characteristics of a Killer Presentation (discussed in the previous chapter).

Playing It Safe Can Be Risky and Costly When Giving That All-Important Presentation

Giving a "good" presentation is no longer (good) enough in our hypercompetitive, fast-changing world. A large construction company we know of recently lost a multibillion dollar bid primarily because its presentation to the client was "fine and acceptable," but it did not *wow* the decision makers, who went with this company's strongest competitor that *did do* a Killer job. Teams of engineers, project managers, and executives in this company spent months working on their proposal and presentation, focusing on a very complex construction and technical solution that they were confident would win the bid. They mistakenly believed that the oral presentation (to the potential customer) would account for a lesser portion of the customer's decision-making criteria and that the presentation was essentially a mandatory rubber-stamp activity to go through. Nevertheless, this construction company spent millions preparing to try to win this gigantic deal.

The construction company had an insular culture with a "clenched state of mind" where outside ("not invented here") ideas and imaginative approaches were shunned and where senior executives felt that their current presentation model, process, and style—which had been relatively successful in the past—would garner them the biggest project in the company's more than 100-year-old history. Well, it didn't. When a fierce, highly respected competitor, just like the construction company's rival, focuses on innovating its presentations to craft an A+ game, it "creatively disrupts" the decision-making score for the buyer—greatly in the competitor's favor. And that is exactly what happened.

The conventional "play-it-safe" presentation that had mostly worked before did not work now. Doing things differently and standing out means taking some risks. But fitting into the crowd of look-alikes means you can't be seen—you can't be viewed as special, unique, or superior. So you incur the danger of being left in the dust. Smart presentation game changers consistently win, leaving their competitors surprised, shocked, and dismayed at their losses. If you don't take some prudent, calculated, and smart risks—if you don't play to win instead of playing *not* to lose—you will never distinguish yourself from the average crowd. As the saying goes, "To get something you never had, you have to do something you never did."

Not only did this bidding company lose the biggest deal in its history, but it lost millions of dollars in preparation time and other costs. The company also lost industry bragging rights that would have won it larger and more profitable deals from others in the future, never mind the demoralizing effect it may have had on certain members of the business development and project team who might have been carving capstones for their careers but now might be thinking more of headstones.

Had this company's executives spent more time and imagination exploring more options to compellingly communicate not just the company's technical excellence, but its overall ability to deliver a best "partnership experience in all aspects" for the customer, it would have increased its chances of winning the deal.

Even when the odds seemed stacked against you, and even though your company might be initially considered the furthest trailing bidder before the final presentation, using our P-XL^2 Model with your iPad or a laptop can snatch victory from apparent defeat. In the fabulous film *Executive Suite* (which we also mentioned in an earlier chapter), famed actor William Holden used strategy, psychology, and some creativity that brilliantly demonstrated how one can make a group of people do a sudden 180-degree reversal from their feelings and intended decision. Get a DVD of this movie and see how he powerfully did it! And as an example that life imitates art, later on in this chapter is a true story that illustrates how a Killer Presentation using our model won a huge deal in spite of enormous odds against it happening.

Four Key Components of the P-XL^2 Model for Killer Presenters

This is an extraordinarily effective model developed, refined, and tested by Ray Anthony and his company over a span of years to give professionals a presentation methodology to achieve the Ideal 10 traits of a winning presentation. What makes it unique and impactful from a communication and persuasive standpoint is its ability to appeal to all people in some way. It brings presentation skills to a new height whether you are using an iPad, laptop, or no computer at all!

With our model, you combine the four key elements of technology, strategy, creativity, and psychology in various ways and degrees (that you decide upon) to superbly inform, convince, motivate, entertain, and inspire audiences as never before. For example, when a presenter uses creative ideas with digital technology (such as video, multimedia, webcasts, Skype presentations) on a platform like the latest iPad, the positive effect on audiences is greatly amped up. Likewise, you can use technology (e.g., showing an emotionally charged video using an ultrahigh-definition television [HDTV]) with the element of psychology and strategy (targeted to elicit specific feelings from the audience) to increase your chances of reaching your presentation objectives. As you experiment and create your own mix of formulas, these four elements will interact in all sorts of wondrous ways to produce breakthrough levels of communication and expanded possibilities. The following will give you more details on each of the four vital components of this Killer-icious, game-changing presentation model.

Technology

The nineteenth-century original thinker, philosopher, and psychologist William James said, "Language is the most imperfect and expensive means yet discovered for communicating thought." Did he have a crystal ball that showed that today's technology—with your iPad at the critical core—will give you an unbridled advantage in helping you communicate immensely more effectively and powerfully *if* you use it smartly? Your iPad is like "Hollywood in a box." You have the raw power to display and discuss anything from abstract concepts to complicated solutions as never before. The trick, though, is to know exactly how to link up this digital genie with your imagination, along with visual and audio resources to make your communication burst out alive in living color.

Slides with bullet points, like spoken language alone, simply cannot convey information, ideas, formulas, visions, and especially emotions as effectively as other forms of media. Over two millennia ago, Aristotle said,

"The mind never thinks without a picture." Technology has enabled multimedia—the ultimate pictures—to come of age. But the power of multimedia is still largely untapped and underutilized in today's presentations. The term *multimedia* means *multi*ple *media* elements consisting of photos, graphics, illustrations, animations, video, music, text, numbers, sound and visual special effects, and even 3-D photorealistic renderings and props. As you have seen in movies, on TV, and in video games, incredibly powerful special effects and 3-D animation software can essentially do whatever one can imagine.

George Lucas and his teams at Lucasfilm Limited and Industrial Light and Magic started the amazing digital special effects revolution with the first *Star Wars* film in 1977. Steve Jobs, who cofounded and served as CEO of Pixar Animation Studios, also knew the unlimited power and potential of computer-generated imagery. As the executive producer of the critically acclaimed film *Toy Story,* he set the bar high for animated features; subsequently many others (*Finding Nemo, The Incredibles, Cars, Toy Story 3,* and more) were given Academy Awards for Best Animated Features. Pixar actually sells the same software—RenderMan Pro Server and RenderMan Studio—it uses to create its legendary animations. Some outrageously innovative and visionary Killer Presenters will surely find ways to use the software for magnificent effects in their presentations.

Just as high-definition (HD) video cameras and televisions are becoming commonplace, new ultrahigh-definition (UHD, also called 4K) video cameras, televisions, and projectors are coming on the scene. These new entrants promise even more spectacular resolution and overall image quality and are now available in large-screen televisions in sizes ranging from 50 to over 80 inches from Sony, LG, Sharp, Samsung, and many others. UHDTV has a resolution of 3,840 × 2,160 pixels, or four times the resolution of HD video (1,920 × 1,080 pixels), giving your visuals, text, videos, photos, and graphics the clearest, cleanest, most vivid images yet.

Presenters can now give their audiences the ultimate immersive, lifelike visual experience as never before. There are videographers using UHD cameras (such as the various RED cameras) that you can hire to shoot absolutely stunning videos for your upscale presentations, and you can project the videos onto giant screens using a Redray player, for example.

While video has been getting a lion's share of publicity, technology in audio PA systems is still a vital component of a presenter's success. Instead of relying on a hotel (or resort) meeting room's ceiling speakers that often produce inferior sound, Killer Presenters use state-of-the-art external public address speakers and quality microphones that produce superb-clarity audio (so necessary but often neglected in one's big event, seminar, or speech) without feedback or distortion. Whenever possible, rent or buy top-quality speakers from JBL, QSC, Mackie, Electro-Voice, Line 6, or Bose. These manufacturers and others have the latest amplifier, digital signal processing, and feedback suppression circuitry and speaker technology that will make a huge difference in how well your voice sounds and projects.

Here are some questions you should ask yourself to ideally leverage technology-related (hardware and software) products in your presentations:

- How can I use stock video (or video from YouTube, Vimeo, and other sites) to help make my points more understandable and help deliver me more (intellectual and emotional) impact? What HD or UHD video might I shoot (with a camcorder, DSLR camera, iPad, iPhone, or RED camera) to customize my message to this audience or potential customer?

- How might I begin to explore and apply gesture-based presenting techniques to navigate and manipulate my visuals (as seen in the 2002 Tom Cruise movie *Minority Report*)?

- What types of animation (both stock and custom) would take my visuals to a new level of effectiveness? How can I use animation software to better illustrate trends, relationships, causes and effects, outcomes of a process or system, or any meaningful change in variables? Learning Apple's Motion or Adobe After Effects will give you a relatively easy and quick way to animate text, illustrations, charts, and graphs and enable you to do impressive special effects aimed at adding meaning and value to your points. Consider contracting with multimedia developers who use more sophisticated animation and 3-D rendering software to create photorealistic images.

- In what ways can I creatively use green screen (Chroma Key) techniques for video and photographs to create unique and stunning backgrounds for my visuals?

- How can I use iPads (handed out) with smaller groups (fewer than five) in a novel approach to deliver "up-close and personal" media to my audience?
- In what ways might I use an iPad to radically improve the way I creatively present multimedia (e.g., place iPads and wireless speakers around a room where I selectively show visuals or photos with voice narration, music, or audio effects)?
- During my presentation, how can I use a live Skype interview with someone in another part of the world to give impact and immediacy to the messages I am communicating?
- How might I use technology to better interact with and engage the members of my large live (and also webcast) audience to answer questions, ask them questions, or otherwise get them more involved in a relevant way?
- What are some impressive and imaginative ways I can incorporate social media into my speech (e.g., have audience members use Twitter to ask me questions or make comments while on stage)?
- For my large-scale events, how can I use multiscreen imaging, computer-controlled lighting, and other stage effects to upgrade the production value of my presentation?

Strategy

Successful companies have well-thought-out, detailed sales and marketing, engineering, manufacturing, R&D, and financial investment strategies, among others. *Strategy* is management's game plan—a road map that serves as a guide to achieve a set of goals and strengthen the performance of the enterprise. So why don't most presenters develop and work their presentation strategy? After all, it is one of the most important factors in determining a winning talk, and yet it is one of the most neglected parts of planning one's presentation. The answer is that most speakers aren't even aware they need such an important course of action in their talk. Not so with Killer Presenters—they are great strategists! Being so gives them a decided advantage over other presenters vying for the same deal or opportunity. Most people confuse choosing and organizing their content for a strategy. That comes under the umbrella of strategy, but it's only a part of it.

Derived from the Greek word *strategos,* a strategy was seen in the narrow sense as "the art of the general." Alexander the Great (356 BC–323 BC) was considered among the greatest commanders of all times because of his use of brilliant strategy, among other things. *Strategy* is a decisive "force multiplier" not only in military and business situations but in presentations as well. *Tactics* are those more detailed and specific steps that support a strategy.

If your goals are what you want to achieve (in terms of specific audience understanding, acceptance, commitment, behavior, or actions), then your strategy describes *how* you intend to achieve your specific aims. With strategy, you are methodically thinking about the ideal (least risk versus gain, quick, effective, easy, most cost-justified) ways to get your desired results at the end of your presentation. Here are some questions to consider asking yourself when using strategy in planning and delivering your presentations:

- Based upon the specific goals I want to accomplish, the audience I am presenting to, and the current situation I am facing with this group, what is my overall strategy and set of tactics to get my planned results? Examining the P-XL² Model, how might I smartly incorporate creativity, technology, and psychology into my overall strategy?
- What actions and activities need to be done *before* my presentation to set the stage and also *after* my presentation to ensure the fulfillment of my objectives?
- What resources (people, equipment, technology, visuals, handouts, other) will I need to support the attainment of my goals?
- Should I use a slow, indirect, and subtle approach with this group, or should I begin and maintain a direct, strong, unwavering advocacy of my position?
- What are the strengths and weaknesses of my competitor presenters? How do I leverage what they lack, and how do I counter their advantages?
- What are the two or three greatest impediments to reaching my presentation goals, and how can I eliminate or mitigate them?
- What is the best content (information and structured messages) I should use to convince the people in my audience and compel them

to act upon my requests? What should I avoid discussing, and how should I handle touchy or risky subjects that might come up?

- What is the singular most important point, fact, or message that I need to repeat and otherwise slam home to my audience?
- What forms of solid "proof" (e.g., statistics, verifiable facts, results of research, historical precedents, demonstrations, success stories) must I provide to give strong credence and substance to my claims?
- What is my approach (i.e., direct, indirect, subtle, or assertive) to ask for audience support, commitment, or action?

Creativity

If you want to transform yourself into a "communication artist" and win an Oscar at the "Presentation Academy Awards," engage your imagination in high gear. At the core of Killer Presentations is creativity that, like a center gear, drives the other gears in the iPad's "transmission." Too many speeches and presentations have predictable rhythms and formats (actually "boremats"). But these enfeebled presentations will never get you the over-the-top results that consummately innovative ones will do. Certainly, not every talk requires the pizzazz of an astonishing meeting-room Cirque du Soleil performance. However, when you want to wow your audience with a terrific performance and experience or when you want to snatch that huge, once-in-a-decade deal away from your strongest competitors, you need to ramp up your presentation with bold and daring ideas that will brilliantly distinguish it from even excellent presentations from others in the bid. Audiences don't expect you to be amazing, but when you are, the results and accolades you get will also be just that—amazing.

Being creative means doing something from a perspective that is (slightly to hugely) original. Whether you call it *clever, ingenious, inventive, innovative, original,* or just *cool,* using creativity in your presentation is about getting the edge over others and making a major splash with your audience. We're often asked, "Where I can I get good ideas to make my presentation come alive?" The short answer is *everywhere!* The essential thing is to be on the lookout for ideas that you can copy and modify from sources that are seemingly unrelated to presentations. One of the best sources for inspiring, amusing, and jaw-dropping presentations can be had by going online and watching TED Talks (TED.com). You will see great examples of speaking skills, fascinating content, cleverly used props, interesting visuals, stage decorations, and more. Other areas to seek out useful ideas include:

- Slideshare (look at the slide content, photos, and visual designs and illustrations)
- Google (search for the "funniest graduation speeches of all time" for humor ideas)
- Interesting websites (look at their designs, videos, and content)
- Magazines and books (with lots of photos, illustrations, and snappy advertisements)
- Museums, art galleries, and craft shows
- Toy stores (online and walk-in stores)
- Catalogs of all kinds (trade show products, signs, gadgets, tools, and others)
- Gift and card shops (hobby, arts-and-crafts, and artist supply stores)
- Department stores (e.g., Sears, Macy's, Dillard's, Kohl's, Neiman Marcus, Nordstrom)
- Office supply, electronics, and gag-gift stores
- Home decorating and big box stores (e.g., Wal-Mart, Home Depot, Costco, Lowe's)
- Supermarkets (look at all the food and product packaging to see how it grabs your attention and interest)
- Comedy clubs, plays, and YouTube to find other humorous ideas

Here are some questions that you can ask yourself to prompt you to add more creativity to your presentations:

- How can I use my iPad as an entertaining and meaningful prop, not just as my presentation device?
- What profound metaphors or analogies would give a new spin and perspective on my main points?
- In what ways can I use the element of surprise, intrigue, anticipation, curiosity, or controversy to add impact and excitement?
- How might I begin my presentation in a highly unusual, attention-grabbing, and interest-generating way that is captivating and yet totally professional in nature?

- What interesting small or large physical props, toys, or novelty items can I use to add emphasis, power, and improved meaning to my messages?
- What clever mixes of humor can I add to my presentation such as jokes, amusing stories and anecdotes, funny quotations or sayings, jocular visual cartoons and illustrations, or belly-laugh-inducing videos (e.g., from YouTube)?
- What professional kinds of "theatrics" might I employ to entertain my audience while reinforcing my key points—perhaps acting, using costumes, or cleverly orchestrating my presentation with a prepared copresenter (who might play devil's advocate, for example)?
- How can I use or adapt ideas or themes from TV shows, video games, or movies?
- What tests, games, or puzzles directly relating to my topic can I use?
- What background signs, trade show–type visuals, special lighting, decorations, props, or stage sets can I use to bolster the theme or tone and mood of my presentation and add more background "eye appeal" to my talk?
- What audio (music, excerpts from historical speeches, special effects sounds, ambient sounds) would make my points stronger and more memorable and add an entertainment value to my presentation?

The boardroom doesn't have to be the bored room. Even conservative businesspeople can't stand to sit through dull, lifeless presentations. So don't be afraid to use new ideas or even aim for a tectonic creative shift to make your presentations more entertaining, meaningful, engaging, and fascinating.

Psychology

Psychology gives understanding, meaning, and direction to our everyday activities. It explains how we think, how we feel, and how we act or react. Killer Presenters, motivational speakers, top-notch salespeople, and those who persuade and influence people use psychology to guide others to make decisions, buy a product or service, or act in some intended way. You don't have to be an Erich Fromm, a Dr. Phil, or a cognitive scientist to use basic street psychology to understand and get the attention of the people to whom you are presenting and to affect their perceptions, emotions, and behavior regarding your topic.

Successful influencers are typically those who learn, possess, and display high levels of emotional intelligence—a valuable empathic skill at reading others' emotional needs, desires, moods, and motivators. They are able to pick the (emotion-influencing or igniting) tactics that are most appropriate and implement them in an effective manner. We cannot stress this enough: psychology is at the very core of persuading, influencing, and getting people to act upon your request. Successful leaders know the raw power of applied psychology to galvanize and move the masses toward a vision, mission, and set of objectives set by the leader. There are psychological triggers and hot buttons that a presenter can attempt to activate in a nonmanipulative way to get his audience to either reinforce that group's set of beliefs, attitudes, preferences, assumptions, or perceptions or to change them (to some needed degree). The psychology element in presentations, like that of the strategy component, is one of the most neglected yet most important aspects on which to focus.

Cognitive affect is a fancy scientific term for how factual information of all kinds is perceived and then processed. It involves attention, understanding, reasoning, problem solving, and decision making—basically, logical and rational thinking by your audience during your presentation. The companion psychological aspect is *emotional affect*, a term for reactions and arousal of human feelings that have a high probability of producing changes in awareness, mood, and behavior. Both cognitive affect and emotional affect will impact and change the way people process information and choose to do something advocated by the presenter

One streetwise psychological principle is this: people often want what they don't need and often need what they don't want. Some hard-core financial businesspeople, for example, will spend exorbitant amounts of money for prestigious, luxury items like a corporate jet, a lavish office, or other extravagant things that others might consider a wasteful, nonproductive investment. Their emotional affect drives them to obtain these expensive perks, while their cognitive affect finds facts to justify and rationalize their decision. The point for presenters to remember is that emotions and feelings almost always trump intellect and logic, even in spite of people saying otherwise about their decisions and behavior. The essence of persuasion or influence is getting people to *want* something (create or make them aware of their desire) and then convince them they absolutely *need* it—perhaps can't do without it!

Another psychological principle to know is that people are much more motivated to eliminate painful, unpleasant, or stressful situations than they are to gain something of benefit or pleasure. Obviously, successful presenters try to show people how to reduce or eliminate their "pain points" while also improving satisfactory conditions and making them aware of getting "pleasure points." The list below identifies feelings that people would want to rid themselves of on their jobs or in their lives. Ask yourself how in your presentations you might show the members of your audience how they can reduce or even reverse their unpleasant feelings.

Pain Points and Negative Feelings

abandoned	dread	intimidated	scared
anxious	envy	needy	shamed
bewildered	fearful	neglected	stressed
concerned	frightened	overwhelmed	trapped
confused	frustrated	panicky	troubled
dejected	guilty	pessimistic	unappreciated
disappointed	helpless	puzzled	unsure
discouraged	infuriated	rejected	vulnerable
drained	insecure	resigned	worried

Psychologists, counselors, psychotherapists, and other students of human behavior know that, as a whole, people crave a deep sense of belonging, meaning, and purpose in their lives and that they need to feel self-worth and self-respect. We want to know that we contribute in some way and degree to what we do at work, at home, and in our communities. Who of us doesn't want to believe that our existence somehow matters on this earth? That is not abstract or esoteric psychobabble, but noble human nature begging to leave behind some worthwhile legacy of good.

Successful motivational, inspirational speakers, for example, are masters at making people feel good and optimistic about themselves and letting them know that they are fully capable of doing the extraordinary. These speakers often appeal to one's higher human principles, benevolence, and noble aspirations and causes. Killer Presenters, in business, psychologically tap into and influence the feelings of those in their audience, getting them to yearn for something new, something better—something within their reach and grasp.

The following questions to ask yourself will help you leverage psychology to strengthen your presentation strategy, content, and delivery style:

- What are some sure ways to get my audience to like, respect, and trust me so I can better utilize emotional affect during my presentation? How can I quickly develop rapport and display credibility with this particular type of audience?
- Have I sufficiently analyzed the people in my audience to find out what they collectively want, need, and expect (intellectually and emotionally) from my speech or presentation? Do I know where they currently stand in terms of their beliefs and general feelings toward my topic?
- What are the specific emotions and their sequence that I would like the members of my audience to feel during and after my presentation? What is the most critical emotion I would like to be able to evoke from them? What is the best way for me to do that?
- How can I appeal to both the (logical, analytical, methodical, detail-oriented) left-brainers and the (emotional, creative, expressive, conceptual) right-brainers in the group?
- What "touching" photos, videos, visuals, metaphors, music, or visual or audio special effects could bring forth the set of emotions I want my audience to experience?
- What stories could I tell that might deeply move people to intended positive or negative feelings such as pride, righteous indignation, hope, fulfillment, faith, confidence, or relief, for example?
- What are the top two or three pieces of cognitive-affect information and messages that I absolutely need to communicate to enable people to justify and rationalize their decision to accept my recommendation?
- Overall, how would I describe my psychologically based persuasion strategy for my group?

■ What type of presentation style is best for this audience: relaxed and conversational? high energy and motivational? serious and all business? or action oriented with a sense of urgency?

How Do You Win an "Impossible" Deal Leveraging Our P-XL² Model? A Brief Case Study

Suppose you had a slim-to-none chance (estimated to be 5 percent or less) of getting one of the biggest deals in your division's history in your company and you wanted to go all out to try to win it, even if you went down in flaming glory? How can you up the odds and, maybe, pull off an incredible upset? Well, the following is a true story that occurred several years ago. While the general concepts and basic strategies are accurately described, we are changing some of the information and parts of the scenario to respect our client's confidentiality. We have also added some new aspects to the story to indicate how we would *now* incorporate the use of the iPad (which was not available back then) to enable this company, a top four accounting firm, to win what people in the industry considered a long shot, at best.

How about this for a challenge: what if your competitor—which is the main service provider for the bank whose project you are trying to win—is willing to provide its initial services, worth several million dollars, for *free* just to keep you and your company out? And what if your competitor is doing over 100 times the amount of business your company is doing with that particular bank? Finally, what if your client is totally satisfied with your competitor, which has been firmly entrenched in that account for many years? Can a "superset" composed of an innovative Killer Proposal and Killer Presentation really snatch a deal that appears all but unattainable? Here's the real story of amazing victory.

Ray Anthony had done Concept Presentation training for the senior partners in New York City for one of the top four accounting firms. A senior partner in the training session asked if Ray was interested in helping the firm try to get an enormous but extremely difficult-to-close deal with one of the world's largest international banks.

His accounting firm was doing about $1.5 million a year in revenues with this bank, while the firm's competitor, another top four accounting firm, was doing over $150 million per year with the bank. The competing firms were initially bidding on about a $2 million deal that would grow to over $100 million in several years. The firm estimated that it stood a minuscule chance of winning—*unless* it took some extraordinarily bold and daring steps to create a proposal and presentation unlike any other it had ever done.

The accounting firm realized that it would have to smartly apply Ray Anthony's P-XL² Model in every aspect of its proposal and presentation to win what would be one of the largest deals in the tax group's 30-plus-year history. The following summarizes the analysis, in the group members' own words and outlines how they designed and delivered their winning Killer Proposal and Killer Presentation.

Goal. Win the deal!

Situation analysis. Our strongest competitor (believed easily favored to win the deal) has been the bank's primary accounting and tax processing firm for the last ten years. They are well liked and respected and have an impressive record of customer service and quality operations. This entrenched firm is willing to do the initial deal (worth $2 million) for free just to keep us and other accounting firms out to get the rich rewards of extended projects, conservatively estimated to approach an extra $100 million within five to seven years. Our competitor's executives have a strong professional and personal relationship with the bank's top management.

Decision-making criteria. The bank will choose the accounting firm that can deliver the best metrics of service including quality, responsiveness, and return on investment with consideration to obtaining the best fee structures. An important decision criterion is for the winning accounting firm to be able to apply continuous improvement in operations (and resulting benefits of savings, quality, and processing innovations) over a five-year contract period.

Strategy. If we are to win this deal, we must:

- Take calculated risks to create an innovative, daring, and bold proposal and oral presentation unlike any other we have done to sharply differentiate ourselves from all other bidders in ways that make them pale in comparison to us.

- Develop and substantiate a vastly superior value proposition for the bank that no other competitor can match.
- Create a compelling visual metaphorical theme (that is psychologically symbolic) that is immediately recognizable and memorable and that encapsulates the powerful solution we offer.
- Impressively quantify our value proposition (including our proprietary IT processing technology) in such a way that it leaves no doubt as to the specific ways and extent our solution can produce both exclusive and superior results in which the bank would greatly benefit.

Here is how the accounting firm leveraged the components of technology, strategy, creativity, and psychology in the P-XL^2 Model.

Theme and Concept

The metaphorical theme the firm chose was "generating powerful results." While the title may initially sound somewhat mild, the visualization and execution of it were not. The people at the firm designed a three-part visual that was the focus of the proposal and oral presentation. The first part was the firm's exclusive, proprietary Digital INTERprise Engine. It powered the service delivery model—the company's accounting process—that was depicted as a generator (the second part). The output from the powerful generator was represented by lightning bolt–type arrows (part three) pointing upward to signify increases in savings, efficiencies, and other important results wanted by the bank. The lightning bolts psychologically symbolized the potential power and blazing speed of the output.

Next, the bidding team came up with a Killer concept (along the lines of ROI, or return on investment) called "72 POI—Points of Impact" (generating results). To quantify how this solution was far superior to its competitors' solutions, the firm objectively identified 33 service delivery functions for tax processing that were *just as effective* as those of the competitors that were bidding, 21 that were *better* than all the others, and 18 that were *exclusive* —that no other provider could do because of the firm's proprietary technology. So not only could the firm match the best that all the others could do, but it identified and quantified the vital "value-added" 39 other—better and exclusive—functions that generated the extraordinary results.

Three-Part Killer Proposal

Instead of giving the bank a traditional, letter-size, portrait-format written proposal (either spiral bound or in a three-ring binder), the accounting firm provided its proposal in three extraordinary "parts," each for a different purpose. The first was a somewhat conventional proposal, but with some creative changes. Written in two columns on a landscape (horizontal) legal-size paper, it was actually elegantly designed using black and blue shades of ink for text and diagrams. This changeover to a horizontal, legal-size format with its two-column printing enabled the accounting firm to include all information in a proposal that was thinner, less intimidating, and more attractive to read than a letter-size, single-column document.

Accompanying the written proposal was a unique "proposal on a chart" given to each of the five decision makers from the bank. It showed the detailed three-part generator diagram of the firm's solution along with the critical proposal points on a foam core board 30 inches by 24 inches. The clients could see at a glance the entire scope and differentiation of the firm's value proposition. The foam core piece was a well-designed, captivating "visual executive summary on a board" for those who chose to view that in place of (or in addition to) a detailed written proposal.

The third part of the proposal set included five iPads to be lent to each of the bank's executives involved in the deal. Using iBook as the proposal platform on the iPads, it contained a voice-narrated executive summary accompanied by some compelling *animated* charts, diagrams, and critical pieces of information. The iBook summary proposal also contained three concise 90-second videos by the senior partners on the bidding team who articulated their value proposition and emphasized their differentiated solution via the powerful three-part visual.

The most important message, though, was of the accounting firm's chairman. That video was actually shot outside the client bank's New York City main headquarters location as opposed to a more traditional (i.e., boring) in-office shoot. Sitting informally on the steps of the bank headquarters plaza on a sunny, warm spring day, wearing a crisp white shirt and classy red tie, the firm's chairman did a splendid, sincere job explaining why his firm's teams would work so well with the bank's employees and how together they would accomplish numerous, impressive breakthroughs in joint operations—setting new standards of productivity, quality, and efficiency. And of course, he vocalized his commitment to his accounting firm's total support and excellence in this project.

The ending of the chairman's four-minute video was the high point, where he recounted a heartfelt personal story. He said that when he was a young manager starting out in his firm, one of his first, most satisfying projects was working with this international bank in Europe; and he noted how well the project had gone because of the chemistry between the people and because of the shared values, principles, and norms of both organizations' cultures. He concluded by saying that he expected the same results and great experience to be duplicated again should the bank choose his firm. His final statement was, "If you give us an opportunity to work with you on this huge undertaking, we will, in turn, give the bank numerous opportunities to maximize your financial returns on this investment. That's our goal . . . that's our deep commitment."

The psychology in designing and delivering three imaginatively designed proposal pieces was not just that each served its unique purpose, but that the pieces symbolized how differently the firm approached situations and the extent to which it was devoted to over-the-top excellence. After all, if it would exert that much creativity, effort, and innovation in creating an extraordinary set of communication tools, then it would certainly channel its out-of-the-box thinking to do the same in an ongoing business relationship with the bank.

The Killer Presentation

The set of proposals greatly impressed the people involved in making the decision for the bank. As a result, the accounting firm easily made the short list. Now two firms would be allowed just 30 minutes to give their oral presentation to highlight their solution prior to being chosen a winner. Two senior partners were selected to be the copresenters for the firm. Again, the strategy—like that for the proposal—was to do something bold, innovative, and fiercely convincing around the value proposition and 72 POI. The presenters focused on demonstrating precisely how their solution was not only vastly *different*, but vastly *better*. And they aimed to give a superbly orchestrated, dual-presenter "performance." Here's how it unfolded:

■ After brief welcoming remarks, they each gave a crisp, one-minute executive summary—backed up with two visuals from their iPads—that encapsulated all the key points critical to making a decision in their favor.

■ PowerPoint was not even considered. They used two forms of "ultravisuals" in an innovative hand-off fashion. The first visual was a large storyboard (60 by 40 inches), which was a less detailed version of their summary proposal board. It had a number of Velcro pieces; one presenter would attach the pieces to build the ongoing process and story of their solution. Once that piece was added to the storyboard and very concisely described, the other presenter, using his iPad, would show a brief animation (projected onto a screen nearby) of how that process actually operated to bring about several of the POI. It took almost three days of countless rehearsals to create smooth segues from one presenter using the storyboard to the other presenter using his iPad to transition to the next part of the story. The storyboard, with its Velcro pieces, made it simpler to understand how the firm engineered its superior solution for the bank; while the iPad, using 3-D animation, captivatingly showed interactions, causes and effects, relationships, and projected trends between the firm's technology and service delivery model to produce the savings, efficiencies, productivity, and quality from their 72 POI.

■ They concluded their presentation with a matching executive summary (as in the beginning) and followed it with their clincher ending with the slogan "ONLY," as in:

> "ONLY our firm has the proprietary technology 'INTERprise' system."
> "ONLY we have extensive experience already with your systems, processes and procedures."
> "ONLY our firm has the '72 Points of Impact,' 39 that are better or exclusive to you."
> "ONLY we can give you short- and long-term solutions that match your most stringent requirements."

■ The closing presenter then showed a new video from the firm's chairman, who said, "I'm so proud of my team for putting together this tax solution for your international group, and I commit to the bank and to each of you [the chairman then actually mentions the five names of the bank's decision makers] to put our entire firm behind this project to make it a resounding success!"

■ Finally, the two presenters reached into a box and gave out the only handout in the presentation, a laminated replica of one of the lightning bolts with a written summary on it of their key points.

The accounting firm was open to trying something daring and bodacious, but always with a focus on being professional. Change is difficult, and not everyone thought it a good idea to create a scheme that some perceived as a radical departure from a traditional, "safe" presentation. But the firm took the chance and *won* big time!

Leveraging the P-XL^2 Model will give you astonishing results compared with what you get with the "traditional" presentations you have been giving. Get ready to win that elusive deal you've been salivating over and prepare for some raucous standing ovations at your future speeches. This model has got serious game and can be the ultimate best practice in the presentation arena. Learn how to work it!

CHAPTER 5

Creating Your iPad Presentation

Now that you've nailed the P-XL² Model structure, this chapter will show you how to combine two of the quadrants—technology and creativity—to produce fabulous presentations that reinforce your strategy and play into the psychology of your audience. If you think of the purpose of a presentation as communicating information, you start to realize there are endless opportunities to make a presentation using the P-XL² Model.

Today's technology takes your presentations beyond bulleted text and simple line graphs, and using your iPad as the means of communication is an efficient and entertaining solution to any presentation, large or small. With your iPad in hand, you can control and manipulate your presentation to respond to the needs of your audience with a simple tap or swipe. To present on the fly, use your iPad as a virtual whiteboard or create Killer Presentations with eye-popping images, graphics, video, sound, and links to websites with presentations like those we discuss in this chapter.

We explain how to move presentations you've already created from your computer to your iPad. We then give you ideas for using the iPad's preloaded apps to add zing to your presentation. The core of this chapter covers our top picks of presentation apps. Last, we explore ways to connect your iPad to a projector or monitor and discuss the physicality of presenting with an iPad, which is to say, we do a quick survey of iPad stands and other options for securing the iPad when it's not in your hand.

Throughout you'll find iPad tips, tools, and techniques to fire your imagination and help you avoid embarrassing snafus. You want your audience to remember *you* and your *message*, not the iPad presentation that didn't work.

Using Computer-Created Presentations on Your iPad

To give a presentation on your iPad, you need something to present. For our purposes, regardless of the media type—slides, videos, photos, music, links—we refer to the media that represents your message as either "presentation" or "visuals." There are two ways you can put a presentation on your iPad: create a presentation on your computer and then transfer it to your iPad or create a presentation on your iPad using a presentation app.

If you're an iPad newbie or prefer taking one step at a time, using a tried-and-true presentation method (i.e., PowerPoint or Keynote) with new technology limits your potential-error factor. Even though your iPad can house hundreds of design, photo manipulation, video, and presentation apps that create Killer visuals, in some cases, a linear PowerPoint or Keynote "slide show" is called for. And sometimes, you just don't have time to create something new and exciting, and so your best answer is to use something you've already made.

In this simplest of examples, there are two steps: (1) Copy your presentation to your iPad, which we explain next, and (2) then connect your iPad to the audiovisual equipment used to project the presentation, which is explained toward the end of the chapter.

Whether you make frequent presentations or it's a nerve-racking once-in-a-blue-moon experience, you've probably encountered PowerPoint, the presentation application part of Microsoft's Office productivity suite. If you work on a Mac, you might know, and even prefer, Keynote, the presentation part of Apple's iWorks productivity suite.

A doctor we know gives about 25 presentations a year at medical conferences. His computer is a storehouse of PowerPoint slides. When he has an

"Why bother?" you ask. Consider the following:

- ▶ The iPad is lighter to tote along.
- ▶ Held like a clipboard, the iPad lets you look at your audience more frequently rather than bobbing your head up and down from laptop screen to audience.
- ▶ Using touch-screen gestures to move from slide to slide is natural and intuitive.
- ▶ Your audience will think you're really cool.

upcoming presentation to make, he usually creates a new master slide (the layout used for all the slides) and then puts together a presentation that comprises new slides and slides from other presentations. He either takes his computer to the conference and connects it directly to the AV system or copies the presentation to an external flash drive, from which it is then copied to the AV system by a conference technician. As long as connecting to the AV system is an option, our fine physician can put his presentation on his iPad, take his iPad and the proper VGA or HDMI cable connector to the conference, and project his presentation from his iPad.

Moving a Keynote Presentation from Your Mac to Your iPad

If you use a Mac and Keynote to prepare your presentation, you can simply purchase a copy of Keynote for your iPad ($9.99 at the iTunes Store), save your presentation to iCloud on your Mac (see Figure 5.1), and then open it in Keynote on your iPad. Make sure iCloud is turned on for Keynote in your iPad Settings by tapping Settings on the Home screen, scrolling down to tap Keynote, and then tapping Use iCloud to the On position (see Figure 5.2).

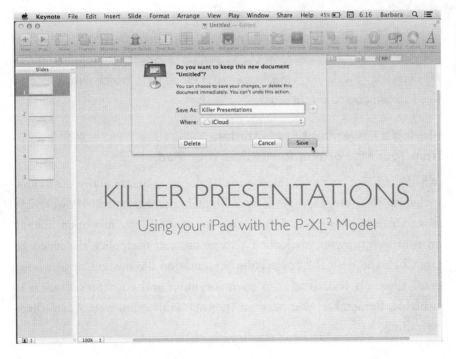

FIGURE 5.1
Save your Keynote presentation to iCloud.

FIGURE 5.2
Activate iCloud
for Keynote in the
iPad Settings.

Are you a Mac user but don't have Keynote? You might want to invest in a copy. At just $19.99 in the Mac App Store, it's every bit as good as the iPad version and possibly even better. It may be faster to develop your show in Keynote on the Mac and then use your iPad to run it.

Keep in mind a few caveats when moving a Keynote presentation from Mac to iOS:

- Recorded audio (voice-over narration) is not imported.
- Comments are not imported.
- Many Mac fonts are unavailable on the iPad.
- Web links and slide-to-slide links are maintained, but all other links are removed.

And refer to Apple's presentation support document, *Best Practices for Creating a Presentation on a Mac for Use on an iPad* (http://support.apple.com/kb/HT4114?viewlocale=en_US&locale=en_US), to learn which templates and fonts are supported on the iPad.

Moving a PowerPoint Presentation from Your Mac or Windows PC to Your iPad

MS-PowerPoint isn't available for the iPad, but there are many iPad apps, including Keynote, DocsToGo, and SlideShark, that convert PowerPoint files to a readable format. If you plan to use Keynote, just open iCloud on your web browser, click the iWorks icon, and then click the Keynote tab. Click and drag the PowerPoint presentation file to the Keynote window. Then, on your iPad, tap open Keynote, and your presentation is available. Remember, you need an Internet connection to perform these operations.

Syncing the Presentation File via iTunes

Connect your iPad to your computer with the USB-to-dock connector cable that came with your iPad or use Wi-Fi syncing if you've turned that option on. Open iTunes and click the iPad tab in the upper right of the window. Go to the Apps tab and scroll down to the File Sharing section of the window. Apps that allow document transfer are listed in a pane on the left. Click the app you want, in this case Keynote, and then click the Add button at the bottom of the Documents pane on the right, as shown in Figure 5.3. Scroll through the directories and files in the Chooser that appears, or type the file name or kind (for example, "ppt" to find PowerPoint files or "key" for Keynote files) in the search field. When you find the document you want to transfer, click it; then click the Open button. Remember, if you want to select multiple files, hold the Shift key to select contiguous files or hold the Command key to select multiple noncontiguous files. Either way, click the Open button after you have selected the file or files you want to transfer to your iPad. When you finish selecting files, click the Sync button to move those files to your iPad.

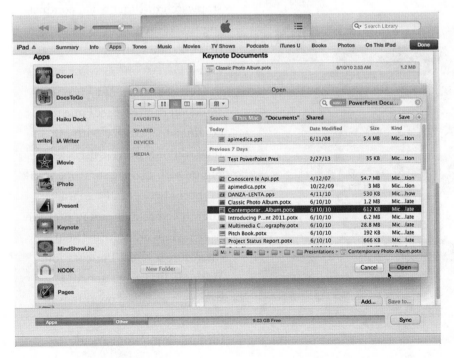

FIGURE 5.3
Sync presentation files from your computer to your iPad using iTunes.

Creating Presentation Elements with iPad's Preloaded Apps

Even without downloading presentation apps to your iPad, you can put together a slide show or play a video using the Photos app to show images you capture with the iPad's built-in camera, but don't limit your presentation imagination to the Photos app. Here, we give you ideas for using iPad's preloaded apps as part of your presentation.

- *Calendar.* Use the Week view to display a conference program or the Month view to plan and discuss deadlines. When dates are set, make the calendar public so the staff can access it from their iPads or computers.

- *Camera.* Capture and edit photos or video that you want to share with others. Use your iPad's camera on the spot to work with the audience or capture images you want to talk about.

FIGURE 5.4
FaceTime brings remote experts to your meeting.

- *Clock.* The world clock can kick off the event by showing the different locations and local times. Use the stopwatch or timer when conducting timed exercises in a classroom or workshop setting.

- *FaceTime.* As long as you have 3G or LTE cellular or Wi-Fi connection, you can use FaceTime to conduct a video chat with other iPad, iPhone, or Mac users (see Figure 5.4). Having someone speak to the audience via FaceTime is guaranteed to make an impression.

- *Maps.* Maps adds great visual interest to a Killer Presentation. With satellite views and 3-D images, you can show things like housing density, or land available for building or for agriculture, or directions of how to get from here to there.

- *Messages.* Anyone in the audience with an iPhone or iPad can send you messages during your presentation. Ask members of your audience to send questions to you during your presentation and then select those you want to answer.

- *Music.* Choose music to accompany your slide show from Photos. Tap the Slideshow button and then tap Play Music to the On position. Tap the Music button, which opens the Music app in a window within Photos. Choose the music you want to play during your slide show.

- *Newsstand.* Grab some of the latest headlines that relate to your presentation and show them to support your point of view.

- *Notes.* In the absence of a whiteboard, this is a great place to make to-do lists or record notes while in a meeting.

- *Photo Booth.* Liven up your meeting with Photo Booth photos or create images that you later use in another app. For example, the photo in Figure 5.5, created using the Mirror effect, could be used to introduce a collaboration idea playing on the phrase "Two heads are better than one."

- *Photos.* Here's where all your photos, videos, and screen captures end up. To use images from another app, create the image you want; then hold the Home button and On/Off button simultaneously to save a screen capture to Photos. If you use Photo Stream, you also have access to photos from your computer or other iOS devices. Take advantage of the Photos editing tools to rotate, crop, and correct your shots. Once all your desired images are saved in Photos, create an

FIGURE 5.5
Photo Booth lets you create funhouse-type photos to liven up your presentation.

album of the images you want to include in your slide show (see Figure 5.6), choose a transition style and background music, and let the show begin.

- *Reminders.* Make a list of all the tasks associated with your project; add deadlines, reminders, and notes about who's responsible; and then refer back to the Reminders to make a status update.
- *Safari.* Your iPad's web browsing app is the gateway to websites that you want to view during your presentation. If you use iCloud, you can access bookmarks from Safari on your computer (as long as you turn on that feature on both your iPad Settings and your computer's iCloud preferences). Save web pages you want to display in the Reading List and then view them whether you're online or offline.

To keep the presentation running smoothly, open the apps you plan to use in your presentation before beginning and then switch between them as needed by quickly pressing the Home button twice, revealing the open Apps bar, which allows you to switch between apps without returning to the Home screen.

FIGURE 5.6
Photos works in a pinch to create and display simple slide show presentations.

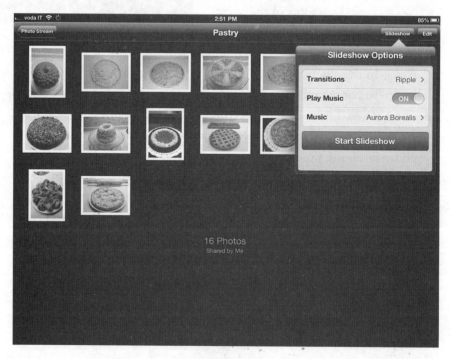

Presentation Apps You Can Download to Your iPad

PowerPoint isn't the only game in town anymore, hundreds of presentation apps are available for downloading to the iPad, and it seems more crop up every day. Some simply convert PowerPoint slides to a format that is viewable on the iPad, and others let you create linear presentations or more sophisticated multimedia HTML5 presentations. At the end of this section, we've included a chart to help you choose the app or apps that best suit your needs.

What You Need to Know About Cloud Servers

Before we turn our attention to the apps that will help you build a Killer Presentation, we want to say a few words about cloud servers. Although some apps mentioned here give you the option of syncing slides or presentations from your computer to your iPad with iTunes, most support cloud servers, and we encourage you to work that way. It's an easier, cleaner way to transfer files, and you always have a backup. Essentially, create presentation files and elements on your computer and upload them to the app-specific cloud server or a remote storage service such as DropBox or Google Drive. Then access the cloud through the app on your iPad and download the presentation. That way, even if you don't have an Internet connection when you make your presentation, you have your media. If you create a presentation on your iPad, you can send it in the other direction too, that is, back to the cloud to be accessed from your computer. Remember, cellular data transfers are limited to 50 MB, so you'll want to have Wi-Fi access when you access your presentations from the cloud service.

Cloud storage gives many people access to the same presentation, and so it is possible for someone in the home office to tweak the presentation to reflect up-to-the-second information and upload the presentation to the cloud while you're traveling to the client's office with your iPad in tow. Download the revised presentation and show up to the client with the most accurate, current information available.

Because they support cloud computing, most of these apps require you to set up a username and account before you can begin using them. We're not crazy about having yet another password to remember, but with online access, usernames and passwords are unavoidable. The plus side is receiving e-mail about new features and app updates.

And now, here are the promised apps that combine creativity and technology to help you create your iPad presentation.

iPRESENT

Free one-month trial; $21 to $50 per month per user subscriptions
http://www.ipresent.com
iPresent takes sales presentation software to a new level. It combines output from traditional presentation media, such as PowerPoint slides, PDF files, and video, and lets the user create gesture-driven menus to navigate seamlessly between the various types of media. Presenters get the best of both worlds—professionally designed interfaces that make it really easy to tell a story, combined with a custom look achieved in just a few minutes.

The biggest difference between iPresent and other presentation tools such as Keynote or Powerpoint is that iPresent encourages you to break up your content into many different areas, any of which you can navigate to quickly and easily. The presenter engages the audience, especially in smaller meetings, and can dynamically respond to audience questions, requests for clarification, or details on an interesting point—digressions that often disrupt and sometimes destroy a conventional presentation.

If your company offers many products or services with literally thousands of variations, you customize your presentation so that you talk about a specific variant in more detail depending on the questions the audience raises. iPresent holds a collection of information from which you pick and choose appropriately, leaving your audience with specific, relevant information and avoiding information overload. Each presentation, while starting from a common point of departure, evolves into a personalized interaction between presenter and audience, resulting in an informed and satisfied audience.

We spoke with Phil Lenton, CEO of iPresent, who gave us some history and insight: "When we started to formulate the ideas for iPresent in early 2011, we were in the privileged position of having worked already with some great forward-looking companies that use the iPad as a premium sales tool. We saw common themes emerging and built iPresent with the following objectives in mind:

- "The need for an interface that was rich, beautiful, gesture-driven—in short, one that felt 'Apple'-y enough to live up to being on an Apple device.
- "The need for access—all the time, not just when connected to the Internet—to a wide range of different material for the salesperson to have at their disposal.
- "The need for companies to be able to frequently update their material; the freshest presentations are always the best. When you present up to date material your audience know you're taking them seriously."

iPresent responds to the needs of twenty-first-century presenters by supporting rich HTML5 content without leaving behind the often necessary, twentieth-century presentation tools such as video, slides, and PDF files to generate interactive, creative content that really wows an audience.

iPresent goes beyond the traditional speaker-audience presentation scenarios with three creative ways for sharing and showing presentations: Kiosk Mode for self-service use; iPresent Multicast, a mechanism for sharing your iPresent screen with many other iPads, in the same room and remotely; and the possibility of e-mailing content from the app.

iPresent provides the right balance of central control, with the corporate office generating presentations while giving the individual salespeople a chance to shine, to be creative and responsive to the audience with the freedom to move around but within a structure designed and approved by the company they work for. Information comes down from corporate quickly and seamlessly, but the Briefcase feature enables users to integrate personalized content and presentations with the company content, all in one package.

Phil Lenton also let us in on some of the plans for new features for iPresent:

- Companion phone app—content, interactive slide controller
- More platforms—Windows 8 tablets, Android tablets, even more conventional access for Macs and PCs through the browser
- Data forms
- Easier ways to build interactive HTML5 content
- More menu customization

After you set up your account, you can begin building your presentation. iPresent refers to the visuals that accompany your presentation as a Content Set, which comprises resources that include the document, slide, spreadsheet, graphic, audio files, and video files. iPresent offers menu templates in several different styles: carousel, dock, and scrolling tiles among them. You choose a menu design that correlates with your business message and then add your logo, color scheme, and background image. The carousel menu works best for about six headings, while others, such as the tile menu, provide space for larger quantities. In a nutshell, first you upload resources (your media files) or a URL to your iPresent account; next you build the content set using one of the menu templates and then link resources to the menu items.

You, or members of your sales team, log in to the corporate account from the iPresent app. The content set appears, and you simply tap it to download. The spinning gear begins to turn, letting you know files are being downloaded. iPresent gives you an ETA for the download time, which we find to be a fantastic feature—you know if you have time to run to the water cooler; or if you're downloading just minutes before your presentation, you know if you have to stall while your content appears. Once the content set is on your iPad, you can view it directly on the iPad screen or connect your iPad to a projection system.

Following are two examples of how companies are using iPresent.

In the first example, a worldwide event producer has a large number of salespeople responsible for selling exhibition space, advertising, and sponsorship for their many events. These salespeople have a wealth of information available, including videos, PowerPoint files, case studies, and ROI calculators, that they can use in presenting to potential customers. They also need up-to-date

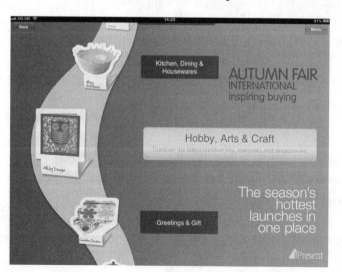

FIGURE 5.7 With iPresent, presentations are customized for each client.

information, as availability on specific events can change on a daily basis. iPresent enables the sales force to organize content in a far better way, ensuring that potential customers aren't subjected to long sequences of standard presentations but instead are shown content relevant to them. (See Figure 5.7.)

In our second example, the executive board and senior management teams of a global airline company have extensive, mostly confidential, information to evaluate at their monthly meetings. Historically, board members would be e-mailed documents, which were then printed and carried around. Any last-minute changes or new documents had to be resent and reprinted. Now the company uses iPresent to prepare extensive "board packs" prior to each meeting. Access to all the content can be carefully controlled, and last-minute changes can be easily pushed out to everyone. The content in iPresent is carefully arranged to match the agenda, and so attendees can spend more time focusing on making strategic decisions and less time trying to find documents.

KEYNOTE

$9.99

http://www.apple.com

For creating presentations on your iPad, Keynote is hard to beat. Apple describes Keynote as "the most powerful presentation app ever designed for a mobile device." A bold claim that's absolutely true in our humble opinions. Keynote was built from scratch for the iPad (and other iDevices), so it's easy to create compelling presentations complete with high-end features

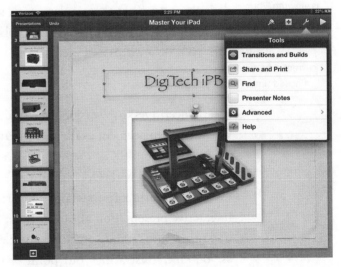

FIGURE 5.8 With a feature set similar to that of PowerPoint, Keynote lets you create elegant presentations entirely on your iPad.

like animations, transitions, and builds. While the feature set is similar to PowerPoint's, the user experience is pure Apple. (See Figure 5.8.) Keynote is a Swiss Army arsenal for presentations and will do more to make you

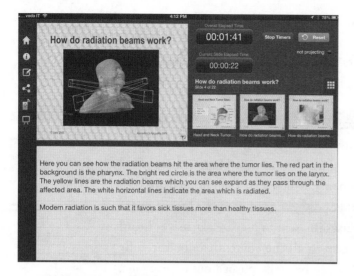

FIGURE 5.9
The Presenters Display lets you see the slide your audience is viewing, your presenter's notes, plus your choice of the current time or elapsed time.

look good than any other app we know of.

You can run your presentation in full-screen view and present right from your iPad or use video mirroring to present on an HDTV. There's even a Presenter's Display so you can preview your slides and notes on your iPad screen while you display the appropriate slide to your audience. (See Figure 5.9.)

If you're a Windows user or use PowerPoint on the Mac, you'll be happy to know that both the iPad and Mac versions of Keynote can import most PowerPoint presentations with little or no loss of functionality.

To make working with Keynote even easier, many developers and designers offer Keynote templates for a small fee. Download the templates app, choose one, and you need only replace the text and image placeholders with your own words and pictures.

DOCERI

Free; Doceri Desktop version, free trial, $30 single-site license. Stylus and watermark replacement available for purchase
http://doceri.com

We're impressed with Doceri's fun, creative user interface. This is a great resource in both corporate and educational classroom settings. Build an interactive presentation ahead of time; or because Doceri is so simple to use, turn your iPad into an electronic blackboard and "write on the board" as you talk, illustrating your point or jotting down questions and comments from the people in the audience while facing them.

One of our favorite features is the proprietary timeline tool, which lets you move back and forth in the presentation by sliding your finger along the timeline (see Figure 5.10). Instead of tapping "Undo" 15 times or erasing, just drag the slider back to the point where you want to start over.

To make a screencast, create your presentation and then record your voice-over separately. Move the timeline tool to the point where you want to insert the voice-over, and if you make a mistake, rerecord pieces as needed rather than starting from the beginning. You can also share your presentation or screencast. For example, if there were exercises or homework problems during your presentation or workshop, students could download them on their computers or iPads at home and work on them.

FIGURE 5.10
Use Doceri's timeline tool to undo whatever you did by sliding back in time.

Add Doceri Desktop to your computer to display your presentation on your computer screen while managing it from your iPad. This also lets you run PowerPoint and Keynote presentations and write on top of them with Doceri's different pen tools. If you have a classroom with a computer at each desk, put Doceri Desktop on each computer; your students or participants see your presentation on the screen, while you see the presentation along with the presentation tools on your iPad. There's a one-time site license fee associated with Doceri Desktop (after the initial trial period), but if you find yourself using Doceri, Doceri Desktop is probably a good addition to the package.

PERSPECTIVE

Free app; fee-based publishing
http://pixxa.com/perspective
Perspective gives you a new... umm... perspective on presenting by turning your data into a story (see Figure 5.11). Granted your data are interesting to you, but making them interesting to your audience is the challenge for all presenters. Perspective takes a traditional slide presentation style and adds color and animation to your mind-numbing, stale charts and graphs.

FIGURE 5.11
Perspective searches for appropriate copyright-free images based on your text.

We love that you can build your story directly on your iPad. The user interface is clean and takes full advantage of iPad technology; rather than trying to recreate how things are done on a computer, Perspective's tools are original yet intuitive. To create your story, tap the Add button and then select a scene that fits the information you want to share. To add graphics or images, Perspective accesses Photos on your iPad, or you can conduct an image search. When we tried Perspective and built the first scene of our story with the title "Presentation Success," Perspective offered a selection of related photos found on the Internet—and did it in an incredibly fast response time. You can integrate existing data from Excel, CSV, or PDF files and add a voice-over so viewers can listen to your story even when you can't be there to tell it.

PREZI

iPad version free with all licenses

http://www.prezi.com

Prezi has received a lot of positive press for its innovative design and free-form presentation style—there's nothing linear about Prezi. If traditional presentations are like a train on the track, each car pulling the next, Prezi presentations are like a painting, a cloud here, a tree over there, a river flowing through the woods. And when you step back, you see the complete picture; and the farther you step back, the more of the picture you see. The iPad version is more limited than the desktop version; it only lets you use text and photos, and there isn't a way to link the frames. The best way to take full advantage of Prezi is to create presentations on your computer and then access them through the cloud service. Aside from the original, free-form design, one of the biggest advantages of Prezi is the number of training and learning resources available on the website. You can even sign up for a webinar to learn how to use Prezi, which is probably your second best learning tool for making presentations (this book being your first!).

If any app here encourages you to go bulletless, it's Prezi. This is more of an intellectual challenge than a tip, but try to create at least one presentation without any bullets. Steve Jobs never used bullets, and he was one of the greatest presenters of our time... so why not try it yourself? It makes you think differently about what the audience sees and might be just what your presentation needs. (See Figure 5.12.)

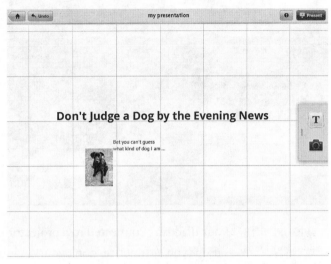

FIGURE 5.12 Create simple text and image Prezi presentations on the iPad.

SLIDEROCKET

Free

http://App.sliderocket.com

You must set up an account on the SlideRocket.com site before you can access SlideRocket on your iPad. SlideRocket is a user-friendly app and website with a smorgasbord of features. You can upload existing PowerPoint or PDF files or create a new presentation on your computer using a SlideRocket template and theme or something you design on your own. Remember, "themes" are the colors, typefaces, and graphic style, and "templates" are the layouts of the elements in the presentation. All these options let you mold and bend a presentation to your liking.

SLIDESHARK

Free with fee-based upgrade options

http://www.slideshark.com

Create your presentations in PowerPoint on your computer and then transfer them to your iPad by uploading or e-mailing them to the secure SlideShark server from your computer or accessing them from a cloud service (SlideShark

FIGURE 5.13
SlideShark reads your PowerPoint files and has great presenter options.

works with the most popular). SlideShark converts your Power-Point file (including hyperlinks) to a SlideShark file, which you then download to your iPad. Use common playback controls and gestures to view your presentation. There are two on-screen timers that are really handy: one shows the elapsed presentation time, and one shows how long the current slide has been open. Being able to use these tools when your iPad isn't connected to a projector is helpful for practicing your presentation (you *do* practice, don't you?). A built-in laser pointer appears when you press and hold on the screen. (See Figure 5.13.)

SlideShark lets you share a link to your presentation so it can be watched online on demand. Built-in analytics track who's watching and where, which helps you measure your client base and the effectiveness of your presentation. The team version of SlideShark is a good option if you have multiple people giving the same presentation. Each member has a personal folder, while the administrator manages shared content. Again, built-in analytics show which presentations are being used most.

2SCREENS—PRESENTATION EXPERT

$4.99; 2Screens Remote, $2.99
http://www.elpstudio.net/2screens/pe/about.html

2Screens offers PDF or PowerPoint file access and web access along with whiteboard creation. Access your PDF or PowerPoint files from several cloud storage services and then store your files locally or leave them in the original remote location. Write on top of your traditional slide presentation or even a web page accessed through the app, or open a whiteboard to illustrate a point to your audience or brainstorm with your team (see Figure 5.14). Notes are saved with the relevant presentation so you find them the next time you give that presentation. There are some nice graphic functions for creating a whiteboard presentation directly on your iPad too.

The strength of 2Screens lies in seamlessly switching between your presentation, websites, and the whiteboard during your presentation; and if you're an iPhone user, the companion app, 2Screens Remote, turns your iPhone into a remote control. The file structure is straightforward, so finding the item you want to switch to is quick and is invisible to your audience. 2Screens nicely blends traditional presentation and new media.

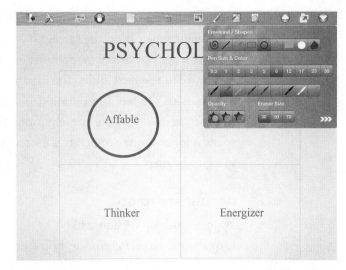

FIGURE 5.14
Emphasize a point by writing directly on your 2Screens presentation.

If you use PDF files to make your presentation, check out PDF Splicer (free with ads, $4.99 without); this nifty app could be a huge time-saver. You can cut pages from your PDF files or merge two PDF files together.

PRESENTATION NOTE

Free, lite version; $4.99, full version
http://www.doxout.com
We like Presentation Note because it's one of the few apps that doesn't ask you to create a username and password since your files, although processed by Presentation Note, are stored locally. You can transfer PowerPoint or PDF files through various cloud services, and icons on the Presentation Note home screen automatically connect the app to your preferred cloud service. If your computer and iPad are on the same network, log in to the Presentation Note server from your browser and upload files directly from your computer; then download them directly to your iPad.

Presentation Note assumes you'll connect your iPad to a projection system, and so the presentation controls—a slide counter, timer, laser, and slide Advance and Back buttons—reside at the top of the screen at all times. A marker icon opens a whiteboard on top of your slide so that you can explain something from your iPad. We appreciate the enhanced laser pointer options: your finger can be a dot or tail, which is active only while your finger is on the screen; or it can create a line, which underlines text or images or draws arrows or circles that remain on the screen until you move to the next slide. The capability to use your iPhone as a remote control with the free Presentation Note Remote app is a handy addition. If you're new to making presentations from your iPad and don't want to spend a lot of money or create a user account, Presentation Note is a good place to begin.

DOCUMENTS TO GO

$9.99; Premium Version, $16.99
http://www.dataviz.com/dtg_home.html

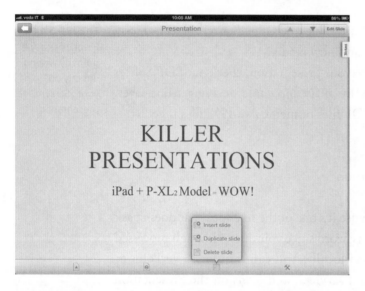

If you rely heavily on the MS-Office productivity suite, Documents To Go is extremely useful since it lets you view, edit, and create MS-Office documents, including PowerPoint. (See Figure 5.15.) The editing is limited for PowerPoint, but in a pinch you can change your text or add a slide at the last minute. The nice thing is that you work in the familiar PowerPoint environment. Docs To Go also lets you view PDF, iWork, and other file types. You can upload files to your iPad from various cloud storage servers, such as Dropbox and SugarSync, or via an iTunes connection; the changes you make will sync automatically between devices if you use the desktop version on your computer as well.

FIGURE 5.15 Documents To Go is the closest thing to PowerPoint on your iPad.

Keep in mind, if you plan on using cloud services to keep your presentations in sync, especially with iCloud, make sure you close your file on one device before opening it on another. If you make changes on one device, leave the file open, and then make changes on a different device, chances are you'll lose the changes you made on the first device.

If you're scratching your head and thinking, "These all sound great, which do I choose?" this chart should help you:

	Upload PowerPoint	Upload Keynote	Upload PDF	Create Presentations on Desktop	Create Presentations on iPad	View on Multiple iPads
2Screens	x		x		x	
Doceri	w/desktop version				x	
Documents To Go	x	x	x		x	
iPresent	x	x	x	x	x	x
Keynote	x	x	x	x	x	x
Perspective			x		x	
Presentation Note	x		x			
Prezi				x	limited	x
SlideRocket	x		x	x		x
SlideShark	x	x	x			x

The Technology Is the Tool...
Design Tips for Killer Visuals

We encourage you to use your iPad as more than a slide projector, but in the end, the iPad is a tool—a really great one—but still just a tool to get your message across. Technology can be a huge help, but the quantity of options can make you lose sight of the objective: getting your message across. The bottom line is to strive to make your content compelling and original by using the new tools that are available.

Although slides still form the basic element of most normal presentations, go beyond ho-hum text and stagnant graphics; integrate appropriate video and audio in your Killer Presentations. Keep the following in mind when creating your visuals, regardless of the app or technology you use to convey your message:

- Use a maximum of 40 words on each visual, preferably fewer.

- Use large, bold sans serif typefaces like Arial or Helvetica and not more than three different typefaces together.

- Use images such as charts, diagrams, illustrations, graphics, photos, and videos to communicate your points, themes, and messages rather than text alone.

- Wean yourself off templates or use them with caution. Choose templates that are simple and clean lined. Busy templates can be distracting, become tiresome during the course of the presentation, and occupy space that is better used to enlarge an image. Look at how Apple's Steve Jobs, Tim Cook, and others presented: just a plain white (or black) background, a few words, and a strong image.

- Use high-quality video and animations to better communicate key ideas, facts, concepts, and, yes, emotions. Animations that show a process, trend, or relationship are more effective than a static visual. Consider having a skilled videographer or multimedia person develop custom animations for important presentations.

- However, make sure your video isn't so amazing that the message is lost in the media.

- Limit the number of elements on your visual. Display an entire complex image and then show pieces of it on the subsequent slides. Some of the worst slides we've seen are charts that list studies or articles referenced in the presentation. Give the audience essential information and provide references on request.

- Each visual should make one point. The primary concept should jump out immediately. For example, showing a slide with a simple title and single image, a presenter might say, "This visual shows you the initial complex design of our older turbocharger. Just look at the 187 parts that are prone to wear and tear and malfunction. Here [next slide] see how we redesigned that equipment, which now has only 35 parts and is 68 percent more reliable and durable!"

■ Use brief, descriptive, catchy titles that encapsulate your visuals. Look at the difference between "Recovering Sales" and "Sales Are Rebounding Strongly" or between "Our New Product" and "Our Competition-Killing New XD5 Laser."

■ Keep it simple. Skip the elaborate transitions between slides (which take up time and are distracting). Just use cuts between slides. Stick to a few colors that work well together; avoid stark contrasts.

■ If your app permits, you can use your fingers to expand or shrink the image on your iPad and move it around so people can better see what you want them to. Many apps have laser functions where touching the screen creates that focusing red dot that draws attention to the area. Some have a feature that lets you temporarily draw on the visual while you are presenting.

■ If not talking about the information on your visual, black it out until you are ready to bring it up again or move onto the next slide. We've yet to find an app that does this, and so your options are to:

▶ Cover the projector lamp.
▶ Put black slides at intervals where you know you take a break for questions or where you tell a story and you want the audience to focus its attention on you and not the screen.
▶ Add a hyperlink to a black slide and click the link when you want to go there; then click back to where you left off.

The blackout slide gives your audience a break from multiple sensory inputs and is a sign that a transition is taking place in the presentation, such as moving on to the Q&A time or handing off to another speaker.

■ Do *not* read any text on your slides word for word. Instead point to the line of text and conversationally explain in slightly different, more detailed words.

■ Be careful not to repeat the same phrase over and over. For instance, vary the way you introduce slides, such as "This slide shows…," and "Now here you will see…," and "Take a look at the chart in this slide…"

■ Tell stories, give vivid examples, share anecdotes, and engage your audience by asking for comments, feedback, opinions, and feelings about your topic. We recently saw a spellbinding presentation given by an engineer and complimented him on his presentation style afterward, intrigued by how he had honed his skill. We learned that acting was his hobby, and he used some of his stage tricks to keep his audience involved and interested. Consider hiring a speech coach or taking an acting course at your local community college to acquire skills that make you that compelling speaker.

Giving Your Presentation Without Tripping Over the Connector Cable

Now that your presentation is available on your iPad, you're probably anxious to show it off. You can view it on the iPad's fabulous screen, although this is realistically practical only when you have one or two people looking over your shoulder. A better way to show your presentation to a larger audience is to connect your iPad to a projector, HDTV, or computer monitor, either via cables or Wi-Fi. In Chapter 7, we discuss apps that give you a third option, which is to broadcast your presentation to iPads that your viewers hold in their hands.

Apple offers a variety of cables and adapters that let you "mirror" your iPad's screen on a larger one. This means that what you see on your iPad appears on the big screen. Presentation apps take mirroring one step further. They show your presentation on the big screen, but you see extra tools such as a timer, presentation notes, and thumbnail images of your entire slide show on your iPad.

Here we give you the information you need to determine the type of cables and connectors you'll want to keep in your equipment bag, and we also give you tips for walking around the stage or conference table.

Connecting Your iPad to a Projector or HDTV

To choose the correct cable, determine which version of iPad you have and what kind of projector or monitor you'll be connecting to. Use the composite AV Cable ($39), 30-pin to VGA Adapter ($29), and 30-pin Digital AV Adapter ($39) for second- and third-generation iPads with 30-pin dock connectors as well as the Lightning to VGA Adapter ($49) and Lightning Digital AV Adapter ($49) for the iPad mini and fourth-generation iPad. Older TVs and projectors are likely to offer VGA or composite inputs but not digital HDMI ports; newer projectors and HDTVs are likely to offer digital HDMI inputs and may also sport VGA and composite video ports.

There are a couple of downsides to cable solutions. The first, which affects all of the above, is that you're tethered to your iPad by a rather short cable. Wouldn't you rather be free to move about with your iPad in your hand? The second drawback applies only to VGA adapters: video purchased from the iTunes Store will generate the dreaded "Connected display is not authorized" error if you try to view it via any of the VGA adapters.

A better, albeit somewhat more expensive and technically challenging, solution is to use a $99 Apple TV (see Figure 5.16), a little black box that lets you wirelessly stream what's on your iPad screen to any HDTV or projector

FIGURE 5.16
Stream what's on your iPad screen to an HDTV or video projector with Apple TV. (Photo courtesy of Apple, Inc.)

that has at least one HDMI port. Apple's AirPlay technology, which is baked into most Apple devices, is what makes it possible. And like so much of what Apple does, it (usually) just works.

If that sounds awesome, it is. The freedom of moving around while maintaining full control of your video and audio is a rush, and we can't recommend it highly enough. Of course, this is what we use when we present, if possible.

But before you get too excited, here's what you'll need (in addition to your iPad) to make it happen:

- An Apple TV ($99)
- A Wi-Fi (802.11a, g, or n) network
- An HDTV or video projector with an available HDMI port

In a perfect world you'd bring all of the above and more to every presentation. There's no substitute for testing, and if you own it, you can test it at your convenience. However, you'll sometimes have to rely on services provided by the venue. Fortunately, many typical meeting spaces, like hotels, convention centers, meeting rooms, classrooms, board rooms, and such, are equipped with gear that fulfills both the network and video requirements; just show up with your iPad, an Apple TV, and an HDMI cable, and you're good to go.

A less expensive solution is to download AirServer (free seven-day trial, $15 for lifetime use on five computers) to your computer. This handy software turns your computer into an AirPlay server. Connect your computer to the HDTV or projector and then tap the AirPlay button on your iPad. Wireless iPad use was never so simple.

If you use a Mac running Mac OS X 10.8 (Mountain Lion) or later, you can use AirPlay to stream your Mac screen to your Apple TV. This is huge, especially if you want to use a laptop and an iPad at different times in your presentation. And it's easy to switch from one to the other and back again without missing a beat.

When it comes to Internet access or Wi-Fi bandwidth, always expect the worst. If your presentation needs Internet access, consider bringing your own. Apple's AirPort Express ($99) is a powerful dual-channel Wi-Fi router that can be set up and administered from your iPad. Or consider renting or buying a 4G hotspot from any wireless carrier. Both fourth-generation iPads and iPhone 5s or later with 4G can act as a wireless hotspot for up to five devices. A 4G hotspot can be as fast as Wi-Fi and just as reliable, but remember that you're paying for the data you consume.

To check your iPad's data usage, tap Settings > General > Usage > Cellular Usage; to enable the personal hotspot feature, tap Settings > Cellular Data > Personal Hotspot.

Using a Personal Projector

As far as video projectors are concerned, neither of us owns one. We've found adequate projection equipment available at just about every venue we've presented in. And more and more facilities these days offer digital (HDMI) input in addition to (or instead of) VGA. While it is easy for us to recommend Apple TV and AirPort Express, which are tiny and inexpensive, you're on your own if you want a video projector, although we have listed suggestions in the Resources. We are intrigued by the pico projectors, which weigh less than a pound and cost under $500. We suggest reading all the reviews you can find and buying from a vendor with at least a two-week return policy and no restocking fee. Then, if the system doesn't perform to your liking, you can take it back and get a refund or try a different model.

Bringing Your Own Audio

Another consideration is audio. Your presentation may include theme or ambient music or video soundtracks. And the audience needs to be able to hear your voice clearly. If the venue has its own sound reinforcement (as many do), it will provide a microphone, but you're responsible for connecting your iPad (or laptop) to the house sound system. VGA connections don't support audio, so if you're using VGA, you'll need to connect your iPad (or laptop) with a cable from its headphone jack to the sound system. HDMI supports audio and video so you won't usually need a separate cable for audio when you're using it. Still, it's not a bad idea to pack an audio cable in your bag of tricks, just in case.

Hardware in hand, keep in mind these tips for glitch-free connections on the day of your presentation:

- *Master your tools.* We have a tendency to dive right in and start using new apps without bothering to RTFM (read the fine manual). That's OK; we understand. But after the thrill wears off a little, you'll be rewarded many times if you take the time to check out the built-in help, watch the tutorial videos, and visit the developer's website to learn about great features, free bonus content, and time-saving techniques.
- *Test everything before you leave your home or office.* Before you walk out, check that you've packed everything you will need.
- *Plan for Murphy's law.* Whatever can go wrong, will. Pack spares for everything you can. Pack a spare dock or Lightning connector cable and video adapter. We've often had to resort to plan B after arriving at a venue where the equipment wasn't what we expected. We carry an assortment of cables and adapters, even ones we probably won't need.
- *Charge your rechargeable devices before, during, and after your show.* Of course, you want your iPad fully charged at the beginning of any presentation. But if you're also using other rechargeable devices like wireless speakers, iPhones, or a Bluetooth keyboard or headset, make sure they're fully charged, too.
- *Turn on Find My iPad, the built-in feature that can locate a misplaced iPad and display its current location on a map and that also can remotely send it a message, lock it, or erase your personal information.* If you wait until your iPad is misplaced, it's too late. So turn that locator on now before you forget. You'll thank us someday. Tap Settings, tap iCloud, and then tap Find My iPad so its switch is *on*.

Handling Your iPad While You Present

Take it from us—using your iPad in a natural, unobtrusive, and poised fashion while maintaining eye contact and connecting with the audience, takes practice. You'll hear us say it again and again, but if a presentation is worth giving, it's worth practicing until you get it right.

If you're using a wired solution, you won't want to move your iPad around much, if at all, because you risk disconnecting the video cable, which isn't at all pretty. Most HDTVs and projectors take anywhere from a few seconds to a minute or more to restore video after disconnection. And nothing will stop your presentation momentum faster than 30 seconds of dead air.

Dozens of different iPad stands are available. Coauthor Bob has tested more than a dozen, and several stand out:

iKlip Studio (http://www.ikmultimedia.com, $29.99), from IK Multimedia, is an adjustable tabletop stand aimed at musicians who need to keep their iPads stable in the recording studio or on stage. It folds flat and is made of lightweight, shock-resistant thermoplastic, so it's easy to transport. It has rubber footpads to prevent your iPad from unwanted sliding, and its design makes it easy to switch from landscape to portrait. (See

FIGURE 5.17
iKlip Studio is a sturdy, inexpensive desktop iPad stand. (Photo courtesy of IK Multimedia)

Figure 5.17.) The same company also makes iKlip ($39.99), an adjustable iPad holder for microphone stands.

In addition to holding your iPad steady, it's perfect for turning your iPad into a teleprompter; just mount the camera on a mic stand and mount the iKlip below the camera lens. Several teleprompter apps are available such as Teleprompt+ for iPad ($14.99), PrompterPal ($4.99), and ProPrompter ($9.99), all of which can be downloaded from the App Store. Best Prompter Pro ($3.99) lets you record yourself so you can practice and play back.

Another solid desktop stand is the NuGuard GripStand GripBase bundle (http://www.newertech.com, $59.99), which includes a pair of interchangeable stands: a sturdy weighted base and a smaller foldout stand that doubles as a handle for carrying or hanging your iPad. (See Figure 5.18.)

Perhaps the most utilitarian option is ZeroChroma's Vario-SC (http://www.zerochroma.com, $49.95), which combines a rotating 11-position stand that folds flat when not being used and a sturdy protective case that can be combined with an Apple Smart Cover for additional protection.

The Vario-SC, unlike the other stands we've discussed, is something you'll put on your iPad and leave on forever, so there's nothing extra to pack, carry, or lose. It's the case Bob uses with his iPad even when he's not presenting. (See Figure 5.19.)

FIGURE 5.18 GripBase (*left*) and GripStand (*right*) offer flexible options for securing your iPad when you speak.
(Photo courtesy of Newer Technology)

FIGURE 5.19
The Vario-SC combines a stand and an iPad case; once you put it on, you'll never want to take it off.
(Photo courtesy of ZeroChroma)

Sanity Check: Is the iPad the Best Tool for the Job?

At some point in the presentation planning process, you'll need to determine what (if any) video, audio, computing, and connectivity gear you'll need to support your show. While this book is about Killer Presentations with your iPad, remember that your iPad is not mandatory for every presentation. There are going to be times when, for whatever reason, a laptop will be a better choice than an iPad. There will also be times when an iPad is a better choice than a laptop. In many (or most) cases, a combination of laptop and iPad will help you deliver the most compelling presentation.

As a sanity check, before you even start to consider which devices to use for a presentation, consider the pros and cons.

Laptop (or even desktop) computers have a proven track record when it comes to presenting. We'd venture that the majority of presentations you've seen in your lifetime involved some version of PowerPoint running on a Mac or PC laptop. As a result, you'll usually find more resources available for a laptop than for an iPad. If you're presenting in a public space, you'll have a better chance of finding help to connect a laptop than to connect an iPad. Our experience has been that if you show up with a laptop, someone there will be familiar with connecting it to the projection and sound systems. Finally, if anything happens to your laptop, there's a better chance of finding a replacement for it than an iPad. Show up with an iPad, however, and you're probably on your own when it comes to getting it up and running, connecting it to the venue's audio and video gear, or finding a replacement if necessary.

Another consideration is that most laptops offer a variety of ports and slots, providing a myriad of options when it comes to peripherals and data. For example, if your presentation includes streaming video, a laptop's Ethernet port provides faster and more reliable Internet access than any wireless connection. The iPad, with a single proprietary connector—either a dock or Lightning connector depending upon your iPad's vintage—limits you to peripherals designed for the iPad and certain USB devices (using Apple's Lightning to USB Camera Adapter or Apple iPad Camera Connection Kit, available for $29 each). Furthermore, with iPad storage topping out at 64 GB, you may not have enough free space for a media-heavy presentation.

The bottom line: don't present with an iPad just because you can. Do it to add dramatic flair and the sense of the unexpected to your show. Consider the technical challenges you'll face and ask yourself whether it's worth it. If the answer isn't an enthusiastic yes, you might want to leave the iPad out of this particular presentation.

CHAPTER 6

Expert's Corner: Advanced Ideas and Tips for Killer iPad Presentations

Now that you understand the basics of using your iPad as your tool for giving presentations, we're going to introduce you to the enhancement apps. We review apps that help you create media on your iPad. We've divided the chapter by category so you can easily find what you need most. Remember, these apps help you create visuals—charts, enhanced photos, videos, voice-overs, animation—that you can then insert as part of your presentation.

117

The end of this chapter presents a Q&A with coauthor Bob LeVitus, who shares his technical expertise about all things iPad. Glance through this section to find answers to your questions and to learn advanced tips that can help you avoid problems that may come up in the future.

Using Media-Creation Apps on Your iPad

The App Store holds millions of iPad apps. To narrow our choices, we checked the release dates and chose only apps that had been updated or released within the last year. We made sure there was an active website so you can contact the developer in the event of a problem with the app (although you will want to double-check since, as we all know, URLs can sometimes change or disappear). We considered the ratings and reviews, reading them with a critical eye to make sure that unsatisfied users hadn't expected more than the app claims offer. We looked at the user interface and picked apps that we like. Of course, these criteria are subjective; your aesthetic preferences and needs could be different from ours. For example, since we're writers and not sketch artists, we tend toward apps that enhance our drawing skill rather than give us free rein.

The following sections are presented in the order that you might use the apps to create a presentation: from planning to making charts to photo manipulation and animation. Don't limit yourself to the apps we present here. Make sure you stroll the aisles of the App Store and read reviews from some of the tech pubs and websites, as you're sure to find some that better suit your particular needs or that you find easier to use.

Brainstorming or Mind-Mapping Apps

Mind maps help us identify patterns in our thinking, link ideas, and find solutions to problems. Whether it's a sales presentation, a staff meeting, or a trade conference, the end result will be better if you have a plan before you begin. Creating a mind map can help you clarify your presentation ideas and create sequential links or hyperlinks between them, as well as identify the type, content, and media that will best support your message. We chose the following apps for their flexibility in mind-mapping style. All allow you to change the colors, shapes, and graphics used. You can work alone, or if you work on a team, hook your iPad up to a projector so everyone can see and contribute to the mind map; then share it via e-mail or a cloud server.

MINDMAPLE

Free, lite version; $4.99, full version

http://www.mindmaple.com

If you're new to mind mapping or want an easy-to-use app, MindMaple could be a good choice. Create the first, central cell. Then all you need to do is drag your finger out of it to create subcells, or "children"; and from those, drag your finger to create more subcells, or tangent "sibling" cells. When in view, the toolbar runs down the side of the screen, and tapping the relevant tool lets you add a note, task information such as the deadline or responsibilities, or a callout to a specific cell, as well as set up relationships or boundaries. If you want to share the map with others, make sure they have the free MindMaple Viewer app so they can open and view the file.

MINDOMO

Free (three maps); $6 a month for single user, unlimited maps and other goodies, special corporate and education pricing—see the website for details

http://www.mindomo.com

Mindomo offers a built-in presentation mode, which means the mind map is the visual of your presentation. You can also use Mindomo to plan your presentation and then create the presentation itself in another app. A neat feature of Mindomo is the ability to store your mind map on a cloud server and provide a direct link to share it with others. The Mindomo website gives great mind-mapping tips, and we paraphrase a few here:

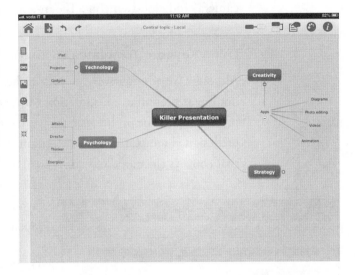

FIGURE 6.1
Before creating any media, plan your presentation using an app like Mindomo.

- Make your desired outcome or call to action the center of the map; everything else on the mind map leads to that outcome either directly or sequentially (see Figure 6.1).
- Use a mind map to support your talk. Your audience will appreciate seeing the entire context at once.
- Start in the upper right corner and work clockwise through your topics or messages.
- Use sections and subsections to break down information, tasks, and facts.

DROPMIND

Free (three maps with limited features), $11.99

http://dropmind.com/pricing/ipad

DropMind is a powerful mind-mapping tool, especially if you work with a team and want an app that's integrated with a desktop and web-based version. The desktop version also offers integration with MS-Office. We appreciated the efficiency of the Next button on the keyboard, which quickly creates sibling cells as you think of them. Another feature we found helpful is the option to select multiple cells so you can color-code them at the same time rather than doing so one by one.

In addition to providing multiple views and sharing the map as an image, PDF, or DropMind (.dmmx) file or putting it on Facebook or Twitter, the full version also allows sharing as an outline, cloning to create another map, printing, inserting images from your Photos library and iPad camera, and cloud syncing. The in-app instructions are well written too.

Using Keynote Templates on Your iPad

Although we promote wowing your audience with a multimedia, interactive, nonlinear presentation, sometimes time or necessity dictates a sequential presentation. One of the easiest ways to create such a presentation is to use a predesigned template. With the options listed here, you can find a template that conveys the mood of your presentation and reflects your style. All offer template themes and then multiple slide layouts within each theme; you need only replace the text and image placeholders.

TEMPLATES FOR KEYNOTE

$1.99

http://www.no8ody.com

With 50 templates that each offer a selection of over 20 slides, Templates for Keynote gives you the biggest bang for your buck. We like the preview layout of the slides within each template—and then simply tapping Open takes you directly into Keynote. You can apply your own color scheme and typefaces or keep the ones provided.

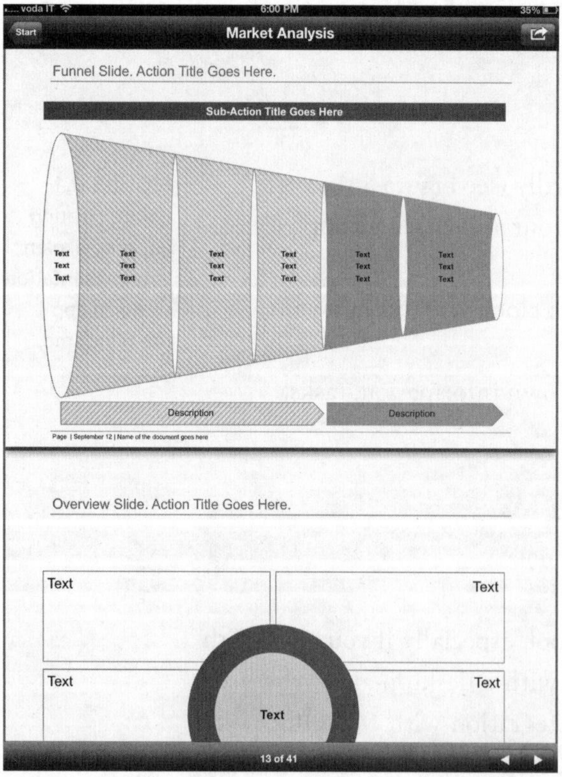

FIGURE 6.2 Templates for Keynote Pro suggests the type of text or image to put in the placeholder.

TEMPLATES FOR KEYNOTE PRO

$9.99

http://www.made-for-use.com/templates-for-keynote-pro.html

The 36 colorful, graphic templates come with more than 725 slides in all. We appreciate the descriptive placeholder text, which offers presentation advice such as "Brief and precise heading" or "This is the Action Title: Try to summarize your slide in one sentence here." (See Figure 6.2.) A variety of tables, charts, pictures, diagrams, and quotes are included.

TEMPLATES FOR POWERPOINT PRO

$9.99

http://www.made-for-use.com/templates-for-keynote-pro.html

Developed by the same company as Templates for Keynote Pro, these 10 templates provide more than 100 slide-ready graphics. The style is all business, and the templates can be imported to the mobile office suite app of your choice. Presentations are divided by context, such as marketing, consulting, sales, and research and development.

TEMPLATES FOR KEYNOTE PRESENTATIONS
AND TEMPLATES FOR POWERPOINT PRESENTATIONS

$3.99 each (if you use other iWork apps such as Pages and Numbers, you might want to purchase Templates for iWork for $7.99 instead)

These templates have built-in special effects like the "magic move" transition from one slide to the next and 3-D charts. The maps and infographics give some options that the other template apps don't have. If you use both PowerPoint and Keynote, a few PowerPoint-compatible templates are included with the Keynote version.

KEYNOTEZONE COLLECTION

$19.99

http://www.keynotezone.com/themes_ios/index.html

Don't be put off by the price; the templates in Keynote Zone Collection are original and edgy. On the website, you can view all 11 themes and the associated slides, along with a video showing the themes in action, before buying so that you know what you're getting. Considering the cost of

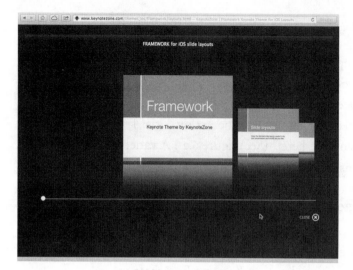

hiring a graphic designer, overall you may find this to be an economic solution to wow potential clients. (See Figure 6.3.)

FIGURE 6.3 View all the KeynoteZone Collection templates online before purchasing.

Apps That Create Diagrams, Charts, and Graphs

Charts and graphs always seem to find their way into presentations. The familiar, modular display of information helps our brains instantly grasp the concepts being communicated: pie charts visually show who or what is getting the bigger slice of the whole, a peak in a line graph can be cause for celebration or alarm, and bar charts make comparisons easy to understand. Diagrams, on the other hand, are where the fun begins. The apps here are creative powerhouses that provide stencils, which you put together to form flowcharts, objects, and instructional schematics.

In the App Store, you'll found a slew of specialized graphing and diagramming apps for creating Venn diagrams, Carroll diagrams, UML diagrams, flowcharts, graphs for tracking stock prices, graphs for analyzing Google Analytics, and depth and pressure graphs for petroleum professionals.

OMNIGRAPHSKETCHER AND OMNIGRAFFLE

$14.99 and $49.99, respectively
http://www.omnigroup.com/products/omnigraffle-ipad/
(See Figure 6.4.)

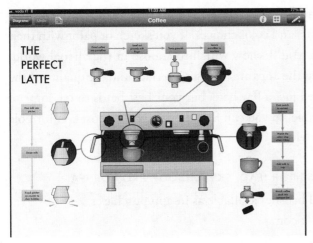

FIGURE 6.4 Create elegant diagrams with OmniGraffle's seemingly endless supply of stencils. (Image courtesy of OmniGroup)

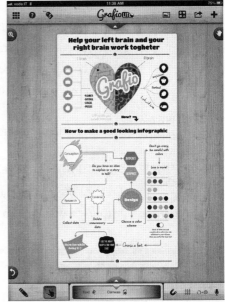

FIGURE 6.5 Create unique diagrams every time with Grafio's built-in shapes library. (Image courtesy of Grafio)

GRAFIO

Free, lite version; $8.99, full version

http://www.tentouchapps.com/grafio

(See Figure 6.5.)

VIDIA

$6.99

http://genarks.biz/Home-en.html

Sketching Apps

The beauty of apps is that if you want an app that's specific to your profession or your audience, chances are you'll find it. In this category, there are apps for engineers and architects as well as medical and automotive professionals, even shoe designers. The small selection here is the tip of the iceberg of sketching, drawing, painting, and designing apps. However, we sorted by rating to bring the top-rated apps to the top of the list and then pulled out those that we think would be useful for creating a presentation, since that's our focus.

FIGURE 6.6
Sketching in
SketchTime
comes close to
real sketching—
just pen, paper,
and an eraser.

All the sketching apps offer a selection of brushes, pens, and pencils in varying widths, weights, and color choices. If you sketch or paint with their physical counterparts, you'll know which to choose in the virtual world. What changes between the apps are the user interface and the quality of the image. We've suggested just a few here, but your best bet is to try some of the free versions available, so you can find the app you're most comfortable working and creating with.

SKETCHBOOK EXPRESS FOR IPAD, SKETCHBOOK PRO FOR IPAD

Free, $4.99; additional brushes available as in-app purchases
http://www.sketchbook.com

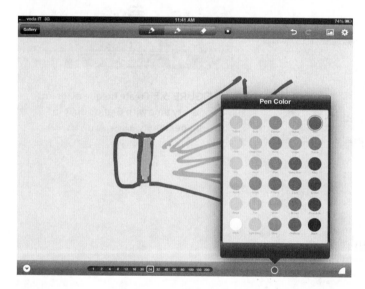

ICANVAS PRO

Free
http://www.satwebapps.com/
ic/wp/

SKETCHTIME

$1.99
http://sketchtimeapp.com
(See Figure 6.6.)

TOUCHDRAW

$8.99
http://elevenworks.com/home

Photo Editing and Enhancement Apps

You can simply use the Camera app that came with your iPad to capture photos and videos, which you then import to your presentation, or you can use any of the myriad apps for photo manipulation. Photo and Video is a category of its own in the App Store. We list just a few that have features we find particularly useful, but your needs, capabilities, preferences for aesthetics, and user interface may be, and probably are, different. Use our comments as a guide to think about what you need in a photo editing app.

SNAPSEED

Free

http://www.snapseed.com

Snapseed is probably the most advanced editing tool of the bunch, with capabilities far beyond what many apps that cost money offer. Its Auto Correct option seems to work better than others, including iPhoto's, making it perhaps the best one-click-fix tool. (See Figure 6.7.)

Most of the tools and filters work the same: just drag your finger up or down to select an option and drag left or right to increase and decrease the strength of the effect. And an omnipresent button lets you instantly compare your modifications with the original.

FIGURE 6.7
Snapseed is powerful, elegant, and easy to use.

PHOTOTOASTER

$1.99

http://www.eastcoastpixels.com/
  cgi-bin/product.php?p=4

For ease of use, PhotoToaster wins hands down. To begin, access the photo you want to edit from Photos and crop, rotate, straighten, and lighten your photo. Lighting brushes let you lighten or darken specific areas of a photo rather than the whole photo. Choose from dozens of global preset filters or edit the lighting, effect, vignette, texture, and border singly and build your own filter presets. The thumbnail images at the bottom of the screen show your selected photo with each effect in that category so you can compare side by side (see Figure 6.8). You can manually set the adjustments with sliders that increase or decrease the intensity of the effect.

FIGURE 6.8
See how each PhotoToaster filter affects your photo.

iPHOTO

$4.99

http://www.apple.com

Another excellent multipurpose photo editor is Apple's iPhoto. It gives you even more control over your retouching with brushes that paint adjustments where you need them and with edge detection to help you apply the corrections more precisely. (See Figure 6.9.)

Other useful tools include graduated filters, beautiful black-and-white conversion you adjust with a finger drag, vignette effects, a tilt-shift filter, and artistic effects including one that turns your photo into a vibrant watercolor.

FIGURE 6.9 iPhoto's brushes give you superb control over adjustments.

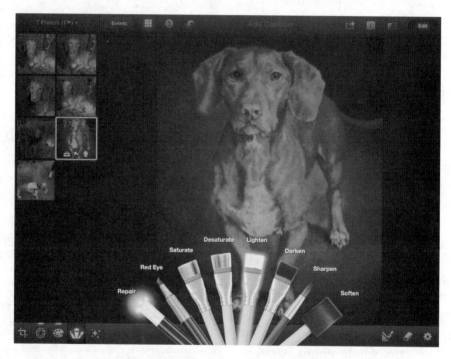

CAMERA PROFESSIONAL EFFECTS

Free; $0.99 to remove ads

http://freshtouch.us/index.php?id=2

This is really two apps in one: filters add special effects to your photos, and manual controls change your iPad into an SLR camera. The Quickshot function shoots rapid-fire photos without stopping to show you the photo you just took. The Slowshutter function lets you set the resolution, shutter speed, and sensitivity, which improves low-light photography; and with the Multishot function you set the number of frames per second and the number of frames you want to take. The countdown timer, useful when you want to put yourself in the picture, can be used on its own or in conjunction with the other functions. Overall for 99 cents, we think this is a pretty neat app for capturing cool images to add to your presentation.

ARTSTUDIO

$4.99

http://www.iphoneclan.com/artstudioipad/

If you're a Photoshop user, you may prefer ArtStudio, which includes a full-featured drawing and painting environment, layers, masks, and a comprehensive array of photo editing and compositing tools. ArtStudio is the most Photoshoplike graphics app we know of for the iPad.

Aside from photo editing, there are hundreds of photo filters available. Most have simple editing features such as panning, zooming, cropping, and rotating; and once your subject is in position, you apply a filter that may be an effect such as aging or pixelating, a color wash, an exposure setting, or an artistic effect, for example, turning your photo into a sketch or painting. Here are just a few we like:

INSTAGRAM

Free

http://www.instagram.com

GLAZE

Free; more filters available as in-app purchases

http://www.the11ers.com/glaze/press/

FX PHOTO STUDIO HD

$1.99

http://www.fxphotostudioapp.com

XNVIEW PHOTO FX

Free

http://www.xnview.com/mobile/

There's nothing to keep you from installing and using all the aforementioned apps and many more. Often one app does a particular task better than another app. And not all presets and templates are created alike. You may prefer the look of one app's options better than the same options in another app. Of course, you could buy every app mentioned for less than a decent dinner for one, so we recommend getting the ones that appeal to you so you have plenty of options when creativity strikes.

Video Capture and Editing

There can be much more to a presentation than just static slides and still images. A frequently seen and effective way of using video is creating an "endless-loop" presentation to occupy an audience's attention before a big

FIGURE 6.10
The precision editor makes it easy to edit clips accurately with your finger.

presentation, workshop, or speech. We usually prefer to create and edit audio and video on desktop computers with multiple displays, but there are times when it's necessary to create video or audio materials with our iPads. So here are just a few of the apps we've found useful for producing movies or soundtracks on iPads.

IMOVIE

$4.99

http://www.apple.com

Apple's iMovie delivers a lot of bang for five bucks. First and foremost, it provides a full-featured HD video editing environment that makes it possible to shoot and edit an entire movie production right on your iPad. You can add video, photos, music, and sound effects to your production; trim the length of individual clips; split clips; and create freeze frames quickly and easily. It even has a precision editor for frame-accurate editing! (See Figure 6.10.)

One of our favorite features is iMovie's "Instant Movie Trailers," which lets you create professional-looking movie trailers in just a couple of minutes.

As an aside, much like the template apps for Keynote and PowerPoint, there are apps that provide styles for iMovie too, such as Intro Designer for iMovie, Scrolling Credits, Extras for iMovie, and MovieDrops for iMovie—all available at the App Store.

CUTECUT

Free; $3.99 pro version

http://cutecut.mobivio.com

CuteCUT is a straightforward app for creating and editing a multimedia video—and no, that's not an oxymoron. You can combine video, still photos, text, and drawings you make within the app, your own music or in-app songs and effects, and voice-overs. Each element is a track or layer of your video. One of the features we found particularly useful is the pinch-and-spread gesture that can expand or compress the timeline so you find exactly the point you want to trim or sync with other tracks. Even dilettante videographers will find CuteCUT easy to use right from the start.

REELDIRECTOR

$1.99

http://www.nexvio.com

Another video editing app of note is ReelDirector, which also lets you edit video; reorder, trim, and split clips; add transitions, opening titles, and closing credits; and apply the Ken Burns effect to still photos to simulate motion. (See Figure 6.11.) The editing interface is straightforward, letting

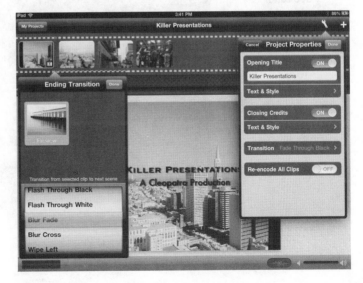

FIGURE 6.11
ReelDirector can automatically create your opening titles and closing credits.

you drag and drop clips to change their order. Trimming clips is also easy, so don't be afraid to let the camera keep rolling.

PINNACLE STUDIO

$12.99

http://www.pinnaclesys.com/

Pinnacle Studio is perhaps the most full-featured and capable video editor for the iPad. It's easy to use with a storyboard mode, in addition to a traditional timeline, and includes one of the best selections of high-quality transitions and effects we've seen. It also includes animated and static titles that are as good as any we've seen, and they look great on the big screen. (See Figure 6.12.)

Pinnacle Studio has a montage mode unlike any other we've come across. Just drag photos onto the template, and the app generates a great-looking animated montage.

FIGURE 6.12
Pinnacle Studio is probably the most advanced video editor on the iPad.

ACTION MOVIE FX

Free with two effects; in-app purchase for more special effect packs at $0.99 each

http://www.actionmoviefx.com

There are thousands of iPad apps that work with video. And while many of them are amateurish or just plain dumb, some, like Action Movie FX, are gems for presenters. Action Movie FX lets you add big-budget Hollywood-style special effects to video shot with your iPad.

Think about trying this: Create a prop box that says "The Competition" and shoot a few seconds of video of it. Now add the Action Movie FX of a giant boulder dropping onto it and crushing it. Add a voice-over that says, "The power to crush the competition," and you've got 10 seconds of video that's sure to make the point. And since the effects are HD, they all look fantastic on a big-screen or projection TV.

COLLABRACAM

$5.99

http://collabracam.com

CollabraCam lets you collaborate on video projects, shooting video with up to four iPads (or other iDevices) and then viewing, recording, or editing the footage in real time. It even has a built-in communication system so the "director" can provide cues such as camera movements or angles to each "cameraman."

Now, here's one last video tip before we move on: if you shoot video with your iPad, make sure you have adequate light. Video shot with your iPad camera looks noticeably darker than the same picture shot as a still. Remember that light is your friend when you record video with your iPad. Experiment with lighting if you can, but more is usually better.

Audio Production and Editing Apps

If you plan to record and run your presentation independently—for example, showing it at a kiosk in a trade show or in the lobby of your company's building, using it as a loop to entertain your audience before the actual presentation begins, or perhaps distributing it via e-mail or through your website—you'll want to add voice and maybe even music to the visuals. The apps here let you create or record audio on your iPad and then edit the recordings to accompany your presentation. Once the audio file is created, you import it to your presentation file to create one master file.

Remember, some presentation apps have the option to record voice-over directly with your visuals. The advantage is that you work with one file; the disadvantage is that your audio editing options are usually limited.

GARAGEBAND

$4.99

http://www.apple.com/apps/garageband/

If you need music for your presentation, GarageBand turns your iPad into a reasonably powerful recording studio. It's also so easy to use that almost anyone can create music, even if you know nothing about music. It's packed with professionally recorded loops and Smart Instruments that play notes or chords that sound good together no matter where you tap! If you need music for a project—from a simple drumbeat to a full orchestra—GarageBand makes it hard for you to fail.

TWISTEDWAVE AUDIO EDITOR

$9.99

http://twistedwave.com/ios.html

For professional-level voice editing options in an easy-to-use app, TwistedWave Audio Editor is worth the investment. Choose to work in mono or stereo and then record your voice, even with the iPad's microphone. After recording, the split screen

FIGURE 6.13 Use TwistedWave Audio Editor to edit your recorded presentation, a voice-over, or an interview.

shows the normal wave pattern at the top and an expandable wave form below so you can cut at exactly the spot you want and edit accordingly using the buttons on the toolbar that runs across the bottom of the screen (see Figure 6.13). A variety of effects allow you to clean up or alter your recording. The dynamics processor and pitch and speed functions give you great flexibility in tweaking your recording. We appreciated the multiple file formats and compression values in which you can save your recording, making it easy to share the audio files with many other presentation apps.

HOKUSAI AUDIO EDITOR

Free; $9.99 Pro Pack; $2.99 each, Tools Pack and FX Pack; $1.99 Fun Pack
http://www.wooji-juice.com/products/hokusai/
Hokusai presents a clean-lined, minimalistic user interface. A tool window holds the buttons needed for recording or importing tracks. Tap and hold to select a portion of the recorded audio. A contextual menu will appear so you can work on the selected piece. You can cut, copy, delete, trim, or add effects such as fading in or out, or even reverse the audio so you can look for hidden messages heard only by you when your audio is played backward (just kidding about the secret messages). Adding synthesizers or white noise is as simple as adding a new track. Hokusai lets you export as a Wave file, as an MPEG-4 audio file, or as a ringtone with various options for audio quality.

Animation Apps

Animation is truly an art of its own that combines drawing capabilities, wit, and videographer and director skills. We mention two apps here, but we admit that unless you have the time and talent to create your own animation, you may be better off buying stock video and animations or contracting with someone to create an animation for you. In the Resources section at the back of this book, we give you a healthy list of stock houses, so you'll want to check that out. In the meantime, if you want to play around with creating video on your iPad, you're sure to have fun—without too much frustration—with either of these apps.

VIDEOSCRIBE HD

$4.99; $1.99 to remove branding

http://www.sparkol.com/home.php

Want to make one of those watch-it-being-drawn videos that are popular for communicating a message or teaching, but you don't know how to

draw? Let VideoScribe do it for you. As soon as you open the app, you can be up and running. Tap the plus sign to begin a new project and then start choosing images that relate to your message from the vast library that comes with VideoScribe. Tap the Text button to add text. Tap the Music button to choose an accompaniment from the VideoScribe music library or record a voice-over. Tap the Playback button to view your work in progress, and when it's just the way you want, tap the Video button (that little filmstrip in the upper right corner) to create and save your video file. (See Figure 6.14.)

FIGURE 6.14 Convey your message in a fun, entertaining way with VideoScribe HD.

ANIMATION DESK FOR IPAD

Free, lite version, $4.99, full version

http://kdanmobile.com/en/

Animation Desk works like a flip-book: you draw a series of sketches with slight changes on each one and tap Play to see the animation. Instead of redrawing each page of a paper flip-book, however, with Animation Desk you can duplicate a frame and make the necessary changes to move forward, or you can use a virtual onionskin overlay to trace the parts of the previous frame that remain the same and only draw in the changes. With the Stamp Tool, you can capture a pattern from one frame and paste it in subsequent frames. The Stamp Tool also has a resizing tool, so you could create an image and then resize it so it appears to shrink or grow during the animation. Overall, even if you aren't Walt Disney, Animation Desk for iPad helps you create a decent animation that could be a fun and entertaining part of your presentation.

Expert's Corner Q&A

For the last section of this chapter, we put ourselves in the presenter's shoes and came up with some questions you might have. The first half of the questions focuses on practical presentation problems that are somewhat likely to happen. The second half looks at up-and-coming technologies that you may not have even heard of and gives you some ideas to think about for using those technologies in your presentations.

I Want to Write on Top of My Slides While I'm Presenting. Is There a Way to Do That?

Yes, we've tried it with Doceri, 2Screens, bContext, and Power Presenter. Just open an existing Keynote or PowerPoint presentation or PDF file from the desired app and use the writing tool.

I Transferred One of My Keynote Presentations to My iPad and Got a Message That Several Fonts Were Missing. Can I Load Those Fonts onto My iPad, and How Do I Do It?

Although you can't load fonts into Keynote on your iPad, there are a few work-arounds that you can consider:

- Design your Keynote presentation directly on your iPad; that way, any font you choose is supported by your iPad.
- When designing your Keynote presentation on a computer, use only fonts from the 50 or so that are supported on the iPad.
- Use the fonts you want, including custom fonts, but export your Keynote presentation to PDF or image files. You won't be able to edit the deck on your iPad, but your presentation will look like you want it to.
- Use an app like Inkpad ($7.99). Upload your font families to Dropbox and then link Inkpad to your Dropbox account. Inkpad can access the font families in Dropbox, and you can create text. That text can

then be cut and pasted into your Keynote presentation. There's a great explanation about how to do this at the Working iPad website (http://workingipad.net/tutorial/2012/2/20/install-and-use-typefaces-fonts-on-your-ipad.html).

Sometimes Images Projected from My iPad Are Blurry. Is There a Way to Correct This?

After you confirm that your projector is focused, make sure your presentation is set to display at 1,024 × 768, which is the iPad resolution. You usually find this in the app settings (the button that looks like a gear).

Can I Transfer Images Directly from My Digital Camera to My iPad Without Going Through My Computer?

Yes, the iPad Camera Connector Kit comes with a USB adapter, also referred to as a dongle, and an SD card reader. Connect the USB adapter to your iPad and then connect the USB cable from the USB adapter to your digital camera. Open Photos and transfer images by choosing the correct option on your camera's display. If your camera uses an SD card reader, pop the SD card out of your camera and into the reader—your images are transferred into Photos.

An added plus of the iPad Camera Connector Kit is that the USB adapter also works for other USB-enabled peripherals such as keyboards, microphones, and headsets.

I Wanted to Use a Song from My Music Library in a Presentation, but Nothing Happened When I Tried to Import It. What Happened (Or Didn't Happen)?

You can only import songs from your Music library that are not copyrighted, which means most commercially recorded and sold music is off limits. We give you some ideas for finding stock music in the Resources section at the end of the book.

I'd Like to Put a Podcast in My Presentation. How Do I Do That?

The easiest way to do this is via iTunes. Download the podcast on your computer and then convert it to an MP3 file. (See the iTunes Help section if you're not sure how to do this.) The MP3 file can then be added to most presentation apps. You could also incorporate a hyperlink to the podcast's web page.

How Do I Switch Between Apps During a Presentation? Do I Have to Build Hyperlinks to the App, or Can I Use the Multitask (Open Apps) Bar During Presentations?

This depends on exactly what you want to do. Hyperlinks provide flexibility in your presentation; when a specific question arises, you can jump to the part of the presentation—slide, video, or website—that correlates to the question. If going to another app is a planned part of your presentation, make sure that app is open before you begin. You can double-click the Home button and then use the Multitask bar to go to the other app, and then you can double-click the Home button again to return to your presentation app and pick up where you left off.

How Do I Connect with Other iPads or iPhones That My Audience Brought or Are Located in Remote Locations?

We talk about this in depth in Chapter 7, but essentially all devices must have the same app installed; then your iPad (or a computer if you prefer) acts as the server, and the guest iPads or iPhones are clients. Some apps provide just viewing privileges; others let your audience interact with your presentation.

Can I Connect a Microphone to My iPad to Record My Presentation While Giving It?

Yes, several manufacturers make USB and wireless (Bluetooth) microphones that connect or pair with the iPad so you can record your presentation. These are great options for recording your presentation while making a video or voice-over; however, if you need to record while you're giving your presentation, you have to use one of the following work-arounds:

- Digitally split the audio inside the iPad so that one side of the split goes to an Airplay-enabled amplifier and the other is recorded by the iPad.
- Record on an Airplay-enabled device with a digital recorder.
- Run your presentation on a Mac attached to an amplification device and control the presentation from your iPad.

That said, you may get better results by recording your presentation with traditional audio and video recording equipment.

How Can I Use a Stylus for My Presentation, and What Kinds of Styli Are There?

Because most of us are more adept at using a writing instrument instead of our fingers to write and draw, a stylus is a great option if you plan to write on your slides during your presentation; or use an app, such as a brainstorming or whiteboard app, where you draw or write. Bear in mind, though, that a stylus does give you one more item to juggle during a presentation, whereas you're unlikely to drop your finger. You'll find both cabled styli that plug into the audio port and USB styli that plug into a USB adapter connected to your iPad's dock, or there are Bluetooth styli that you pair with your iPad.

We've compiled an (almost) exhaustive list of available styli in the Resources section. Before you make your purchase, think about how you'll be using the stylus—to write, to sketch, to paint—and choose the tip style accordingly: fine line, thick, brush, or even crayon. Personally, we prefer a wireless stylus, as it keeps the dock and audio port free for other peripheral devices and is one less wire to get tangled up in!

What Other Devices Can an iPad Control?

More than you might imagine. Here's a brief list of things you can control with your iPad:

- Projectors (e.g., Epson)
- Quadcopters (e.g., AR2)
- Televisions (e.g., Samsung)
- Audio devices (e.g., Denon)
- Musical Instruments
- Vacuum cleaners
- Thermostats (NEST)

What Are Some Options for Remote Sound?

With remote sound apps, use your iPad to control the sounds emitted from another device, such as an iPhone, iPod, or another iPad. Apps such as

Sound Ninja or Remote Sound Box come with sounds, whereas Sound Remote controls the Music app playing audio installed on another iOS device.

If you want to get your audience up and moving, you could install a remote sound app on iPhones or iPads hidden around the room and then control the noise that comes from them for your audience members to find the devices. You can also use them to direct your audience's attention to a certain part of the room.

Can Siri Participate in My Presentation?

With her dry wit and signature voice, we think Siri would be a terrific foil to many types of presentations; just make sure you do a test run of your requests if you don't want any inappropriate surprise responses.

How Can I Use Gaming Interfaces or Gestures as Part of a Presentation?

Think about using an actual game in your presentation. Games often have spectacular animation and visuals that take advantage of the iPad's retina display. Colorful and fast-action games can be a compelling intro or example. And don't limit yourself to commercial games like Bad Piggies. There are also motivational and team-building games available for the iPad platform.

Consider using gaming hardware, such as the Fling (http://tenonede sign.com/fling.php), to manipulate your presentation.

Remember, the accelerometer detects your iPad's movements, and so you can creatively turn or rotate images by turning your iPad during a presentation.

How Do You Use Gesture Recognition with the iPad?

Gesture recognition lets you control your iPad without touching the screen. Without getting too technical, your hand or body motion is detected by the iPad's camera, triggering an action. For example, Wave-o-rama is a photo album app that moves from one photo to the next when you wave your hand in front of the iPad screen, and FoodSteps offers touch-free navigation of recipes so you don't sully your iPad screen with flour-covered fingers.

Keep your eyes open for more apps that use gesture recognition—it's the next big thing in device control.

How Do I Use the Accelerometer to Do Creative Things?

The accelerometer detects motion and can be used to rotate images or your screen orientation. The best use of the accelerometer that we've seen is in the presentation that promotes the city of Stockholm, which has gone viral on YouTube. Check it out (http://www.youtube.com/watch?v=53_qvMQf vOE) if you haven't looked at it, and you'll see what we mean about Killer Presentations. In this presentation, a bottle of wine appears on the iPad, the iPad is tilted, and the bottle tilts as if to pour a glass of wine; here, the presenter, who is a street magician, uses some sleight-of-hand moves to actually pour wine out of the iPad! Again, this is a custom presentation designed by a programmer, but the end result is mind-blowingly memorable.

Aside from Using My iPad to Control My Presentation, What Are Some Clever Ways I Can Use It to Connect with My Audience?

If you think of your iPad as a prop, there are lots of ways you can incorporate it as a visual. Here are just a few ideas to get you started:

- Take ventriloquism to a new (and easier) level and use your iPad as a sidekick. You can create an animation or video with one of the apps we discussed earlier and then time it so you ask questions and the image on your iPad answers.
- Use it as a sign or even as a graphic; if you are presenting with another person, you could display a giant arrow on your iPad when you pass the mic.
- With multiple iPads, construct an image, putting a part of the image on each iPad. Think of an Eiffel Tower displayed across five iPads; you could pull the first one to metaphorically talk about the foundation (of your business), the second to talk about structure, and so on, to the apex of the tower.
- Take photos or video of the audience and display the images instantly as part of your presentation.
- Use an augmented reality app to bring your audience into your presentation (see the next question).

What Augmented Reality Applications
Are Available for the iPad?

Augmented reality apps access your location using the iPad's GPS, and location services show you more information about what's around you or pick up on QR codes in printed advertising. For example, open an app like juniao and see information about the office supply store down the street; or open Layar and point your iPad to a page in a magazine, and the website of the article on the page opens in Safari.

In ViewAR, augmented reality gets most interesting for presentations. By placing virtual objects in your present setting, we think ViewAR would be a fantastic addition to a presentation. (See Figure 6.15.) You can use the ViewAR library of 3-D images and impose them on what you see through your iPad's camera, or you can upload a gallery of your own images. Imagine your t-shirts or your products have your logo; now imagine turning your iPad toward the audience and projecting a picture of the audience wearing the t-shirts or holding your project in their hands.

FIGURE 6.15
ViewAR inserts virtual 3-D objects into your surroundings.

How Presentations Are Evolving Now and into the Future

We are on the cusp between the present and the future of presentations and its incredibly exciting possibilities. On the basis of various trends and projections of technology that we researched, we can forecast with a degree of certainty that the future of presentations 5 to 10 years from now will likely involve these amazing innovations:

- There will be total interactivity with audiences as opposed to a one-way pitch or speech.
- Virtual and augmented reality will be commonplace at work, at home, and at play.
- The use of ultrahigh-resolution video and photorealistic 3-D animations will increase greatly.
- There will be a vast improvement in holograms and projected holography that will result in "almost real" 3-D images.
- Full gesture-based recognition will be used to bring up information and control all aspects of the presentation and equipment.
- Artificial intelligence will be able to sift through enormous amounts of data to detect, and show trends, relationships, cause-and-effect correspondence, projections, and other meaningful implications and results drawn from raw data.
- Virtual meetings with vastly improved capabilities will significantly reduce in-person meetings and improve communication productivity.
- Entire walls will turn into ultrahigh-resolution *interactive* video systems, with glasses-free 3-D to follow.
- Video thin film (with wireless capability) will enable presenters to unfurl various sizes of "video posters" as 3-D visuals to use with gestures to present information.

Latest Video and Visualization Systems

Most major TV and high-end projection manufacturers are now coming out with higher-resolution presentation projectors and televisions. Called UHD or 4K (3,840 pixels × 2,160 pixels for a total of 8.3 megapixels), this new format has a resolution four times greater than our current HD systems. The major benefit of this higher-resolution video occurs when larger images are projected or shown on TVs bigger than 70 inches—pixilation is dramatically minimized, and the sharpest details can be easily seen. Even as this technology is entering the market, 8K UHD, which is 7,680 pixels × 4,320 pixels (for a total of 33.2 megapixels) is being developed and is projected to come onto the scene in a few years.

GIGAPIXEL PANORAMA IMAGES AND VIDEO

Gigapixel panorama images (1 billion-plus pixels) offer outstanding-resolution digital image bitmaps. A specially made panoramic robot camera takes thousands to tens of thousands of photos sequentially to cover a 360-degree panorama, if needed. Photos of a building's interior, for example, can be seen from floor to ceiling, front to back, in incredible detail just by scrolling.

A 320-gigapixel photo of London is the world's largest panorama, comprising more than 48,000 individual frames collated into a single panorama by a powerful computer system (go to http://www.360cities.net/ to see it and other fantastic photos). A software program perfectly aligns and "stitches" together the images. These images can be displayed on the Internet and viewed within seconds using a special viewer. This technology is being used in some presentations for sales and marketing, architecture, tourism, virtual tours, and more. For your presentations, you can actually buy panoramic and gigapixel stock photos and vector art from companies like Shutterstock (http://www.shutterstock.com), Stockfree Images (http://ww.stockfreeimages.com), and Big Stock Photo (http://www.bigstockphoto.com).

There are companies doing 360-degree panoramic *moving* videos, the latest innovation of this type. A panoramic video enables viewers to actually "experience" a real location or setting as if they were there. Imagine giving a presentation to potential buyers of a luxury resort condominium in the Caribbean. You hand out iPads offering interactive tours of the resort's lobby, swimming pools, dining rooms, recreation areas, and beaches, where you see real people eating, playing volleyball in the water, sitting at a beautiful lanai bar, and otherwise having a fabulous time.

Because they are panoramic moving videos, the individual participants can tilt the iPads and look upward, for example, at the balcony on the seventh floor suite they are interested in buying or tilt the iPad downward to see—up close—the beautiful tile designs and lush landscaping surrounding the swimming pool and hot tubs. The location-based 360-degree video panoramas can include other numerous applications for architecture, city planning, geographic mapping, and other "tour-type" experiences right from the iPad!

HOLOGRAMS FOR THAT EXTRA PRESENTATION IMPACT

Holograms can add a rich, new dimension to your iPad Killer Presentation. A hologram is a 3-D image produced by two beams of light by holography. One company at the forefront of holographic visualization technology with more than 40 patents is Zebra Imaging (http:www.zebraimaging.com). It produces some of the most realistic 3-D color images on sheets of plastic up to 24 inches by 34 inches (600 mm by 850 mm) that are ideal for architecture, engineering and construction, advertising, retail, and sales.

These are true 3-D holograms that when rotated or tilted display components as if they were solid in shape and form. Holograms use regular light sources at any angle allowing you to see the hologram without special viewing equipment. To create these detailed and accurate images on lightweight plastic sheets, you download Zebra Imaging's software and "frame" your data (from programs such as Autodesk 3Ds Max, Autodesk Maya, or Sketchup) for 3-D holographic printing. Zebra Imaging helps you engage clients with rich, realistic 3-D presentations that enhance collaboration. For big deals you are trying to close, you can create compelling leave-behinds along with your proposals or oral presentations.

3-D Virtual Reality Interactive Walk-Throughs Using Your iPad

There is another visual revolution under way for giving presentations about and exploring new commercial properties and industrial facilities—it's 3-D virtual reality. This is a perfect application for an iPad, because it can act as a remote control device to take a tour. You can be at home, on a construction site, in your car—just about anywhere—and view a realistic presentation that you fully participate and involve yourself in.

As opposed to panoramic video, virtual reality offers immersion into a photorealistic, computer-generated environment developed using 3-D rendering software (such as 3ds Max, Maya, Lightwave, SolidWorks, Daz3D, and RealFlow) to create realistic-looking interior and exterior scenes. Some of the everyday things that take on extraordinary realism include subtle light reflections and shading; detailed textures of wood, marble, leather, glass, and fabrics; fully furnished areas; trees, shrubs, grass, and water; and people—all of this only adding to the virtual touring experience.

With interactive 3-D virtual walk-throughs comes the ability for iPad users to control their own journey (including a "flyover") around the outside and inside of a new home, a resort community, a factory, a refinery, or anywhere else using computer gaming technology. These walk-throughs are ideal for showing a property or industrial facility's design, layout, size, dimensions, and spatial relationships.

With your iPad, you move forward and backward, look up and down, and look right and left to virtually tour and explore a fully realistic, fully furnished and decorated home or any other building or even a complex, computer-generated environment like a planned amusement park. The iPad's gyroscope and accelerometer provide precise motion-sensing accuracy and measurement in the direction you are moving or rotating it in space, as well as the speed and angle of the movement.

With its touch-screen features, you can even use your iPad (within this virtual environment) to activate interactive ("hot") areas within the animation to, say, operate factory controls or open the curtains of a 3-D resort home to see the golf course. You can do it from your iPad anywhere or any time at your convenience!

When it comes to communicating, 3-D interactive animated walk-throughs are the next big "high-impact" presentation tool. To see what we mean by photorealistic 3-D renderings, animations, and walk-throughs, check out iCreate (http://www.icreate3d.com), from a firm based in the United Kingdom, that does a variety of 3-D renderings, animations, and virtual tours. Download iCreate's free iPad app "icreate 3d" from the Apple App Store and use your iPad to experience the future.

Example of Walking Through a Refinery with Your iPad

Epic Software Group (http://www.epicsoftware.com) in The Woodlands, Texas, created a walk-through project for a company that builds large infrastructures. The company came to Vic Cherubini, the owner of the animation and multimedia production firm, to create a virtual reality walk-through iPad application for a 3-D drilling rig to be used for safety training purposes. Epic's 3-D artists and animators created the pieces for a drill rig from photos they shot on rig sites. Epic chose the Unity 3D game engine to build the simulation because it had attractive features for the iPad. For example, when you move around the rig with your iPad, as you get closer to a piece of equipment, you can hear the sound of machines get louder, then softer as you move away.

Epic Software Group went beyond the iPad walk-through by including interactivity throughout the virtual tour. As you move through, around, up, and down the animated rig with your iPad, it features interactive elements: videos, animations, 3-D graphics, photos, web links, and PDF files about technologies for that part of the rig. Epic added a number of rig workers whom you can interact with (see Figure 6.16). If you pass by an animated worker, he will stop, turn, and begin telling you about his job on the rig.

FAR-OUT AUGMENTED REALITY CAN BE AN *AH!SOME* PART OF YOUR PRESENTATIONS

Another ideal application powerfully suited for your iPad is augmented reality (AR), which is still a relatively unknown development to most peo-

FIGURE 6.16
An animated rig worker describes what he does on the oil rig.

ple and is in its infancy stage. Some futurists are calling it the "new Pow-erPoint" when it comes to widespread use for presentations. Google Glass is leading one of the charges in implementing AR, which enables anyone to view a real, physical world combined—"augmented"—with computer-generated graphics, video, animations, 3-D renderings, and sound that is composited over a real view, enhancing what we hear, see, and feel.

AR works by using a particular app for your iPad. When you open that app and point your iPad's camera at a "hot" area that has been "augmented," your iPad combines what the camera sees with a new virtual display from the app. Let's say an architectural magazine has its major advertisements prepared as hotspots. If you had an app that read those advertisements, your iPad might show a video about that architectural company; or it might take a flat drawing of a floor plan on that page and show you a 3-D render-ing of it or give a virtual tour of the building.

You can move your iPad to see different sides and views of this 3-D model of the floor plan. You could be on a subway station or at a bus stop and see a billboard that tells you it is AR enabled; if you point your iPad or iPhone at it with the appropriate AR app opened, that billboard (which may be an advertisement for a new movie) can turn it into a video trailer. IKEA jumped into AR with its 2013 catalog app that featured an AR viewer, enabling people to look at furniture in 3-D and to see video and other digital content for readers.

CHANGING THE MEANING OF PRESENTATION "GESTURES"

Another emerging technology involves touch-free gesture recognition. Machine vision algorithms track your hand gestures and finger-pointing from your iPad's camera and convert them into commands for your iPad. Gesture recognition works with other devices and TVs. You can control many of your iPad's functions and applications during presentations using this technology. Gesture recognition can track your fingertips to allow you virtual mouse functions such as touch-free point and click, tap and drop, and wave and grab on your iPad. With a wave of your hand or a lift of your finger, you can operate your iPad or laptop!

The Leap Motion Controller (http:www.leapmotion.com) is a small piece of hardware selling for less than a hundred bucks that does an impressive job of gesture recognition. Another company to look at is *eye-Sight* (http://www.eyesight-tech.com), which is completely software based. Gesture recognition is developing rapidly and will continue to become more sophisticated in its ability to naturally and effectively manipulate all kinds of digital devices, not just the iPad. We recommend you begin checking out this technology for selective use in your presentations. Take care: if it is used inappropriately, a presenter might come across as a "talking mime," with hands and fingers flailing about in a distracting mode.

CHAPTER 7

Presenting at In-Person and Virtual Meetings with Your iPad

In this chapter, we show you how to effectively use your iPad—and those of your attendees—in meetings. We explain how you can communicate, interact, and collaborate with other iPads, iPhones, or smart devices that audience members have, whether they are in the room with you or across the globe. If you consider that possibility when creating your presentation, you can choose apps that let your audience participate from their iPads.

First we talk a bit about facilitating a meeting and engaging your audience. We also explore a few of the whiteboard apps available, which can be projected from your iPad to the big screen and sometimes shared with other iPads in the room. We talk next about presenting at in-person meetings, where you and your audience are physically in the same room, and we review interactive apps that are suitable for those situations. From there, we segue into the increasingly frequent and important virtual situations such as webinars and virtual meetings. We give you some statistics about webinars and provide tips for creating a presentation that your audience watches without you, such as on your website, by opening a file from an e-mail or viewing at a kiosk. We discuss the etiquette of virtual meetings and present a few of the videoconference apps that are a key component for many corporations that have worldwide offices or permit remote and work-from-home situations.

Whiteboards: The Backbone of Collaborative Planning

If you teach in a scholastic, corporate, or continuing education setting or facilitate meetings, you've probably encountered the whiteboard. If your experience is anything like ours, the markers are dried out and pale, the eraser is missing, and the board itself has a faint shadow of what was written on it before. Your iPad as a virtual whiteboard has none of these problems and has added features that a physical whiteboard can't provide, such as the ability to print the contents or share them via e-mail, a cloud server, or a social network.

Whiteboard Apps

Your iPad as a whiteboard lets you facilitate your meeting by writing main points and then incorporating comments from others at the meeting. Some whiteboard apps have interactive functions that allow iPad users with the same app installed to write on the board projected from your iPad. Before your meeting begins, keep in mind these tips:

- Even in an informal meeting, outline your agenda at the beginning and include how long you think the meeting will take. People like to know what to expect and are more likely to pay attention when there's a schedule to follow.
- Virtual whiteboards let you incorporate photos, images, diagrams, drawings, and text. Use these items to guide the discussion or communicate your message.
- Leave time for your participants to speak, either to ask questions or to express a related experience or idea.

BAIBOARD
Free
http://www.baiboard.com
Although you need an Internet connection to use it, this is a great whiteboard app, and it's free! In addition to classic whiteboard functions, Bai-Board provides diagramming stencils, and it offers the possibility to add photos from Photos or Camera and to take snapshots of your work in progress. A number is assigned when the board is created and your meeting begins. Other meeting participants open BaiBoard on their iPads and access the same board by number. Participants working from a computer can sign in to the URL assigned to the board. Work singly or in presentation mode and open a text or voice chat with participants who are in remote

locations. Save your board to a cloud server or share via e-mail or social networks.

WHITEBOARD GURU

$4.99

http://www.whiteboardguru.net

Whiteboard Guru is the most whiteboardlike of the apps we tried. The lines, shapes, and stencils are always blue, although you can choose a red, blue, black or green pen to write or draw. Use the keyboard instead of the pen to write something, and text appears in a neat handwriting font. The video recording feature works smoothly, and the audio pickup is good. We

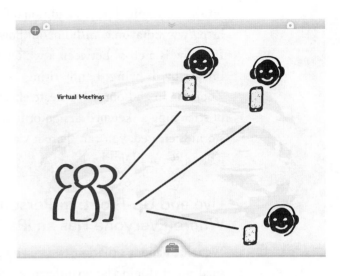

FIGURE 7.1 Use Whiteboard Guru to create instructional videos.

can see using this to create a short instructional video, which you can then edit in Photos. (See Figure 7.1.)

STICKYBOARD2

$4.99

http://www.qrayon.com/home/
    stickyboard2/

If you like to plan or manage your projects with sticky notes on whiteboards, you'll love Stickyboard2. (See Figure 7.2.) This app mimics its physical counterpart perfectly with the added advantages of being able to e-mail the board as a PDF or text file, zoom out to make a bigger board when you run out of space, and provide a keyboard to type your

FIGURE 7.2 Create color-coded plans with virtual sticky notes.

notes, which is especially helpful if your penmanship is less than perfect.

INKFLOW

Free; $7.99 for Plus version, which adds a color palette, pencil, eraser and brushes, unlimited pages, additional fonts, and other functions. http://www.qrayon.com/home/inkflow/

InkFlow is a cross between a whiteboard and a notepad. Add text and images by drawing, handwriting, or typing text and inserting photos. Zooming in and out helps create effects such as bolding handwritten text or stretching a sketched design or figure. After your design, list, or brainstorm is created, you can share it via e-mail, tweet it as a photo, or export it as a JPG or PDF file.

Live and Up-Front: In-Person Meetings Where Everyone Has an iPad

We talked about situations where you present information one-on-one, in small groups, or in a large conference. Often, however, the purpose of a meeting is to discuss something with your audience or to plan something or solve a problem with a client, partner, or your staff. Each attendee needs to refer to the same information and often contributes documents or, at minimum, comments, and your role may shift to that of meeting facilitator rather than principal presenter. With each attendee participating on an iPad with a meeting app, the group interaction becomes dynamic and efficient.

The idea of all the people in the meeting seeing your visuals on their iPads is enthralling, and your first thought might be "I've got their attention now," but the opposite may be true. If your participants are bored, with iPad in hand what's to stop them from drifting over to their e-mail accounts or, worse yet, putting up a Facebook post or tweeting "Trapped in a dark, boring conference room…" Your visuals need to be interesting, but as with any presentation, you want your audience or participants to focus on you and your message. Here are a few general facilitating tips to keep them engaged:

- Dale Carnegie once said that the key to giving a message is to "tell them what you're going to say, say it, then tell them what you've said."
- Consider the outcome you want from the meeting or training and make sure each visual or point supports that outcome.

- Use interactivity to your advantage. Since everyone has access to the presentation, ask frequently for input. While you're doing the talking, ask someone else to take notes. It can be interesting to see if the key points someone else picks up are the key points that you wanted to convey.

- Prepare questions for your participants that can be used throughout your presentation or meeting. One of the best ways to engage people is to ask questions, even if you are the one giving information. Questions about the topic at hand move participants' focus to the meeting instead of to thoughts of whether they put enough money in the parking meter. Questions such as "What do you know about worm composting?" (or whatever your topic is) give you, as presenter, an idea of the participants' knowledge of the material at hand; if they already know the basics, you can skim that part and get into the more interesting, advanced, and new-to-them information. Perhaps the most important effect that questions can have on participants is making them feel considered and affirmed, letting them know their presence in your meeting is valued.

- Think back to your schooldays when the teacher always seemed to know when you weren't paying attention and called on you in that moment. Develop the skill of looking around the room at each person. Make eye contact with each attendee; and if you see a perplexed face, ask, "Does this make sense to you, Jim?" or ask a headshaker, "What do you think about that, Sara? Do you agree?"

Meeting Apps

With the meeting apps below, you create a meeting and upload any documents you want to present or discuss at the meeting. Attendees must have the attendee version of the app on their iPads. Then when they open the app, they log in to the meeting. Some apps require each user to create an account, which is usually an e-mail address and password. After the meeting begins, everyone can see, point at, and sometimes write on your presentation from their devices. Some apps have an, ahem, Android version as well, and most offer the possibility to log in to a URL from a browser on a computer. Think of a meeting where each participant presents an idea ahead of time. The supporting documents for each idea are uploaded, and during the meeting as the individual participants talk about their ideas, they open their supporting documents and can circle or highlight key points; then they can pass the presenter role to other participants to write on the open documents and to present their ideas as well.

TACCTO—INTERACTIVE MEETING PLATFORM

Free for meetings limited to 15 minutes, one document per participant and nine recorded meetings; $49 a year unlimited duration, documents, and recordings
http://tacc.to/site/

This is an easy-to-use, nicely organized meeting app that literally keeps everyone on the same page. When the meeting begins, each participant logs in via the Taccto app or through a web browser using the assigned meeting URL— you have to have an Internet connection to use Taccto. The organizer begins the meeting by opening a document from

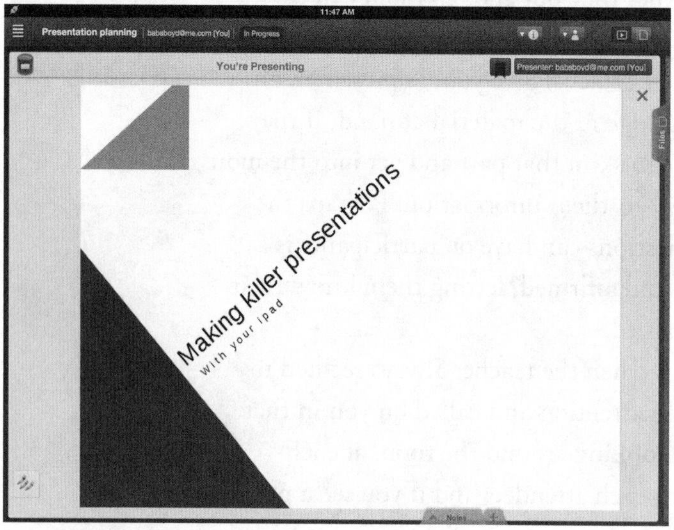

FIGURE 7.3
Taccto lets you collaborate in real time with multiple presenters.

the collateral manager or opening the in-app whiteboard. Participants see the same on their iPads, on another device with a web browser, or on a large screen connected to the organizer's iPad. By switching the presenter role among participants, everyone can write on the same document or whiteboard. Perhaps the most useful elements of Taccto are that it records the audio and visual of your meeting and that you can insert a bookmark at key moments to quickly return to that interaction or topic. (See Figure 7.3.) We see Taccto as a great tool for many types of team efforts.

MIGHTYMEETING

Free for attendees; various price levels for hosting after a free 14-day trial
http://www.mightyhd.com

The benefit of MightyMeeting is that it works for both in-person and remote participants in your meeting. We tried it during an international connection, and it was quick to set up and easy to use. You can also send invitations via e-mail from the MightyMeeting app, which provides a URL that gives invitees access to your meeting from a web browser. If you use MightyMeeting with remote participants, it's a good idea to simultaneously conduct a conference call so you can have a conversation while everyone is looking at your presentation. All participants can add documents to the meeting from their devices as well as mark up the document being displayed. A blank "whiteboard" page is added to the end of each PDF file so you can add notes, and you can also open a Sketchbook page to create a new document within MightyMeeting.

LILYPAD

Free for a limited time; meeting costs start at $0.99
http://www.lilypadapp.com
Tap Set Up a Meeting, and the meeting wizard takes you through setting up the time for the meeting; adding items to be used during the meeting including PDFs, URL links, and polling questions; and inviting attendees. You can also instantly invite someone after the meeting begins or open a document and create a meeting on the spot. If you want to share more documents while the meeting is in progress, tapping the Agenda list accesses your docs. The best part about LilyPad is the way you can interact with your attendees by conducting live polls (see Figure 7.4). When the meeting is finished, a follow-up e-mail is automatically sent to anyone who was invited, along with any attachments from the pond (the area where LilyPad stores files related to the meeting) and your meeting notes, if you wish. Your meetings are stored on the LilyPad server so you can review your past meetings anytime.

FIGURE 7.4
Use LilyPad's meeting setup wizard to create a new meeting.

FEEDBACKFRUITS

Free

http://www.feedbackfruits.com/

If you want a way to gather feedback after a presentation or course, take a look at FeedbackFruits. Although still in the development stage, this free app is one to watch. It was developed for university students, but we think it could be a simple way to receive feedback on any course you teach. Download the app, create an account, and add your course. People who attend your course download the app, create an account, and enroll, after which they can send feedback about your course.

You can also use the apps mentioned in this section in a situation where you are the presenter to a captive, noncontributing audience. But interactivity, when it's available and it works, can be awesome when you want to interact with your audience . If you do decide to interact with your audience, you can also simply use social media. Your audience members send Facebook posts or tweets to you, and you access them directly from the iPad you're presenting with. Keep in mind, though, that while this can be a spectacular tool, it can also be a train wreck. Think long and hard about how it would improve your show before you blithely ask your audience to tweet their opinion.

Virtual Meetings: Videoconferences, Webinars, and Webcasts

The meeting apps we just described let people sign in remotely, but they don't transmit voice. If you want to have a live interaction with people who aren't in the room with you—a virtual meeting—you want to set up a conference call, which could be audio alone, or audio and video, or a webinar.

Videoconferences are mostly used for meetings where the objective is to have input from and interaction between each of the attendees, such as a staff meeting with people in several remote locations or a client and service provider meeting. The difference between a videoconference and a video call is that in a video call, such as Skype or Apple's own FaceTime, only two people are involved. With a videoconference more than two people in different locations are involved, and that's why you need a service and the associated app that coordinates the incoming "calls" from several different locations to one common place.

During a webinar—or web-based seminar—the presenters transmit their information, and the attendees watch and listen, asking questions at the appointed Q&A times. Some webinars are conducted via a call-in service. Many people call a conference-enabled phone number while viewing the visuals on a browser. Questions are asked audibly from the telephone.

Mind Your Ps and Qs—Virtual Meeting Etiquette

Whether you conduct a videoconference, webinar, or webcast, a little etiquette can go a long way. The bottom line is respect for the other presenters and attendees, but here are a few dos and don'ts you should remember:

► Show up on time.
► Turn off your phones, both cellular and office. If you're expecting a call you absolutely can't miss or your young children are home alone, set your phone on vibrate and turn the ringer off. If you must respond, mute your audio-video and leave the room. You might want to remind other meeting attendees to do the same at the beginning of your meeting.
► Turn off instant messaging and audible e-mail alerts on your computer.
► Microphones are sensitive, and noises that you don't notice, such as shuffling papers or clearing your throat, will be amplified, and potentially disruptive, to other participants. Mute all microphones except that of the speaker.
► Remember you're on camera; behave as you would at an in-person meeting. We wish we didn't have to say this, but we've seen the worst: don't pick your nose, twirl your hair, or chew with your mouth open. One frequent webinar presenter we know goes so far as to drink from a nontransparent mug so viewers can't see down her throat when she takes a sip.
► Stay present. Don't read e-mail or exchange text messages while you're in the meeting. People will see that you're doing something else.
► If there's more than one presenter, don't hog airtime. The purpose of a videoconference is usually exchange of ideas and conversation; let each person have her say. Here again, at the beginning of the videoconference, you can set some ground rules about time limits for speaking.
► It goes without saying, don't interrupt—and for Pete's sake, don't yell.

A webcast is a limited version of a webinar. The presentation or video is broadcast live in streaming, but the attendees, who can number in the thousands, submit questions via text chat. The telephone isn't involved. A larger number of people may attend, but the interaction with the audience is more limited than in a webinar.

Technologically, there's not a big difference between webinars and videoconferences, but the objective is different. In both cases you and your invited audience members sign in to a website at the pre-established time. You may or may not need a specific app to do this, but you do need a service provider; many service providers offer both videoconference and webinar technology. Webinar service providers often offer analytics about attendees, and some offer pre-event and post-event marketing support as well.

Apps for Virtual Meetings

The videoconference and webinar apps for the iPad are free, but the host pays to rent the virtual conference room. The services and functions of the apps here are very similar. You can share slide presentations, work on spreadsheets or reports, design documents, and accomplish many productive tasks with your remote colleagues in real time. The apps discussed here lend themselves to hosting a videoconference or webinar remotely and displaying what you want the audience members to see on their screen (PC, smartphone, or tablet), with the ability to answer questions posed by the audience. If you work in a large corporation, your company may already have an account with a meeting and webinar service provider, and so you'll probably want to use that app and service. If not, go to the service providers' websites and compare prices and services to determine which one is right for you. Most providers offer tiered service, so you can pay for as many or as few features as you need. A few offer a free trial period. Think about the following when comparing service providers:

- How often will you conduct a videoconference or webinar? If you conduct frequent virtual meetings or webinars, consider a flat monthly fee; for once-in-a-while events, a per-use fee may be more convenient.
- Do you want to stream an event (webcast) without audience call-in features?

- How many attendees do you anticipate? Some services limit the number of attendees; others have unlimited attendees.
- What kinds of statistics or polling services are included? You probably want to know where your attendees come from and if they stayed for the whole event or disconnected midway through, and you likely also want to have an interactive Q&A portion and maybe even a follow-up survey, which some service providers manage.
- If you're planning a webinar, do you need help marketing it? Some service providers offer an online marketing strategy and service.
- Do you want a recording of your meeting that can be stored, distributed, or accessed after the meeting?
- Do you need a distribution site for your webinar, or will you keep it on your own website?

CLICKMEETING

http://www.clickmeeting.com/pricing.html

WEB EX

http://www.webex.com/iphone/

GOTOMEETING

http://www.gotomeeting.com/fec/

NETCONFERENCE

http://www.netconference.com/about/netconference/

E3 WEBCASTING

http://e3webcasting.com

BRIGHTTALK

http://academy.brighttalk.com

INTERCALL

http://www.intercall.com

Remember, you can use these tools in your in-person presentations as well. One of the most powerful collaborative features that your iPad offers is the ability to bring in a remote guest to participate in a one-to-one videoconference on the iPad via FaceTime or Skype; or you can have more than one remote participant join you in your presentation through one of the other videoconferencing apps mentioned here, which allow multiple video connections. When you need an expert opinion, it can be ever so much more powerful to see and hear that expert speaking to your audience live.

Webinars as a Marketing Tactic

According to a study from October 2012 conducted by MarketingProfs and the Content Marketing Institute, 59 percent of B2B content marketers will use webinars, ahead of print magazines (31 percent) and podcasts (27 percent); the most used tactic is social media (nonblog) at 87 percent. The data we found interesting identify which tactics marketers believe are most effective. The top three are in-person events (67 percent of those polled believe them to be effective), case studies (64 percent), and webinars and webcasts (61 percent).[1]

Any size business can benefit from the interaction and immediacy that a webinar can offer; one of the greatest advantages of online marketing of any kind is that you can create a big presence even if you're a one-person operation. People sign up for a webinar to learn something, which means a webinar is a great venue for sharing information relevant to your field but is less effective for introducing your company, so information about your company should be subtle and implicit.

Take advantage of the current "give it away for free" marketing trend, which translates into the more knowledge you share with your potential customers or business partners, the more likely they are to buy something

---

[1] "B2B Content Marketing: 2013 Benchmarks, Budgets and Trends-North America" was produced by MarketingProfs and the Content Marketing Institute and was sponsored by Brightcove. A survey was mailed electronically to a sample of B2B marketers from among members and subscribers of Marketing-Profs and Content Marketing Institute. A total of 1,416 responded, in August 2012, from North American companies, representing a full range of industries, functional areas, and company sizes. Read more at http://www.marketingprofs.com/charts/2012/9184/2013-b2b-content-marketing-benchmarks-budgets-and-trends#ixzz2OYTGq7Fo.

from you. It's not enough to show your product—in fact, sometimes you shouldn't show it at all—you need to share your expertise, which is inherent in your product or service. Your customers and partners need to view your business as something that will add value to their business (B2B) or life (B2C). Your initial response may be "But I worked hard to invent my secret sleuthing formula. I want to be paid for it" or "My competition will steal my ideas and sell them as theirs." You won't survive as a one-hit wonder; give away what you invented yesterday, and you're more likely to sell what you invented today as well as your future inventions.

Webinars or webcasts are Killer ways to give stuff away. Whether you provide a service or procedure or sell a physical product, think about information and added value that you can provide. For example, let's say you sell mattresses. You offer a webinar on the latest research in polyphasic sleep or on dream interpretation. People come to think of you as the sleep expert, not just the mattress seller. You begin to build a relationship with potential partners and clients, and that's the way business is done today.

Remember, although we've focused our discussion on client or partner communication, webinars are an excellent outlet for limited-access press conferences, board meetings, or industry-specific events with a smaller, discreet audience.

Tips for Creating Killer Webinars

You want to use the same attention and professionalism in planning your online events as you would for an in-person presentation. Take these steps when planning your webinar:

- Create an agenda that incorporates introduction time, periodic Q&A breaks, and closing. Webinars usually run from 60 (informational) to 90 (tutorial) minutes.
- A moderator (this might be you) can help keep everything on track, especially if your speakers are in different locations. Even with only one speaker, a moderator can introduce the speaker and screen and choose and read questions from the audience to the speaker, leaving the speaker to concentrate on the presentation at hand.
- Take advantage of any technical support your webinar service provider has to offer.

- As with all presentations, rehearse, rehearse, and rehearse again. While you can create a script for practicing, you don't want to read from it the day of the webinar. You need to convey an expertise that shows the information is part of your cellular makeup.

- Choose a location that's quiet and free of audible and visual distractions (some webinars broadcast in voice-only, conference-call style, but for our purposes, we presume you are presenting visually as well). If you or your speakers are going to be on screen, make sure the lighting is good, probably brighter than you think necessary, and the background is neutral. We've seen too many webinars with grainy talking heads, a problem that could have been improved, if not solved, with good lighting.

- Avoid clothes with busy patterns, which can create focusing problems for the camera.

- Use a quality microphone or headset connected to your computer or iPad.

- Sit or stand about an arm's length from the videocamera lens.

- When referring to your visual support, in a webinar even more so than an in-person presentation, don't read your bulleted slides. This leaves your audience wondering why you bothered with the webinar instead of just sending a PDF.

- Your visuals should support what you're saying, whether with a phrase on a clean background or with a graph or diagram. Think about using builds where information is added as you talk about it and results in a complete image that you can recap at the end. This keeps your audience focused on what you're saying in the moment rather than trying to interpret what's displayed.

- Keep in mind that some may be viewing the webinar on the smaller screen of an iPad Mini or even iPhone or other smart device, so your visuals should be clearly visible on these types of screens.

- Use a sans serif font, such as Arial or Helvetica, in 24 points or larger and use a background that is in high contrast with the text. Make sure you have a margin around the visual to allow for letterboxing.

- Explain the interactive controls to your attendees in the beginning.

- Use on-screen pointers and overlay features to highlight specific parts of your visuals.
- We particularly liked these two tips from Ken Molay, president of Webinar Success and author of the white paper "Best Practices for Webinars": Address your audience in the second person *you* so that each listener feels you are speaking directly to him or her, and use names when answering attendees' questions. When talking about dry, technical data, add value statements such as "Here's an interesting fact…" or "What's curious about this is…"

Presenting in Absentia: When Your Presentation Must Speak for Itself

While webinars and videoconferencing are situations where you are present to give your presentation to people in remote locations, you may have more opportunities to present when you aren't there—for example, in a video embedded in your website, sent in an e-mail, or displayed at a kiosk. The visual impact and voice inflection of a recorded presentation are perhaps more important for videos than for in-person presentations. Your viewer may be making dinner while your presentation is running in the background, or listening to voice-mail, or drinking a morning cup of joe and absentmindedly watching your video online. Your visuals need to be so eye-catching, your words so stirring, that viewers will stop what they are doing, pay attention, and really listen to what you have to say. Be passionate; if you're bored with your presentation, your audience will find you boring. If appropriate, add something completely silly and out of place and then tell your viewers you wanted to see if they were paying attention.

Apps for Video Presentations

Here are two apps that cater specifically to the needs of this type of presentation.

9SLIDES

Free; upgrade to gold, $9.99
http://www.9slides.com/ipad

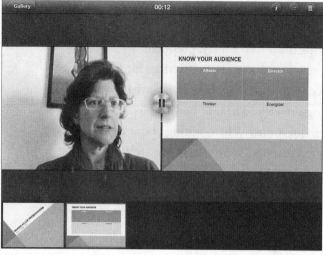

FIGURE 7.5
9Slides
combines video
and visuals for
online viewing.

Given the power of the app, we were amazed at how easy 9slides is to use. Essentially, 9slides displays a split screen: on the left is the video of the presenter; on the right are the visuals (see Figure 7.5). The visuals move ahead in conjunction with the recorded presentation. Once your presentation is on the 9slides site, e-mail the link to people you want to view your presentation or add the URL link to your website. You could also house your iPad at a kiosk and open only your presentation or a series of your presentations, which people can watch as they wish. 9slides is also a great way to distribute your presentation after you give it.

Download the free version if only to access the public 9slides presentations, including Guy Kawasaki's commencement speech, "10 Hindsights," given to the Menlo College class of 2012. The visuals are fantastic—this is a Killer Presentation!

PENXY
Free
http://penxy.com
Penxy lets you record and/or broadcast your PowerPoint or PDF files and accompanying audio, so it's an app that works for live and recorded presentation (see Figure 7.6). You then

FIGURE 7.6 Penxy offers live broadcast of your presentations.

create an event and upload content to that event. You can broadcast the presentation and audio live while recording simultaneously, or you can record only. The user interface is stylish and easy to understand. If you plan to broadcast live, you obtain a link to your broadcast and share it. Broadcasts can be viewed in any browser or accessed from Penxy.com. One of the features we like is the immediacy created with your audience with broadcast presentations: field questions from the audience during live broadcasts and poll your audience with a multiple-choice question and see the results live.

The hardest thing about recorded presentations is not seeing your audience's reaction. If you post a video on one of the social networks or your website, you can obtain analytics to see who watched your presentation, when, and from where, but analytics can't measure the reaction of the viewer, which is important to know. Engage your viewers by giving them a call to action. Marketing guru Marie Forleo produces a weekly vlog to share her knowledge and drive business to her seminars and coaching business (http://www.marieforleo.com). Each one ends with a specific call to action, which may be as simple as answering a question related to the content or a more involved prodding to do something and then write about the results. Each week, there's a string of comments on her website following the vlog. She's created a community.

In the end, regardless of the technology you use, your presentation should create a connection between you and the viewer. Go for an emotional pull, and your chances of creating that connection increase considerably.

CHAPTER 8

How to "Prop Up" and "Model" Your Presentation

You can really spark up your presentation or speech by using props to slam your points home and wake up and grab the attention of your group. They can add variety, drama, interest, and entertainment to your talk so your group will vividly remember your key messages or information. Some special props can also activate an emotional effect upon your audience. Props are one of the most underutilized tools and yet one of the best ways to put more punch in your presentations while setting you apart from other speakers.

Here's a rather over-the-top example of "prop-agating" interest in one's event right from the start. About 700 people from start-up technology companies are gathered in a major conference in a hotel ballroom in Austin, Texas, waiting to hear a well-known expert and showman speak on "disruptive innovation." The elevated stage is decorated with some awesome visuals and cool-looking props. On the projection screen a clock with a second hand ticks down the time from 30 seconds, getting louder as it reaches 10 seconds to showtime. The lights dim.

A recorded voice simply announces the "disruptor's" name. A spotlight shines on the back of the room. A man dressed in Western clothes and cowboy boots pedals a tricycle furiously up the aisle toward the stage. He jumps up onto the stage and shouts, "I'm tired of riding this silly old, slow thing." He disappears behind a curtain and flies back out, riding a Segway scooter and doing figure eights on the stage as the audience erupts with laughter, surprise, and applause.

Twin iPad minis in "holsters" are attached to his cowboy belt. He walks up to stage center, pauses, looks around the room, and begins, "You guessed it. I'm a maverick and a technology Wild West cowboy. If you want to rev up your company, I'll show you how to get off your trike and onto a new platform that will move you ahead at warp speed." That was a fictionalized example of an unexpected, creatively theatrical opening presentation scenario that applied a series of props along with a costume!

Props Can Impart an Urgent Tone to Your Talk

Let's say a vice president of strategic product development for a manufacturer of construction equipment is giving a presentation with a serious undertone. He decides to take a calculated (big) risk that he feels is warranted. A leading consulting firm has almost convinced his top management to go a certain route in developing different vehicles—a course that he strongly opposes. Shortly into his presentation, he pulls out an interesting and shocking prop—a realistic-looking, backward-firing pistol (see Figure 8.1). He holds the gun in his hand in such a way that, if fired, he would shoot himself in the head.

He tells his group of high-level engineering, manufacturing, and marketing executives, "I so strongly oppose the new product direction we are being advised to take, I'm willing to go to the extreme of using this prop to make an urgent point: in less than six months, we will be shooting ourselves for doing it. The pain and damage will be irreparable." With that, he uses his iPad to bring up a visual animation of the reverse-firing gun

FIGURE 8.1
Real-looking
reverse-firing
pistol

shooting with a loud *crack* as flame and smoke erupt from the barrel. A bullet from the gun whizzes toward a three-dimensional word PROFIT that appears to be made of solid glass. It impacts the animated graphic, shattering PROFIT to pieces as another audio file interjects the shrill sounds of glass breaking.

He tells the group, "I will explain and justify why we should not take this deadly course of action. I will give you a new product strategy that will save us from harm in the years ahead." This dramatic, theatrical use of a prop to emotionally and visually emphasize his contrarian message helps him ultimately reverse the group's decision. In this fictionalized example, what made the "performance" even more impactful was how the presenter used some simple acting techniques to creatively handle the gun as if it were real and dangerous and loaded!

Mike Rayburn (http://www.mikerayburn.com) is an award-winning motivational speaker, entertainer, and guitar virtuoso. He uses his guitar as a prop in his inspiring talks. He masterfully plays the guitar unlike anyone you have ever seen, playing just with one hand (you have to see this!) and then playing with the other only on the neck of the guitar, but *not* by picking the strings! He uses his radically unique, superb style to illustrate that we can and should consider doing things differently. You may later forget his name, but not his artistic, entertaining, and humorous performance, totally driven by his guitar as a prop for his insightful messages.

What really is a prop? The term *prop* is a shortened version of the theatrical term *property*, used to describe any typical stationary, portable, or handheld object (e.g., telephone, remote control, chair, umbrella, window) used by an actor in a performance. The same concept of props applies to a presenter or public speaker.

Getting Suited Up to Express and Impress

An outfit, costume, uniform, or disguise is also considered a prop of sorts. Something as basic as a themed hat, even if used briefly, can add some variety to a presentation. Ray Anthony's company built a custom construction helmet (see Figures 8.2 and 8.3) that is worn by one of his clients (a business development professional) when the client talks about how innovative his company is.

Another example: In a video about organizational change management, Lori, a corporate trainer, talks about "policing" the plan to change one's culture and organizational structure. Dressed as a New York City police officer, she uses directional sign props to make her points about following the right directions (see Figure 8.4). Later she moves to sit in a director's chair (also a good prop) with some additional prop items around her, rather

FIGURE 8.2
Construction helmet with rubber novelty lightbulb

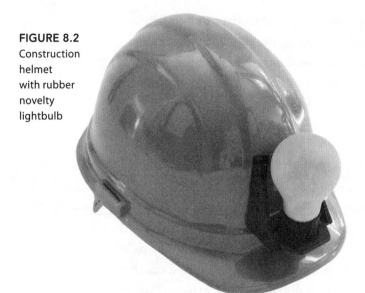

FIGURE 8.3 Custom-made bracket to hold lightbulb on helmet

FIGURE 8.4
Police outfit (costume) with props has an added effect.

FIGURE 8.5
This shows that props are great for use in videos.

than just standing up and talking to the camera for her other video presentations (see Figure 8.5).

And still one example more: Christie, a trainer and consultant, conducts "experiential training" where she and her team teach people about navigating organizational change and innovation by having them play a competitive game. She first gives a one-hour presentation on the basics of "navigating" change. Then participants drive a remote control truck through an obstacle course filled with dinosaurs, robots, roadblocks, brick walls, and bridges. To make the session even more realistic, thematic, and fun, Christie and others get dressed up in racing suits for her presentation and the game (see Figure 8.6).

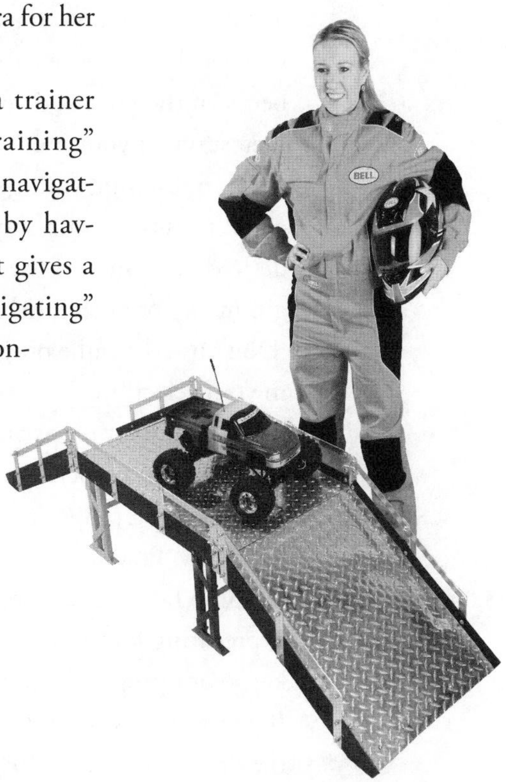

FIGURE 8.6
Another example of wearing an outfit to add spice to a training presentation

Tips on Selecting and Using the Right Props

When deciding upon meaningful props to help illustrate your topic, use them—but don't abuse them by having too many that clutter your talk. In conservative organizational cultures, acceptable props can be product prototypes, scale models of buildings, miniature die-cast models, or 3-D printed objects, all designed to give a more accurate and deeper perspective on the information being conveyed. Motivational and professional speakers generally have greater leeway than other presenters in using a wider variety of props in a more animated, fun, and theatrical way. When it comes to effectively selecting and generally using props for business, sales, and technical presentations or speeches, consider the following seven guidelines:

1. Ask yourself where and when in your presentation a prop would add real value and interest to your talk and how you can smoothly integrate it into the flow of your talk. Don't use a potentially distracting prop that doesn't contribute to the presentation.

2. Think through how you would best use that prop. While the prop will get the audience's attention, it's up to you to create that *connection* between the prop and your important point.

3. Determine if your props will likely strengthen your credibility and assist in reaching your goals with that particular audience or if they could possibly diminish your professionalism and endanger your desired outcomes. If used improperly, props can be seen as being gimmicky or amateurish or somehow trivializing a point.

4. Don't use the same props others might be employing. Be imaginative in your selection.

5. Make sure your props are large enough to be seen and are easily visible to all in your audience.

6. If operating a prop, explain what you are doing step-by-step, if necessary. Practice with it, especially if it requires skill. If your use of the prop fails unexpectedly, have a backup plan to recover or a self-deprecating joke to make so you can easily move on. As a general rule, keep your prop hidden until you're ready to use it.

7. If you want people in the audience to be part of showing or operating the prop, ask them beforehand and instruct them on what you want them to do. They need to know what you're going to talk about, how you want them to act and react, where you want them to be when you are presenting, when you want them to come on, and when they should leave the area.

More Ways Presenters Effectively Use a Variety of Props

Here are some creative examples to demonstrate how various props can be used for effect:

1. A consultant who was talking about creating a clear, enticing vision for organizations bought an inexpensive pair of eyeglasses. During his presentation, he "accidentally" knocked them off his face and stepped on them as he was looking for them. "If I can't see where I'm supposed to go, I won't get there," he said, effectively reinforcing his message on the value of creating a crystal-clear corporate vision.

2. An author of creativity books who was giving a talk on that topic to an association pulled out a replica of the human brain made of a flexible substance. He then took a very large set of pliers. When he tightened the pliers around the model with both hands, you could see the replica brain ("painfully") being squeezed. He wanted to emphasize that we do this to our creativity by censoring our ideas "tightly."

3. An accomplished amateur magician and professional speaker to corporations was talking about his topic, "Using the Full Magic of Technology in Your Job." While he was using his iPad to show photos, illustrations, and video to support his topic, he was also doing magic tricks from his iPad such as pulling objects (e.g., round balls, paper documents, photos, and toys) seemingly right out of the screen.

4. A sales professional selling commercial-duty drills to prospective buyers at a free seminar asked for a volunteer in the audience. She handed the person two seemingly identical black rubber balls (which she bought online from a novelty gift site) and asked the volunteer to carefully inspect each one. After the volunteer said that he found them identical in every respect, she then asked him to drop one ball on the table in front of the group. He did, and it bounced about two feet. She then told him to drop the other "identical" ball. He did it, but this ball fell totally flat with a quiet thud, without bouncing. She explained how commercial-duty drills may look alike, but it's what's on the inside—like the two balls—that determines how they perform. Bringing home the message, she said, "Our brushless motors inside give our models 40 percent more torque and 65 percent more durability than any other brand. They will never fall flat while operating."

5. A financial advisor was giving a presentation about her firm's investment products to a group of about 80 potential clients. She was using her iPad and her iPresent app to show video testimonials, animated charts, and graphs of investment returns and other captivating visuals that spelled out smart strategies to get high returns on one's money. One of the props she gave out to each person in attendance was a bunch of real-looking $1 million bills. At a point in her talk, she asked the attendees, "Who thinks they are good at grabbing money?" Three eager people raised their hands. "Come up here and bring your millions with you. I need you as volunteers." With that she

took one of their bills and asked the first person to try to grab the bill as she dropped it from her fingers (see Figure 8.7). It went right past the volunteer's fingers. She did this three times with each person, and only once did one of the volunteers even come close to snatching it as it fell.

She made her point, saying, "It often looks easy to keep from losing money, but unless you know how to grab it and keep it and build your fortunes, millions can be lost by all of us." Go ahead and try this exercise to make your own different points, especially in sales situations. You will be amazed how difficult it is to grab a piece of currency!

FIGURE 8.7
A simple bill used creatively makes for a memorable activity.

6. An expert in organizational problem solving was talking to an audience of professionals responsible for corporate change management and mergers at a large association convention. His focus was on how to prevent damaging organizational "fires" from occurring and also how to stop them once started. On stage were three 60-inch TVs displaying visuals from his iPad, in addition to the large projection screen. He discussed the major types of fires that most organizations cause themselves.

On one of the TVs, he showed a video of a raging inferno. Behind his podium, he grabbed a carbon dioxide fire extinguisher and aimed it toward the TV. With a theatrical flair, he let loose a cloud of white gas, and out went the fire on the screen. He did this with the other types of company fires on the other two TVs. That prop and how he used it made a memorable impression on his group. As a gift to each person attending, he gave out a miniature red fire extinguisher with his name and contact information to garner more business as a result of his "hot" performance.

7. A friend of ours, Peter H., is a successful consultant, trainer, and dynamic speaker on creativity topics. With some of his speeches, he talks about the need to "shout out loud" to management when it starts neglecting critical innovation that jeopardizes the company. He will pick up a megaphone

and "shout" (not too loud, though) for about 20 seconds to make his point (see Figure 8.8). His branding on his business card is a laminated, die-cut-shaped megaphone.

Impressive Architectural Models for Your Presentation

While the magical iPad will do wonders in creating your Killer Presentation, there are other tools that are better suited for your intended purposes and can wonderfully complement your iPad-based presentation or sales pitch. Architects know that nothing beats an actual physical model when selling a project or making an important presentation. The higher the quality of the model, the more impact the message will have. These impressive models are used for making sales, evaluating a design, and doing planning and development work. They also make wonderful permanent displays.

Myles Burke (http://mylesburke.com) is a producer of premium-quality architectural models. In an interview with David Myles, one of the firm's founders, he told Ray Anthony that detailed models are critical for giving a Killer Presentation. Real estate developers, he noted, put a great deal of effort and money into a project. Along with graphically rich poster boards of suite layouts, renderings, and material boards, they will often use a highly detailed scale model as their primary display tool for ratcheting up sales.

"Renderings can be visually attractive, but are limited to two-dimensional media. They can't begin to convey the full story, while a model communicates three-dimensional space and objects. At a glance, a viewer can visualize length, width and depth, perspective, context, and relationships of design and structure," says Myles. Just look at Figures 8.9 to 8.14, which show stunning architectural designs produced by the skilled model makers of Myles Burke, to appreciate the presentation power of true-scaled, realistic depictions of the real thing.

FIGURE 8.8
This presenter used a megaphone to emphasize his key point.

Myles said, "Our intent is to accurately and compellingly portray the project in its entirety—this is how many stories the building is… this part is red brick, this part is green tinted glass… this is its relationship to the street. We put a great deal of effort into making the model 'believable,' so that when the viewer looks at it, little is left to their imagination as to what it would be like to live or work there. For example, you can make a model out of brown cardboard and say it still resembles the real building, but when you have textured brick, and layered facades that cast shadows on themselves, these important visual cues supply the viewer with an abundance of information as to understand the project completely."

When it comes to presentations, the more visually interesting and fascinating something is, the longer a viewer observes, studies, and perhaps marvels at it. Myles sums it up: "This is the reason why a scale model is usually found to be the visual centerpiece of an important presentation. Scale models present themselves."

FIGURE 8.10 Accurate and detailed building materials show realism.
(Copyright Myles Burke. Used with permission.)

FIGURE 8.9 Models can be huge!
(Copyright Myles Burke. Used with permission.)

FIGURE 8.11 This model shows the layout and scope of a project. (Copyright Myles Burke. Used with permission.)

FIGURE 8.12 Models make for impressive displays. (Copyright Myles Burke. Used with permission.)

FIGURE 8.13 Incredible detail shows sizes, dimensions, and relationships. (Copyright Myles Burke. Used with permission.)

FIGURE 8.14 Lighting adds important perspective. (Copyright Myles Burke. Used with permission.)

Oversized Props for "Big" Effect

We occasionally use big props on stage (or in the front or side of the room) either as decoration or for our use in certain parts of the presentations. They are effective for larger audiences where a smaller prop would have less visual impact. These oversized items are also great for use in videos, in photographs, at trade shows, and in training workshops. Go to http://www .greatbigstuff.com to see some interesting everyday items that are "bigger than life." Below are just a few examples of big and really big from that company:

- Baseball bat and ball
- Computer keys
- Can opener
- Candy bars
- Pink eraser
- Six-foot wooden ruler
- Calculator
- Chess set
- Monopoly pieces

Ray Anthony uses large Scrabblelike letters (see Figure 8.15) that he builds in various combinations, mostly as background display for his videos and also as a static display on stage for keynote speeches. You can also buy these from the Great Big Stuff website and even make complicated arrangements of the wooden letters by attaching them to wooden strips on the back with screws and glue. One favorite prop that audiences like is the giant lighter (see Figure 8.16), which actually gives off a big flame when you put lighter fluid in it.

FIGURE 8.15 Use giant letters for your key messages.

FIGURE 8.16 This lighter serves as a multiuse prop for presentations, videos, and photos.

FIGURE 8.17 A popular big prop for many uses

FIGURE 8.18 You can use props like this to emphasize.

One big prop that people who teach creativity techniques, or talk about product designs, or focus on anything related to ideas, use is the giant plastic lightbulb (see Figure 8.17) that has an optional electric light inside to illuminate it. A popular professional speaker who talks about brainpower and ideas uses the large lightbulb to take photos with attendees holding a copy of his book. He then puts the pictures on his website for people to download them. Another presenter (see Figure 8.18) uses an arrow made of plastic that he employs selectively—maybe only two times during a speech or presentation—to emphasize (especially in a humorous fashion) key points or parts of an illustration, map, or diagram. Other examples of these impressive oversized items are shown in Figures 8.19 and 8.20.

FIGURE 8.19 Props can be visual metaphors.

FIGURE 8.20 An example of a prop used for a fun training video

Models of All Kinds

Presenters use various types of models as static display props (e.g., set out on a table close to them) or ones they pick up and handle. Some are detailed die-cast models of trucks, construction equipment, cranes, fire trucks, or farm tractors with which they illustrate their points. There is a large collection of impressive (including museum-quality) die-cast models for those presenters in the construction and building industries. However, most detailed die-cast models are only one-sixteenth scale at their largest. They are useful primarily with small groups who can easily see them. But they are fine for display in meeting and presentation rooms. TWH Collectibles (http://www.twhcollectibles.com) and 3000 Toys (http://www .3000toys.com) are great sources of intricate, high-quality die-cast models.

Fun-type models that we have seen some presenters use in illustrating their topics are attractive, laser-cut cardboard pieces of famous buildings and landmarks (see Figures 8.21 to 8.23). Amazon sells these buildings,

FIGURE 8.22 These paper models can be very impressively detailed.

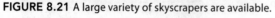

FIGURE 8.21 A large variety of skyscrapers are available.

FIGURE 8.23 Models like this cathedral are great for travel or architectural presentations.

called 3-D puzzles and made by companies such as Daron. You can find famous bridges, cathedrals, memorial buildings, palaces, skyscrapers, towers, and other landmarks from around the world. Most only cost between $6 and $15 each, and you can assemble these rather impressive-looking models in 30 to 60 minutes or less. Depending upon your presentation topics, you might find myriad uses for them as talking points in your presentations and training courses or as props in your videos or photos.

Even more compelling are highly detailed plastic model kits that are typically used in big G-gauge train layouts. We have seen some presenters use these as displays (including making detailed dioramas) in their meeting rooms or use them as props when talking about topics related to them. For example, one manager in the energy industry shows a model of a refinery (that his team built) to discuss the operation of today's complex industrial processes (see Figure 8.24). A human resources specialist who gives presentations to new hires shows a large, old-time detailed model of her company's brewery to illustrate the company's rich history (see Figure 8.25). And a college instructor of agricultural topics might show a model of a grain building to add some realism and flavor to her talk (see Figure 8.26). Piko is a company that sells numerous model kits you can use as not only props in your presentation, but as

FIGURE 8.24
This model would be impressive as a display in a presentation room.

FIGURE 8.25 You can turn models into presentation dioramas.

FIGURE 8.26 This grain building model has a lot of visual impact.

attractive static displays in your meetings, trade shows, or training events. Check out http://www.piko-america.com/Model-Buildings.html for more information.

3-D Printing for Prototypes, Conceptual "Products," and Props in Your Presentation

Imagine a future in which a device connected to a computer can "print" a solid, complex object made of different materials, colors, finishes, and textures just like the real thing—even an operating product with precision gears, slides, levers, wheels, and many other detailed movable parts. Well, 3-D printing is at the stage where it can do that right now. Cathy Lewis, chief marketing officer for 3D Systems Corporation (http://www.3dsystems .com), one of the world's largest manufacturers of powerful 3-D printers, told Ray Anthony in an interview that product developers, engineers, inventors, medical professionals, manufacturers, marketers, and salespeople who need to precisely communicate their ideas by showing realistic concepts and prototypes need to learn more about 3-D printing and how to use it for impressive effect in their Killer Presentations.

It is easy to understand why 3-D printing—by which a digital file from design software such as AutoCad, Autodesk 123D, Cubify Invent, SketchUp, or Solidworks is translated into a physical object by a 3-D printer—is considered an "additive" form of fabrication or manufacturing. The piece is made by building up multiple layers of material. The printing head moves back and forth over a flat surface and builds an object, using hundreds or thousands of layers.

Because a wide variety of materials can be used, high-resolution 3-D printing has altered the product development landscape forever. If you are a sunglass manufacturer, for example, and you want to show major buyers new, impressive designs as part of your sales presentation, rather than show them three-dimensional renderings or animations, use a 3-D printer to create several samples of the real thing within a day or two. Your buyers can see your product, feel the material, explore the designs up close, and even try on the glasses for fit and feel. That may be compelling enough to land the deal right then and there.

You can print your product prototype today and place it in the hands of a customer focus group or your company's internal evaluation team tomorrow as part of your presentation of new product plans. When people can touch, hold, try out, or operate these realistic prototypes at presentations, you have opened up a new dimension that far exceeds the best visuals one could show. Cathy Lewis says, "3D printers can create almost anything from smartphone and tablet accessories to finished jewelry and toys, from custom hearing aids, individualized prosthetics, and Invisalign clear orthodontics to functional airplane, UAV, and car parts. In the twenty-seven years of 3D printing, perhaps ten million people have actually used this technology to advance their products, companies, and careers. Now hundreds of millions will be able to take advantage of this marvelous capability." Smart companies are therefore using sophisticated 3-D printers to show "real" products as part of their Killer Presentations.

Companies recognize that being first to market is critical in the battle for revenue. You can greatly compress your design cycles by printing multiple (each slightly different) prototypes on demand and identifying design errors and inadequacies much earlier. Engineers and designers in all sorts of industries—automotive, defense, tools, electronics, aerospace, consumer goods, sporting equipment, and others—have the intention, during their working presentations and brainstorming sessions, to fine-tune their new product designs with the feedback from their group. So having a quickly available, accurate prototype to examine, test, and refine can be invaluable in making decisions on how to best proceed.

Amazing Results with This Powerful Technology

Look at Figures 8.27 to 8.31 from 3D Systems to see the impressive functionality and capabilities of today's leading 3-D industrial machines. Many commercial models can use multiple materials at once, creating some intricate models with complex geometries that offer a variety of colors, textures, and attributes. Machines from 3D Systems can even print text labels, logos, design comments, or images directly onto the models being printed!

Industrial-quality machines such as those from 3D Systems and Mcor Corporation can offer several hundred thousand to over a million colors with a high resolution. Intricate designs for architecture, action figures, and character models are rising in popularity with this capability. Another leading manufacturer of impressive commercial-duty 3-D printers is

FIGURE 8.27 You can print an entire assembly like this. (Copyright 3D Systems. Used with permission.)

FIGURE 8.28 An example of an accurate prototype design. (Copyright 3D Systems. Used with permission.)

FIGURE 8.29 Architects are using printers for small buildings and parts. (Copyright 3D Systems. Used with permission.)

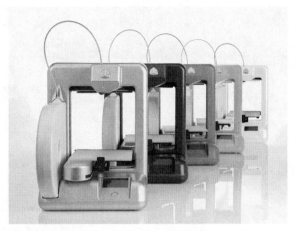

FIGURE 8.30 Looks exactly like the real thing! (Copyright 3D Systems. Used with permission.)

FIGURE 8.31 Printed prototypes showing a variety of true colors. (Copyright 3D Systems. Used with permission.)

Stratasys (http://www.stratasys.com), which offers a wide variety of printers from small desktop models to its largest Production Series models. Visit the Stratasys website to find out more about applications and case studies that can ultimately support your Killer Presentations with prototypes, models, and props.

Whenever people attending a presentation can see ways to better evaluate for themselves the form, fit, and function of real objects or product or engineering prototypes, it is the most convincing and compelling way to have them understand what you are communicating. If your business and job would benefit by it, learn more about how 3-D printing will add more Killer to your presentations.

Prop(el) Your Presentation Far Ahead of Others

While your iPad is the main engine powering your Killer Presentation, don't forget to consider using some interesting and compelling props, models, prototypes, and displays in your presentations and speeches. They will help you better communicate your ideas and messages and add that extra important "flavor" to your talks.

CHAPTER 9

Riveting Openings and Killer Conclusions

The introduction and conclusion are the most important parts of a Killer Presentation. People are affected more emotionally, intellectually, and behaviorally by the very first and last things they see, hear, smell, touch, taste, sense, or experience than they are by almost anything encountered in between. It pays to spend extra time preparing, rehearsing, and fine-tuning your presentation's introduction and conclusion. Throughout the following pages, you will discover great tips, techniques, observations, and even valuable scripted examples on starting and ending your presentation with a bang. Or in the words of old-time movie mogul Samuel Goldwyn, a movie (like a presentation) should start with an earthquake and build to a climax.

Grab 'Em from the Start: Crafting Your Riveting Opening

Why a riveting opening? You only get one chance to make a favorable, all-important first impression. It's the reason you need to make a splash with your audience right from the start of your presentation. In an April 2012 *Harvard Business Review* article titled "Use Your 118 Seconds Wisely," the author noted that the average elevator ride in New York City takes 118 seconds. He says this is the ideal timing of an effective "elevator pitch," with the first 8 seconds the key to grabbing the attention of the listener. The same applies to a more lengthy presentation, only you have a slightly longer "grace period."

187

The introduction is a like a delicious appetizer—setting anticipation for the delightful entrée (the main body and substance of your presentation) next on the menu. It should be like the exciting blast-off of a rocket ship or the takeoff of a jet. It should give the audience an exciting and enticing snapshot of what will follow. It sets the tone, quality, intent, and perhaps the urgency of the presentation. It communicates so much so quickly about your credibility, image, and speaking style. Done well, it says you are prepared, poised, and confident. If your first two or three minutes of speaking come across as lifeless, rambling, or anxious, the audience will tune out in a heartbeat. But if the opening remarks and your engaging style evoke the curiosity of the people in your audience, spark their imaginations, stir their emotions, and captivate them, the audience will be motivated to concentrate on your entire presentation. Blow the introduction, and you will have a mighty tough job trying to recover the audience.

Before we dig into what makes an opening a riveting "Killer," let's look at a few examples:

Imagine sitting in an audience of hundreds waiting for a renowned motivational speaker to present "Let's S-O-A-R to New Heights." At the back of the room is a larger-than-life cardboard cutout of a man and woman with wings, flying together among the clouds. On either side of the room are freestanding seven-foot-tall signs. One says, "Your Attitude Determines Your Altitude," and the second reads, "Why Walk or Run When You Can Fly?"

The lights dim, and the energetic theme music swells to a crescendo, but instead of a traditional introduction, the projection screen plays a stunning video of eagles flying: soaring and diving in spectacular displays of aerial mastery. Then the screen fades to black, the stage lights come on, and the presenter is standing center stage, smiling at the crowd with an iPad in his hand.

"Let's *soar*!" he says. As he taps his iPad screen, the spotlight picks up a remote control hovercraft rising on the right side of the stage. Easily controlling the craft with his iPad, he flies it down the aisle to the cutout in the back of the room. All eyes are on the drone as it hovers over the flying man and woman. He continues, "Today I'm going to show each of you how to lift your wings and fly high in your career and life." Still controlling the nearly silent remote drone with his iPad, he sends it across the room above the heads of the captivated audience, coming to a stop and hovering over one of the freestanding signs. "The main focus of my speech today is how changing your attitude will change your life," he says. The craft again flies over the audience, this time hovering above the second sign. "You'll discover it takes the same energy to fly as it does to walk, and you *will* soar if you want to."

"Just look at the screen," he says, flying the drone over the audience again, but this time activating an HD video camera and transmitting what it sees—a top-down view of the audience—to the large projection screen above the stage. Finally, iPad in hand, he flies the drone around the room a bit and then has it hover two feet above his head as he says, "If I can soar, you can soar. Now let's learn to fly high together!" The audience erupts in raucous applause. What a beginning!

Jennifer R., a financial advisor, is giving a presentation about retirement income to 45 people in a closed room in a restaurant. She welcomes the group and starts off by unveiling an oversize replica of a slot machine she is using as a prop. She says, "Many of us enjoy a bit of gambling as a form of entertainment, but none of us would ever consider seriously chancing our hard-earned lifetime savings, would we?" as she jerks the handle and the wheels spin, but with no resulting win. The audience members nod their heads in agreement. She then takes her iPad, walks to a table, and asks a woman to look at the iPad screen (which has the face of a slot machine). "Push this *special* button," she tells the woman.

Smiling, the woman touches the iPad, the wheels spin, and the audience sees the action projected on the 60-inch LCD television in front of the room. "Three sevens!" Jennifer shouts, above a perfectly timed, loud audio of coins crashing. "You win!" She then walks to another table and asks a distinguished-looking gentleman also to push the button on her special "always a winner" slot machine app on the iPad's screen. As all eyes focus on the TV in the front of the room, the reels spin, and three winning cherries are displayed on the big screen, accompanied by the sound of more coins shooting out. "Another winner!" she enthusiastically yells out.

Jennifer transitions, saying, "We all know that slot machines pay out about 95 percent of what they take in. So the house always wins—over a period of time. But my company has developed a rock-solid, proven financial system that consistently pays out between 110 and 115 percent or more of your investment over an extended period of time, an impressive accomplishment, indeed, in these low-yield times. No gambling. No risk. No taking a chance. Instead, a guarantee of steady wins over time. According to *Conservative Investor's Weekly*, our investment model has provided the highest rates of return for the most people of any investment firm in the world. Tonight I will show you conclusively how to invest and win with your hard-earned money." She uses her iPad slot machine app to bring up three jackpot symbols, along with the loudest sound yet of a real slot machine winning, to slam her point home. That's the way she starts off, and her group can't wait to hear what she has to say!

Lori, an account manager from a leading open innovation firm, is about to give her first presentation to the R&D group of a leading multinational consumer goods company that is interested in learning how it can connect with worldwide innovators who have already developed specific technologies. She found out that the head of R&D is an avid fisherman.

Soon into her presentation introduction, she pulls out a miniature (but fully functioning) fishing rod and reel (called the fish-

FIGURE 9.1
Presenter using her two props for an impressive beginning

FIGURE 9.2 Clever acronym with a metaphorical graphic

ing rod pen, which she bought on Amazon.com) and takes her iPad and holds it up to show this visual (see Figures 9.1 and 9.2). She says, "Today is about catching F.I.S.H., and that stands for 'Future Innovations Served Here.' I will introduce you to a process that will triple the effectiveness of your already highly productive research activities and double your ability to commercialize your innovations through teaming up with our tens of thousands of scientists, researchers, and engineers who are in our database."

FIGURE 9.3
An example of the origami fish that Lori gave to each person in the group. (Artwork and design by Won Park)

Next, she grabs the handle of a small fishing net and pulls out 10 small fish—each an impressively intricate origami piece of art made from a dollar bill (see Figure 9.3)—and gives one each to the attendees at the presentation. She discovered the fish in the book *Dollar Origami: 10 Origami Projects Including the Amazing Koi Fish* by Won Park. Because of the complexity and elegance of the origami dollar fish, she had an experienced origami artist create them. After gifting each of the attendees, the account manager adds, "Our F.I.S.H. are all designed to give you superior revenue opportunities and unprecedented returns on your investment. Let's talk about great F.I.S.H.ing for you!" as she launches into the main part of her presentation.

After Lori finishes her presentation, she performs an impressive "matching conclusion" by pulling out her fishing rod and reel (see Figure 9.4) and saying, "Let's go F.I.S.H.ing together to get a big catch!" With that she hands out a novel gift—that miniature fishing rod and reel she bought from Amazon.

FIGURE 9.4
Presenter reminding people to go "F.I.S.H.ing"

FIGURE 9.5 Gift of real fishing equipment within a "pen"

com (see Figure 9.5)—to each of the people attending her presentation. What an impact!

Not all presentations launch with the kinds of *wow* illustrated in these three examples. And you don't need a $300 Parrot AR Drone quadricopter, a cool slot machine replica and iPad app, or fishing props to craft a Killer opening, either. But what a difference an exciting, creative introduction can make. How often have you seen a business presenter or public speaker start off in a lackadaisical or making-it-up-on-the-spot way that invites you to tune out, daydream, or concentrate on something else entirely? No matter how compelling the content, if you don't grab people's attention from the start, you can't expect them to still be with you 30 minutes later.

This next section will give you tools, insights, information, and ideas to help you craft and deliver compelling and captivating introductions every time using the four components—technology, strategy, psychology, and creativity—of the P-XL² Model (covered in Chapter 4).

What Do You Want Your Introduction to Accomplish?

Consummate presenters know the art of teasing and tantalizing their audience by building up suspense, curiosity, anticipation, and eagerness to hear or see what happens next. Besides riveting your audience's attention and starting to build rapport and credibility as a subject-matter expert and competent speaker, other goals of your presentation's introduction may include:

- An overview of things to come
- The significance, benefits, and value of the information you're about to provide
- Promises or commitments
- A call to action: what you want them to do when you finish

Building Block Approach for Designing Your Killer Introduction

There are a number of parts—communication components—you can use to create quality introductions (and conclusions). Think of them as links in a chain or building blocks (like Legos) that can be snapped together as needed. You can join any number of building blocks in any combination or order you wish. How you create your building block introduction depends upon the nature of your presentation, your audience, your speaking style, and the time you have to prepare. The blocks in the examples of the following pages are by no means the only types of building blocks you might use; additional building blocks you come up with are limited only by your imagination. Consider the following building blocks (with scripted examples) for your next presentation.

Introduction Building Block 1. Amenities

The purpose here is to greet the audience, start building rapport, and get off to a friendly, smooth, and natural start. Look at this example:

"I'm delighted to talk about our multifaceted solution for your project. I'd like to thank Fred W. and Joan R. for their support in providing the relevant information we needed and for brainstorming terrific creative ideas with us. I've enjoyed working with all the fine professionals in your company and look forward to a close and beneficial relationship with all of you here today."

Introduction Building Block 2. Team Member Introductions

If giving a team presentation, introduce yourself and other members of your company's team who will be presenting or contributing information from the sidelines. Here is an example:

"For those of you who don't know me, my name is Paul K. I'm your account manager and the team leader for this presentation. I've been in the automated controls industry for over 15 years in the areas of engineering, technical support, and marketing. Like many of you, I have a degree in electrical engineering. Let me introduce the members of my presentation team and tell you how they will be contributing to our presentation today. Starting from the left is ..."

Introduction Building Block 3. Theme

If you have a theme, you might want to unveil it in your introduction and then play off it throughout your presentation to support your key points. As an example:

"Our theme for this presentation—that I've just displayed on the screen from my iPad—reflects the impact it will have on your profits and competitive edge. WINNER stands for With Integrated Networks—Numerous Excellent Returns. The integrated network we design for your future will give you exceptional returns on your investment. Our partnership in this project will, indeed, be a WINNER for both of our companies."

Introduction Building Block 4. Objectives and Expectations

In this part of an introduction, you tell the members of your audience what they can expect from you and also what you would like to get from them, as this example illustrates:

"We have three objectives. The first is to give you a detailed overview of the solution we're proposing based upon the requirements you gave us. Our second objective is to have a constructive dialogue during our presentation where you share your opinions and feelings about the solution we developed for you. Our third is for us, as a group, to reach a decision on whether this solution should be implemented, how, and in what time frame."

Introduction Building Block 5. "Housekeeping"

Often called "housekeeping" in standard business presentations, this optional building block communicates the structure and logistics of one's talk, as this example shows:

Mention your agenda and review it: "To reach our objectives, I've created an agenda of topics. You have a copy in front of you. I'll start out by summarizing our project goals, operational needs, and support requirements to ensure we are addressing all your key issues. Next, we'll cover..."

Gain acceptance of the agenda from your audience: "Is this agenda acceptable?"

Discuss presentation duration and process: "My presentation will last about 45 minutes. Feel free to ask questions at any time. I invite your feedback and comments as well."

Let your audience know how to access additional information: "At the end, you will get a DVD with more details about our leading-edge products that includes [describe contents]. We will also give you several links to our website and others that you will find useful in evaluating how our products best fit your needs."

Introduction Building Block 6. Verifying Needs and Findings

If you are selling a big-ticket product or service or presenting a complex project, consider summarizing the needs, wants, priorities, requirements, and preferences that your group expressed to you. Confirming this in a concise, accurate way will boost your credibility and help ensure that your presentation will meet your audience's expectations. Here is an example:

"You've provided us with information regarding your new program. I'd like to quickly summarize what I understand that you've told us and confirm that we're on track. Then, my team will discuss the details of this major project.

"What's most important to this implementation is . . .
"Your top priority is . . .
"Two major technological requirements driving the success of this
      project are . . .
"During our presentation, you want us to focus on . . .
"Have I accurately summarized the big picture? Is there anything that
      has changed that we need to know about before we continue?"

Introduction Building Block 7. Relevant Quotation

You can use a quotation that makes a strong point and ties into the major thrust of your presentation, such as the following:

"The new currency of this digital age and economy is ideas. The futurist Denton Redman said, 'I can't fathom why so many people are frightened of new ideas and concepts. I'm really afraid of the old ones.' And Mary Calter, an innovator in aerospace, wrote, 'We should assume not that the old way is wrong, but that there is a better way now we should consider.' For our organization to fast-forward ahead in the industry, we mustn't be frightened of new, even radical ideas."

Introduction Building Block 8. Startling Facts or Statistics

There is nothing quite as effective as surprising or shocking statistics or facts related to your topic. Notice how the following example does this:

"Our start-up firm is on the cusp of developing a working prototype of a quantum computer, so revolutionary, that in about 10 years, we will have a model the size of my iPad that will be more powerful than all the world's supercomputers combined! While even the best computer quickly works on one computation at a time, a quantum computer—using single atoms in a parallel processing mode—will do a million computations at once and even do it faster! Quantum computing will bring about more changes in the next 20 years than *all* the technological breakthroughs we've experienced over the last 100 years *combined*! In my presentation, I will give you a nontechnical overview of this supertechnology based on quantum mechanics and the stuff of science-fiction-turned-reality."

Introduction Building Block 9. Rhetorical Questions

Rhetorical questions are those that are asked solely, not to elicit a reply from your audience, but to create curiosity, suspense, or even drama. Done right, these questions nicely set the stage for your answers to those questions. Look at how this example offers a series of rhetorical questions in this sales presentation introduction:

"How is it possible that a 'disruptive technology' like ours can be significantly more reliable, efficient, and productive than even the best current technology that costs four times as much? Why are we the only one in our industry that has developed the radical innovations you'll hear about in our presentation? And how can you trust a relatively small company like ours to meet your most demanding requirements now and far into the future? The answers you hear will impress you!"

Introduction Building Block 10. Clever or Amusing Anecdote

An amusing anecdote or short, relevant piece of humor (though not necessarily a joke) will help to spotlight your topic, as the following example shows:

"Tongue-in-cheek comedian George Carlin said, 'There are only two places in the world: over here and over there.' Well, we are 'over here,' providing the largest selection of products along with fanatically great customer service that enables our customers to grow and prosper. Our competitors are 'over there,' trying but failing to imitate our exceptional business model. I will tell you how being 'over here' with us will make all the difference in the world for you and your organization."

Introduction Building Block 11. Executive Summary

If needed, give your audience an enticing big-picture overview of your product, proposal, or idea and effectively highlight its benefits. The most effective executive summaries use enumeration to help the audience absorb each distinct point, as the following illustrates:

"In the next 60 seconds or less, I'll tell you the essence of our proposal and how it will reap impressive rewards for our reality TV production company. There are three significant reasons why we need to make this investment in transitioning from film cameras to all video cameras from BLUE Corporation:

"One: Improved workflow and savings. We measured the increase in productivity in shooting three of our weekly 30-minute programs with the new cameras we rented: 40 percent reduction in work-hours across the board with about 25 percent less reshoots needed. That translates into savings of at least $62 million per year.

"Two: Leapfrog the competition. While other networks are currently shooting for high-definition TV, we will shoot in 4K resolution—way ahead of those—so we can develop programs now that are ready for the new ultrahigh-definition TVs.

"Three: Increased functionality. With these new BLUE cameras, we can now do so many more types of shoots, and do them so much more easily and quickly and with greater abilities than ever before, enabling us to produce even more innovative programming for our viewers.

"When you add up these three significant benefits of buying BLUE cameras, you will likely come to the same conclusion we did—this is a superb chance to leap ahead. Over the next 30 minutes, I will give you specifics on what I've just summarized for you."

Introduction Building Block 12. Transition Statement

This brief (transition) statement acts as a bridge—a segue—alerting the audience that you are now finished with the introductory remarks and will be getting into the detailed substance (body) of your presentation, as these two examples illustrate:

"Let's now get into the details of how our product will meet or exceed every one of your requirements and specifications." Or "You heard our executive summary. Now it's time for us to back up the impressive benefits we've projected for you. We'll begin by talking about…"

Implement the Introduction Building Block Approach

Let's take a look at an introduction that uses the building block approach to create a riveting beginning that powerfully sets the stage for the information that follows. Read the following fictionalized example, and see if you can identify which specific building blocks were combined.

Scenario. Ryan W. is an executive vice president in charge of advanced R&D for a major automotive company. He is giving a presentation to his company's board of directors to present the findings from his department's recent development of a prototype of a revolutionary new car and truck engine. His objective is to get the board's approval for funding to put the engine into mass production. He had his engineering department use a color 3-D printer to create a one-tenth-scale mock-up of a half cross section of the new engine and cut a piece out of the cross section to place his iPad inside (as a case for it) for stunning visual and theatrical effect. Here is his introduction:

"Sixteenth-century statesman Francis Bacon smartly said, 'A man must make his opportunity as oft as find it.' We did both: we found it and made it! Over the next 30 minutes, I'm going to tell you about a radical breakthrough in engine design that will be a financial bonanza for our company and guarantee us industry leadership far into the future. It is an opportunity we must not pass up."

From behind the lectern he pulls out the iPad with the realistic engine backing and shows it to the group. He touches the iPad screen to bring up a photo along with an audio file and says, "Listen. This is the sound of the world's quietest engine—running at low speed. Not our engine, though." While it is quiet, the group can clearly hear its sound. He touches his iPad screen, shows a photo, and activates another audio file, telling them, "That's the sound of our new engine—at full throttle—8,000 rpms!"

The board members look puzzled because the sound is quieter than the low-speed running engine! "No mistake," Ryan emphasizes. "This is the smoothest, quietest engine on the planet," he proudly boasts. He looks at the screen and says, "Now the sound of horsepower...," as he uses his iPad to display a video of four wild horses galloping; the sound this time is the loudest so far. "That's like the horsepower of current cars." He pauses and says, "But here is the horsepower of our superengine," as he touches his iPad screen to bring up a new video of a much larger pack of horses running at full gallop. The sound of hooves crashing against the ground is temporarily deafening, if only for a few fleeting seconds, but it definitely makes the comparative point in a most dramatic, auditory way—this engine is unbelievably powerful!

He continues, "Six months ago, my R&D team produced a quantum-leap breakthrough in nanotechnology and ceramics engine design. Our exhaustive lab tests show it will produce 80 percent more horsepower per pound than any engine in production, average over 135 miles per gallon in a midsize car, reduce engine emissions by 97 percent, and improve reliability by at least 85 percent. Astonishing isn't it? As impressive as the engineering wizardry is, so are the financial implications with this engine for our company:

"Over the next four years, we can grab five extra points of market share, giving us $71 billion in additional revenues during that time.

"Return on investment for the first year of production is estimated to be between 35 and 40 percent, far exceeding our investment hurdle rate of 16 percent.

"We can get this engine to the marketplace within 18 months, leapfrogging over our competitors and keeping them from copying us by at least four years.

"We will reduce our warranty expenses by approximately $1.2 billion per year because of significantly increased reliability.

"We must capitalize upon this opportunity. I will ask for your approval for the budget and for your ongoing support in three other ways to ensure the complete, successful outcome of this stunning breakthrough. Now, I will get into detail on this exclusive window of opportunity available to us…"

Tips for Crafting Captivating Presentation Introductions

Here are a few more things to consider as you're assembling your Killer intros:

- *Be creative.* If using your iPad, think of how you can use it not only as a controlling device but also as a clever prop. Also think of unconventional or entertaining ways you can introduce your talk with photos, illustrations, animations, stirring videos, audio special effects, narration or music, props, or theatrical effects.

- *Make it impressive.* Nothing is worse for the members of an audience than to hear a presentation start off dry and boring and feel they have to put up with 30 or 45 minutes more of yawn-filled pain. Ask yourself how you might immediately start off to impress the people in your group and how you could stimulate them intellectually and even emotionally in that first critical minute.

- *Keep it concise.* Get to your salient points quickly or risk losing your audience. Your lead-in should be concise but not rushed. Generally speaking, the introduction and conclusion should each take between 5 and 10 percent of the total time of your presentation. If your presentation is 30 minutes, the introduction and conclusion would each be about 1½ to 3 minutes long.

- *Show confidence and energy.* Begin your introduction with enthusiasm, poise, and passion. Use a strong voice volume, a slower speech rate, a smile, and good eye contact.

- *Avoid credibility killers.* Don't project false modesty or brag. And never apologize or make excuses as in these examples:

    "I'm sorry I'm not the person scheduled to give this presentation. They called me at the last minute, and I threw something together real quickly. So if the information is a little incomplete or a few slides have spelling errors, please excuse that." Or "I'm so honored to address this group. I feel almost inadequate since you are distinguished executives, many with credentials far more impressive than mine."

Make It Memorable: Crafting Killer Conclusions

Creating a standing ovation-quality conclusion is as critical to the success of your presentation as is a terrific introduction. The conclusion is the capstone, climax, and finale of your "performance." If an introduction is the presentation's appetizer, then the conclusion is the dessert—that last delicious part of a fine meal (presentation body) that lingers on one's (intellectual and emotional) taste buds. An impressive conclusion cements the speaker's credibility at its high point and shows consistent presentation excellence, right to the very end.

We remember the final things that are said much more than anything mentioned in the middle. It's the reason trial lawyers spend extra time preparing their summation remarks to the jury. Their goal is to create such an overwhelming impression of innocence or guilt that it steers the jury's decision making toward the desired verdict.

Building Block Approach for Designing a Memorable Conclusion

A great conclusion also has building blocks you connect together, with stunning results. You can use most of the building blocks relevant to crafting an introduction, but with some exceptions and variations. Remember that the following examples are only a partial set of building blocks. Let your imagination come up with others.

Conclusion Building Block 1. Transition Statement

Use transition statements to signal and announce that the end of your presentation is imminent. This will alert and perk up your group for an extra dose of concentration. Examples:

"In conclusion . . ."
"I'll conclude by briefly summarizing key points made during the last
   30 minutes."

"At this point, I'd like to wrap up by quoting something a famous [e.g., statesman] said that shines a spotlight on this issue. He said…"

Conclusion Building Block 2. Summary of Key Points

Summarizing your important points in a simple but compelling way will help your audience to vividly remember. Enumerating your points facilitates understanding. Here is an example of a sales presentation summary:

"Today we gave you an overview of our system's solution including the features, capabilities, implementation, and operational benefits for your company. Our industry-leading order processing system will ensure your explosive growth in the next decade for four vital reasons:

"*One.* It will easily and cost-effectively grow with your company even if your transaction volume skyrockets to 800 percent over the next five years.

"*Two.* It is the quickest system to implement on the market. We can get it installed in two months, which is five months sooner than any other supplier.

"*Three.* Its remarkable online reliability is unmatched anywhere—99.95 percent average.

"*Four.* Your return on investment will be between 25 and 35 percent, far exceeding your expectations and financial requirements.

"These are the four quite compelling reasons for you to partner with us right now."

Conclusion Building Block 3. Challenge to Your Audience

This is used to encourage an audience to surmount obstacles or inspire and motivate the audience members to take specific action. Here is an example of a challenge:

"It won't be easy for us to turn our company around. Our survival is at stake. I challenge each of you to stretch yourself to find and implement radical ideas. Together, we will lead this company—and your future with it—into the most exciting era we have ever known. I call upon you to test just how good you really are when the going is the roughest—to show your right stuff and your best stuff. That is my challenge to all of you!"

Conclusion Building Block 4. Relevant Quotation

The right quotation adds punch to your concluding remarks. You can even repeat the same quotation throughout your conclusion for dramatic effect. Here's such an example:

"General Douglas MacArthur said, 'There is no security on this earth, just opportunity.' Blistering technological, economic, social, and political change can erode our security. But we can maintain security in our lives if we take advantage of possibilities hidden within our tumultuous world. They abound for hands outstretched to snatch them first! General MacArthur was right—there is no security on this earth, just opportunity. So let's become eager and tireless opportunity seekers."

Conclusion Building Block 5. Fascinating or Startling Facts or Statistics

Consider leaving your listeners with a "shocking" statistic or fact that helps them to tightly focus on your main theme or dominant message(s). Look at this example:

"As I said, all of us can better tap into our brains to come up with incredible ideas to catapult the company light-years ahead of competitors. Computers are used as an analogy for the power of our brains. One scientist noted that if we took the latest computer chips and stacked them together 10 stories high and built them the size of the state of Texas, the unimaginable computing power still wouldn't equal that of the human brain! Each of you has more brainpower than a Texas-size computer. Unlock its full imagination potential—use it for awesome effect!"

Conclusion Building Block 6. Reference to a News Article

Use a story from a news source, website, or magazine to add impact to a final point. Example:

"The *New York Times*, in the business section, recently ran a story titled 'Flat-Out Change Is Driving Profits Through the Roof.' It told the stories of two successful large companies along with two thriving start-ups. The article highlighted how each company created a vibrant climate of continuous improvement with spectacular results in productivity, efficiency, quality, and profitability. These four very different companies had returns on their investments that were 40 to 65 percent greater than their nonchanging industry counterparts! Flat-out positive changes will supercharge your business too. The results will be unmatched, unbeatable, and, yes, unbelievable!"

Conclusion Building Block 7. Humor or Amusing Tale

"Leave 'em laughing" has long been the motto of entertainers. When people leave with a smile or chuckle, they are more likely to remember the message spotlighted by an amusing quip like this one:

"In our design of new products, we've got to do our homework and pass the test with our customers. It's like the story of five college students taking organic chemistry. Because each had done well on previous quizzes, they were so confident that they decided to party hard that weekend. They did... and slept through the morning of their final exam. They put together a quick strategy and, as a group, explained to their professor that they went to a friend's house to study, but on the way home they got a flat tire, making them late. The professor agreed to give them a make-up test. In separate rooms, he handed each a final exam booklet. The first problem, worth 50 points, was a simple and easy question. 'This is going to be a cinch,' they thought. Each finished the answer, then turned to the second page and read with dismay: 'For the other 50 points: Which tire went flat?' Now, I don't ever want our customers to catch us off guard and ask 'Which tire?' Doing our product design homework and passing their tough test is our way of getting straight As. No excuses!"

Conclusion Building Block 8. Trial Closes and Close

If you desire a winning pitch, you often need to use *trial closes* and a *close*—terms common to the sales profession. Unfortunately, most presenters who want to persuade their audience to buy or do something, when finished with their presentation, say, "Are there any questions?" Then the presenters thank the audience and leave, not knowing how people reacted to their presentation and, most important, neglecting to ask people to do what the presenters wanted.

A trial close is a question that doesn't seek commitment, but instead it asks people for an opinion to gauge their attitude and motivation to act upon something. How people respond to trial close questions will help you test their receptivity to your presentation.

General trial closes are nonthreatening questions used to engage your group to check for overall reception regarding the points discussed in your presentation. Examples:

> "Ladies and gentlemen, what's your overall reaction to this concept?"
> "What are your gut feelings about the makeup and projected results of this plan? Do you think it's the best one for us to implement now?"
> "Exactly how close is our proposed solution to what you told us that you need and want? Is there anything that doesn't hit the target dead center?"

Specific trial closes assume that the people in your audience are already favorably inclined to what you are proposing and asking of them. They focus on the mechanics of going forward, as these examples show:

> "When is the earliest we might get our respective staffs together to begin?"
> "Before we deal with moving forward to the next step, which is discussing contract preparation, is there anything else we need to discuss or resolve?"
> "What does the group see as the next steps to possibly start implementing this strategy?"

The *close* is a question that asks for a decisive commitment from a person or group to agree to buy some product or service or support and fund a program or project you are advocating. Once you have "taken the temperature" of your audience with general trial closes, followed by specific ones, and determined that their "heat index" indicates "hot" (very interested), then it is time to try to wrap up the deal using closing questions that ask the audience for decisive commitment and action. Look at these:

> "Sounds as if you want to go ahead with this purchase. Is that correct?" (You see nods and vocal agreement.) "I'm delighted! Here is what we need to get the order processed."

"Can we get the contract approved from you for us to begin?"

"I'll need the funding, personnel, and your commitment—as I've described in detail—to support this plan. Can I get your OK to proceed?"

Implement the Building Block Approach for a Killer Conclusion

As with a great introduction, a compelling conclusion should be carefully crafted with specific objectives in mind that make a lasting impact upon an audience. Read the following fictionalized examples and see if you can identify which specific conclusion building blocks were used.

Scenario. A leading nanotechnology scientist gave a presentation using her iPad to a large association of government and corporate researchers who were familiar with nanotechnology. In her conclusion, she wanted to stress the vital importance and opportunity potential with nanotechnology and appeal to them to accelerate nanotechnology innovation in their organizations. Here is how she finalized her presentation:

"It's time for me to conclude. As I mentioned, nanotechnology is the amazing creation of things at the atomic level to develop amazing new products, devices, chemical compounds, and much more. Soon, we will have materials 50 to 100 times stronger than steel but one-sixth its weight." She holds up her iPad over her head and continues.

"Using nanomaterials, my iPad would weigh less than one-half the weight of a business card, have incredible new capabilities, and be practically indestructible! There are three key points to consider as you continue in your basic and applied research:

"One: Enormous industry. Even though a nanometer is 1/80,000 the diameter of a human hair, nanotechnology is going to be the biggest industry in the world. In the United States alone, nanotechnology is projected to be a $3 trillion business, employing from 750,000 to over a million people by 2020.

"Two: Tremendous investment. The U.S. government will be investing over $100 billion in nanotechnology research and commercialization, while cor-

porations and venture capitalists will quadruple that amount over the next five years.

"Three: Massive impact. Nanotechnology breakthroughs will force you to radically rethink your research efforts in practically every regard because they will eventually alter the landscape of all industries like a giant tsunami hitting land.

"Robert Smalley, a Nobel Prize winner in chemistry, said, 'The impact of nanotechnology on the health, wealth, and lives of people will be at least the equivalent of the combined influences of microelectronics, medical imaging, computer-aided engineering, and man-made polymers in the twentieth century.'

"I encourage and challenge each of you to master the magical properties of nanotechnology and apply it in the most imaginative ways. I'll leave you with just one final thought." She smiles and says, "Think small—*really small!*"

As she gets laughs and chuckles from that remark, she puts a visual on the screen filled with word SMALL and then pinches her iPad screen to reduce the word to a miniscule size for a dramatic effect to support her vocal ending.

Scenario. A well-known sales trainer was giving a two-hour public workshop to about 150 people. He made his money not only from charging attendance fees but also from selling his books, DVDs, newsletter subscriptions, and other materials at the back of the room. Before the session began, he hid two Wi-Fi speakers under the chairs in the last row of seats, where people would not notice them. (The chairs had coats and other items on them so others would not sit in those rows.)

As he was wrapping up his conclusion, he activated an audio file on his iPad to transmit an audio track to the speakers. A male voice was heard from the back of the room: "Hey Mr. [his name], how about giving us a bigger discount on your books and other stuff?" Seconds later, a female audio voice calls out, "Yeah, how about it? You said 20 percent before on certain items, but how about a 40 percent discount on *all* your stuff?" The sales trainer played off the voices, and the audience quickly caught on as the trainer then said quite cleverly, "Okay, I *won't* give you a 40 percent discount . . . I'll take half off everything! Obviously you folks know that I had two speakers blurt out their voices from my iPad. I wanted to amuse you and also reinforce how creativity helps get the point across in a surprising and helpful way. I'll see you at the back of the room for your 50 percent discount!"

Tips for Crafting Killer Endings

Here are a few more tips for a strong ending:

- Tell them what you told 'em. Always encapsulate your presentation in a simple, concise, and memorable way to remind the people in the audience of the most compelling points.
- Leave them on a high note. Make sure they walk out feeling better about your topic (more hopeful, more positive, more confident) than when they came in.
- Do it! Few things irritate an audience more than a long-winded, drawn-out conclusion. Some presenters may say, "... in conclusion" several times and ramble on before they actually get to it. The audience is eager to have you finish once you've announced your intention to do so.
- Do not introduce new information. The conclusion is not the place to bring up something you forgot to say during the main portion of your presentation. If it's not important, why bring it up? Besides, you will lose credibility—people will think you did not prepare adequately if you could forget such a key piece of information.
- Avoid an unprepared conclusion. Mediocre presenters approach the conclusion in an unprepared, disjointed, and often abrupt way. Plan and structure your conclusion ahead of time and rehearse it several times so it is strong and smooth. Know exactly what you will stress and how you will put extra voice projection, passion, and body language dynamics into conveying the final messages. Avoid off-the-cuff rambling, weak, or indecisive remarks such as:

"Well, that's about it. I'm finished."
"Sorry it took so long, but I'm finally done now."
"This kind of concludes the presentation. Ah ... any questions?"

- Have a crisp summary. Succinctly review the most important points for your group to remember, make a decision about, or act upon immediately. An effective summary typically has four to six key points. If possible (without diluting important items), boil everything down to its sheer essence in *three points* or less.

- Appeal to your audience for justified action. Whether it is to approve your plan, program, or project, or to ask for funding to implement a solution, or to buy something, always finish with confidence, conviction, and optimism. Project an assumptive attitude that the audience will buy into your idea, plan, or request.

- Explain specifically what you want the members in your audience to do and the exact steps they should take to do it. Never make a vague request, such as "We need your support." Spell out exactly what type and degree of support (specific activities, commitments, money, resources, time, etc.) you require.

- Justify the need for immediate action. Restate the benefits that people will receive when they act decisively or describe the negative consequences of inaction without it sounding contrived.

Like an introduction, your concluding remarks should take about 5 to 10 percent of the total presentation time. As noted earlier, if you have 30 minutes to speak, that means your concluding remarks might take about a minute and a half.

Ah!some Executive Summary Handouts

Want to really impress the people in your group and deliver a final, memorable *wow!* reaction? Then consider giving them a special executive summary handout that contains key pieces of information to assist them in making a decision to buy your product or service. These types of exclusive handouts will reward you with a competitive advantage, especially when your presentation's goal is to sell, persuade, or otherwise convince an audience to take a particular action. While effective presenters always verbally summarize the key points either orally or in combination with a visual from their iPads, an imaginatively designed giveaway (a type of "handout") can be just the novel tool to propel your group to make a decision in your favor. We have helped many clients design these for a most impressive effect against their toughest competitors.

Design and Construction Tips

Following are several (fictitious but based upon real) scenarios of creative executive summaries, some of which are powerful visual metaphors. Many are made from printing a summary of key messages and information on paper, laminating the paper, spraying it with an adhesive like 3M Super 77, and then mounting it to a white or black foam core board. Then, using an X-Acto knife, you can cut the board into various shapes.

Have your graphic designer visit places like Michael's and Hobby Lobby or other arts and crafts, toy, and hobby stores for terrific ideas and materials. When creating these summary handouts, it's important to understand the personality profile of the key decision makers who will be getting these. Look at the following examples to see what we mean to get ideas.

Large "Pill"

Scenario. An account manager gave an informal presentation regarding her company's sales training program with highlights on how it would increase

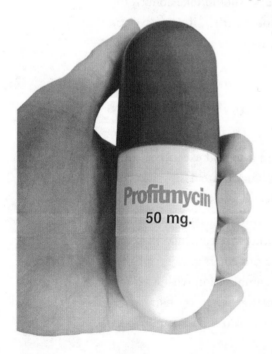

sales for the client. To further emphasize how her firm's program would affect revenues and profits, at her presentation's conclusion, she handed out four of these "summary props" (see Figure 9.6) to each of the sales and marketing people and asked them to open up the "pill" for the amusing but important "prescription" inside (see Figure 9.7), which addressed many of their stated needs and problems. This was designed to appeal to each of the four creative types of personalities that the account manager identified.

FIGURE 9.6 Interesting handout with clever name

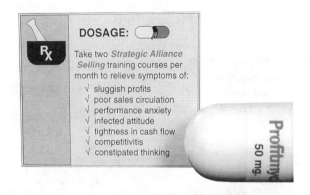

FIGURE 9.7
This amusing "prescription" addresses serious points.

Keep on Truckin' to a Sale

Scenario. The vice president of sales for a major manufacturer of trucks and customized trailers gave a presentation to a leading maker of computer and electronic components with the intention of closing a $60 million deal. Potential customers from purchasing, manufacturing, and operations were in the audience.

After giving a comprehensive and compelling presentation from his iPad using video and 3-D animations of the design, engineering, and operation of his commercial trucks, he wanted to leave an executive summary (see Figure 9.8) of the company's superior value proposition for the decision makers and recommenders attending his presentation. Since many of the people involved in the decision were of an analytical type of personality, the summary handout was designed to have detailed information.

The employees in the seller's graphic design department printed the sheet, laminated it, glued it to a foam core board, and bought an eight-inch die-cast model truck and epoxy-glued it to the board. Finally, they customized the trailer with a slogan and the name of the prospective customer on the side of the trailer.

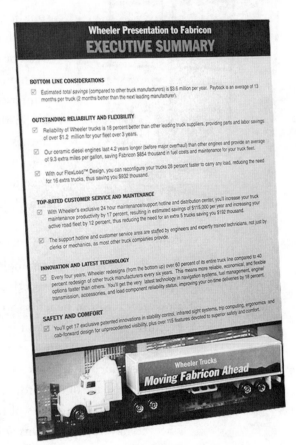

FIGURE 9.8 This impressive handout summarizes key points.

Picture This!

Scenario. A partner in a small technology consulting firm just finished a presentation outlining how her firm could help a potential client improve its engineering designs through implementation of 3-D printers. After her conclusion, she said, "We *framed* our solution toward four major benefits for you. We want you to *picture* the impact we will make for you if you select our firm for this project." The CEO of the engineering company was a typical bottom-line "just-tell-me-the-results" personality, who was not concerned about the technical details of the 3-D printer that the company was considering buying; he only wanted to know the major operational and financial results that the printer could deliver.

So the presenter handed out identical picture frames (see Figure 9.9) to each of the people attending, conveying the simple and concise but powerful benefits. What a great "bottom-line" summary presented in such a clever and visually elegant way!

FIGURE 9.9
A simple, elegant, and powerful summary

Pointing Out Key Information

Scenario. An advanced technology engine company wanted to symbolize that its offering to a prospective customer—a boat builder—would deliver a quantum leap in benefits. So the engine company decided to create an executive summary handout in the shape of a vertical arrow, signifying an upward "leap" in features and functionality. The printout was laminated and spray-glued to a black foam core board and cut out with an X-Acto knife in the shape of the arrow. At the end of the presentation, five "arrows" were given to the attendees of the presentation (see Figures 9.10 and 9.11), with very favorable reactions and ending in a sale.

The decision maker for this purchase was identified as a detail-oriented, analytical type of personality, so the presenter included fairly comprehensive information in the summary handout, while also noting the bottom-line benefits on the lower part of the arrow to make sure that everyone saw the ultimate (strategic) outcomes of the products. Think of the various

FIGURE 9.10 The arrow summary is a visual metaphor.

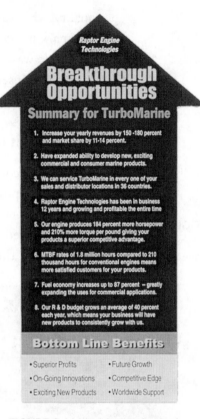

FIGURE 9.11 The handout has both a detailed and "bottom-line" summary.

geometric shapes (circles, hexagons, triangles, others) you can develop for an executive summary handout.

Opening the Door to More Revenues

Scenario. The founder of a small but innovative firm gave an interactive presentation using her iPad to *Solix,* a company in the residential construction industry. She was pitching training, organizational change, and innovation development to the company.

The executive summary she gave out right after her presentation conclusion (see Figure 9.12) focused on seven key benefits for the founder's

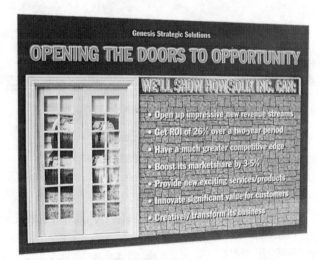

FIGURE 9.12 Creative handout with real miniature wooden door

personality, who was interested in just bottom-line results. The design of the summary handout was printed, laminated, and glued to a foam core board. A hole was cut out, and a real wooden dollhouse door with window panes was inserted and glued in place. Behind the door, you could see three rolled stacks of money!

Customers Want It Fast

Scenario. The account manager of a marketing communications company focused on providing superior results quickly to a client with whom he was trying to close a deal. The metaphor in this executive summary handout was speed of execution in advertising, promotion, and multicity events. Since the account manager talked up how creative his firm would be in developing marketing programs for the client, he wanted to demonstrate his own creativity by delivering an imaginative iPad-based presentation and by providing an executive summary that was specifically designed to appeal to the fun-loving, imaginative, and bold-thinking personality types that defined the clients at the presentation.

FIGURE 9.13
Symbolic and unique "handout"

The account manager's graphic designer found and purchased four metal cars that opened up (see Figure 9.13). The designer developed a small five-page booklet that summarized all the key aspects of the proposed marketing and event programs. The executive summary

FIGURE 9.14
Concise presentation summary booklet of key points

booklet fit perfectly within each car that was given to the attendees of the presentation. Notice in Figure 9.14 how the key message on the front of the booklet highlighted the two critical goals stated by the potential client: "Fast Marketshare Gains and Big Profits."

They Got a "Hot Sale"

Scenario. A company called Incredible! Ovens sells commercial ovens to restaurants. The account manager had finished her iPad-based presentation to the owners of a family-owned business, Crazy Pizza, which is expanding into other markets. The patriarch, who started the business 30 years ago, grew up in an Italian town about 20 miles from Pisa (famous for its leaning tower) and sat in on the presentation. The close-knit family of owners are all warm, gracious, and affable people, who value close and personal relationships with those they do business with. The account manager, knowing her audience, gave a professional but cordial and informal type of presentation. She ended her presentation with a Killer surprise.

FIGURE 9.15
Apron and custom handout designed to impress and endear

She brought along her company's young marketing intern, who came in wearing an Italian-made pizza apron and carrying both a specially designed executive summary (see Figure 9.15) and a 3-D paper model of the Leaning Tower of Pisa, which she assembled from an $8 kit bought on Amazon.com, to present to the founder of the company. The high-quality paper model (see Figure 9.16) only took 30 minutes to assemble, and it added a lot of emotional capital to the presentation.

The executive summary had eight key points to show how Incredible! Ovens had a superior value proposition not only in its technology but in its projected financial results for the customer. When the Crazy Pizza family members saw the line at the bottom of the executive summary page ("Want a 'Pizza' the Action?"—see Figure 9.17), all smiled, some laughed, and the patriarch nodded his head yes.

FIGURE 9.16
A gift for the company's founder who came from Pisa

FIGURE 9.17 This presentation summary was brief but compelling.

FIGURE 9.18 Only a Killer Presenter would develop something like this.

The executive summary, in the shape of the seller's company logo, was made of several layers of different-color foam board and had a porcelain figure of a pizza maker glued to a cutout pizza, giving this executive summary an impressive 3-D appearance (see Figure 9.18). The creative touches, especially provided by the apron-clad, friendly young woman, added a delightful human touch to the presentation, bringing big smiles to the five family owners who attended it. Guess who warmed up to the deal right away?

Having a terrific presentation introduction and conclusion is the mark of a consummate Killer Presenter. Those two things will elevate your presentation above others, boosting your credibility and your professional image. And when you add in giving out imaginative executive summary handouts for your special presentations, you might just be on the verge of being incredible!

Stock Photos, Illustrations, and Vector Images

The websites in these pages show millions of royalty-free photos, illustrations, clip-art, graphics, and 3-D models in thousands of categories that are invaluable for inclusion in your presentations. Photos are offered in various sizes (e.g., small, medium, large, full size, ranging from about 1 megapixel to over 16 megapixels. Remember, vector images are fully scalable and resolution independent, so you can create giant (projected or printed) images that remain crisp and sharp without any blurred or distorted pixelization.

123RF, http://www.123rf.com
Absolute Vision, http://www.absolutvision.com/
Bigstock, http://www.bigstockphoto.com/
CanStockPhoto, http://www.canstockphoto.com/
ClipDealer, http://us.clipdealer.com/photo/
Colourbox, http://www.colourbox.com/
Corbis Images, http://www.corbisimages.com/
Digital Juice, http://www.digitaljuice.com/
Dreamstime, http://www.dreamstime.com/
Fotolia, http://us.fotolia.com/
Gettyimages, http://www.gettyimages.com/
iStockphoto, http://www.istockphoto.com/photo
Pixmac, http://www.pixmac.com/
pond5, http://www.pond5.com/
Shutterstock, http://www.shutterstock.com/

Video Clips and Animations

Typically called stock video footage, there are millions of video clips and animations available in HD (1,920 × 1,080) in thousands of categories just like stock photos. These captivating visuals, if used (full screen and high resolution) in Apple's Keynote presentation software on your iPad, can add tremendous visual and communication clout to your presentation.

a Luna Blue, http://www.alunablue.com/
CallOuts, http://www.callouts.com/
ClipDealer, http://us.clipdealer.com/video/
Daily Motion, http://www.dailymotion.com/video/xq32k8_sci-fi
    -machine-artloops-royalty-free-video-background-in-hd_shortfilms
Digital Juice, http://www.digitaljuice.com/
DVarchive, http://www.dvarchive.com/stock-footage-collection/1323/1/
    animationofbusiness/animationsofbusinesspresentations
Footage, http://www.footage.net/
Fotolia, http://us.fotolia.com/Info/Videos
Gettyimages, http://www.gettyimages.com/footage
Gmanvideo, http://www.gmanvideo.com/
iStockphoto, http://www.istockphoto.com/video
MammothHD, http://www.mammothhd.com/
Motionelements, http://www.motionelements.com/
pond5, http://www.pond5.com/
revostock, http://www.revostock.com/
Shutterstock, http://footage.shutterstock.com/
T3Media, http://www.t3licensing.com/video/home/hd.do
Wavebreak Media, http:// www.wavebreakmedia.com/

Animated Backgrounds and Effects

These resources for your presentations consist of a wide variety of animated and video backgrounds and mattes, special effects, shapes and patterns, lower thirds, character animations, swipes, transitions, motion backgrounds, and more in hundreds of categories much like those for stock photos and videos.

ActionBacks, http://www.actionbacks.com/
Animation Factory, http://www.animationfactory.com/en/
AniStock, http://www.anistock.com/animated graphs and illustrations
Cartoon Solutions, http://www.cartoonsolutions.com/
Digital Juice, http://www.digitaljuice.com/
IgniteMotion, http://www.ignitemotion.com/
Motionelements, http://www.motionelements.com/
Photobucket, http://photobucket.com/
pond5, http://www.pond5.com/stock-video-footage/1/animation.html
Studio 1 Productions, http://www.studio1productions.com/
Wavebreak Media, http://www.wavebreakmedia.com/

Music and Sound Effects

Music, audio special effects, excerpts from famous recorded speeches, and other audio venues can add much value to your presentations. You can get various-length royalty-free music in dozens of categories such as pop, corporate, cinematic, comedy, country, soul, R&B, blues, folk, world beat, and many others. There are also shorter music passages known as bumpers, stingers, intros and exits, and logos that act as brief (e.g., 5–10-second) music-based segues, similar to what you hear on the radio as a transition from one segment to another. In addition, there are hundreds of thousands of all kinds of sound effects to add interest and emphasis to your presentations and videos.

Audio Jungle, http://audiojungle.net/
Audio Network, http://www.audionetwork.com/
ClipDealer, http://us.clipdealer.com/audio/
Digital Juice, http://www.digitaljuice.com/
iStockphoto, http://www.istockphoto.com/audio
Music 2 Hues, http://www.music2hues.com/
pond5, http://www.pond5.com/
RoyaltyfreeMusic.com, http://www.royaltyfreemusic.com/
Shockwave-Sound.com, http://www.shockwave-sound.com/
Sound-Ideas, http://www.sound-ideas.com/
Stock Music Boutique, http://stockmusicboutique.com/
Stockmusic.net, http://www.stockmusic.net/

Other Presentation and Proposal-Related Resources

Depending upon the type of your presentation, you might benefit from other diverse resources such as displays and racks, paper products, tables, product merchandising, props, toys, theatrical supplies, gags, promotional items, AV equipment, and other support materials that you use either before, during, or after your presentation (including back-of-the-room use, display or sales as props, display items, stage and room decorations, giveaways, or other). Check out the following eclectic sources to give you insights and ideas on things that might add value, interest, and meaning to your presentations, training workshops, or speeches.

Amusitreonix 3D, http://www.amusitronix.com/, virtual reality games

Aurora History Boutique Models, Props, Costumes, Replicas, http://www.aurorahistoryboutique.com/Historical-Props.cfm

Backdrop Outlet, http://www.backdropoutlet.com/

Beemak Display Products, http://www.beemak.com/

Big 3D Productions, http://big3dproductions.com/

Bits and Pieces, http://www.bitsandpieces.com/

BuyOnline Now Binding Machines, http://www.buyonlinenow.com/binding-machines.asp

Creations & Collections Ltd., http://www.CreationsAndCollections.com

Crestline, http://www.crestline.com/

Custom Movie Props, http://custommovieprops.com/, mechanical props, models, miniatures, and prop fabrication

Custom Prop Shop, http://www.custompropshop.com/

Dino Rentos Studios, The Prop Magician, http://dinorentosstudios.com/home.php

eHow Stage Props, http://www.ehow.com/stage-props/

Entertainment Earth, http://www.entertainmentearth.com/

Genuine Hotrod, http://www.genuinehotrod.com/

Great Big Stuff, http://www.greatbigstuff.com/home.html

How to do street magic, http://www.howtodotricks.com/howtodostreetmagic.html

Illumivation Studios, http://www.illumivationshop.com/, custom stage props

K-Log, http://www.k-log.com

Lamination Depot, http://www.laminationdepot.com/

Landmark Creations Premier, http://www.landmarkcreations.com/, custom inflatable stage props

Lilliput, http://www.LilliputMotorCompany.com

Magic 4 Speakers, http://www.magic4speakers.com/

MyBinding.com, http://www.mybinding.com/

Norcostco Costume Rental, http://www.norcostco.com/

Office Playground, http://www.officeplayground.com/

Paper Direct, http://www.paperdirect.com/

Peachtree City Foamcraft, http://www.foamcraft.info/foam-props.php, 3-D foam props

Penguin Magic, http://www.penguinmagic.com/

Philadelphia Theatrical Supply & Props, http://shop.ptsonline.biz/

PrizeWheel Games, http://www.prizewheel.us/

Production Advantage Inc., http://www.productionadvantageonline.com/

Prop Warehouse, http://www.prop-warehouse.com/stage.htm

Quill, http://www.quill.com

Scenic Arts Studios Backdrops, http://www.scenicarts.com/, theater props

Schenz Theatrical Supply, http://www.schenz.com/

Siegel Display Products, http://www.siegeldisplay.com/default.aspx

Signals, http://www.signals.com/

Stage Backdrops, http://www.perryscenic.com

StageLightingStore.com, http://www.stagelightingstore.com/

The Costumer, http://www.thecostumer.com/, theatrical supplies and equipment

The Magic Tricks Homepage for Speaking, http://www.magic-tricks.ws/magictrick126.html

Theatre House Theatrical supplies, http://www.theatrehouse.com/

Theatre Services Guide, http://www.theaterservicesguide.com, props, costumes, equipment, accessories

USI, http://USI-laminate.com/

Wall Street Gifts, http://www.wallstreetgifts.com/

Western Stage Props, http://www.westernstageprops.com/

What on Earth, www.whatonearthcatalog.com/

Wireless, http://www.thewirelesscatalog.com/

Trainer Resources

Business seminars, workshops, and presentations can be greatly enhanced by playful materials, games, signs, awards, icebreakers, prizes, e-learning, crowd warmers, recognition products, presentation equipment, and toys, even though they might be more typically used for corporate training events.

Baudville, http://www.baudville.com/?home=new

Crown Awards, http://www.crownawards.com/StoreFront/indexmain .html

Epic Engraving Awards and Recognition, http://www.epicengraving.com/

Games for Trainers, http://www.gamesfortrainers.com

Gamethingy, http://www.gamethingy.com

Glasstap, http://www.glasstap.com

gNeil, http://www.gneil.com/solutions/MotivationRecognition/default .aspx?sessionid=6008.221m4c-412

Successories, http://www.successories.com/

Terryberry, http://www.terryberry.com/

Trainers Warehouse, http://www.trainerswarehouse.com/

Trade Show Resources

One of the tricks of effective creativity in business is using ideas or things from seemingly unrelated areas and applying them in most unusual ways. You can do this by exploring trade show resources, some of which might prove very useful in certain types of presentations and speeches, especially as background displays, props, promotional items, novelties, prizes, games, or other giveaways. Explore some of the following websites and think of ways that the products, typically used at trade shows, might spice up your presentation from various perspectives.

4imprint, http://www.4imprint.com/

Abracadabra Magic, http://www.abra4magic.com

Branders.com, http://www.branders.com/

Camelback Displays Trade Show Games, http://www.camelback displays.com/Games.htm

Displays2go, http://www.displays2go.com/

Gimmees.com, http://www.gimmees.com/

Godfrey Group, http://www.godfreygroup.com/

Infinity Exhibits, http://www.infinityexhibits.com/

M.F. Blouin Merchandising Solution, http://www.mfblouin.com/

Plan It Interactive Trade Show Games, http://www.interactivegame.com/

Prizewheel.us, http://www.prizewheel.us/

Quality Trade Show Products, http://www.qtsp.com/

The Inside Track, http://www.theinsidetrackinc.com/

Trade Show Advisor, http://www.trade-show-advisor.com/, ideas
    and strategies

Trade Show Marketing.com, http://www.tradeshowmarketing.com/
    tradeshow-ideas, ideas, news, and articles

TradeShowAttractions.com, http://tradeshow-attractions.com/

Tradeshowdirect, http://www.tradeshowdirect.com/

Audio, Video Lighting, and Photography

As a presenter, professional speaker, or trainer, you might need to buy, rent, or set up microphones, public address systems, stage lighting, projectors, video and still cameras, screens, AV carts, or other gear and accessories to support your presentation development and delivery.

AV, http://avequipment.com/services.php

B&H Photo, Video, Pro Audio, http://www.BandH.com

CheapLights.com, http://www.cheaplights.com

Creative Stage Lighting Co., http://www.creativestagelighting.com/

Full Compass, http://www.fullcompass.com

IDJ Now, http://www.idjnow.com/

Markertek, http://www.markertek.com

Musician's Friend, http://www.musiciansfriend.com

ProAudio.com, http://www.proaudio.com/

ProAudioMart, http://www.proaudiomart.com/

Projector Central, http://www.projectorcentral.com/

PSSL, http://www.pssl.com/

SLD Lighting, http://sldlighting.com/

StageLightingStore.com, http://www.stagelightingstore.com/

Sweetwater ProGear, http://www.sweetwater.com

Timewalker Toys, http://www.timewalkertoys.com/

Magic Books and DVDs

It is amazing how captivating and compelling simple magic tricks can be in adding meaning and persuasive effect to your presentation or speech. You don't have to spend months learning and practicing "magic" to incorporate elements of it in your performance. The resources below are a great way to start your sleight of hand.

All New Tricks for Trainers: 57 Tricks and Techniques to Grab and Hold the Attention of Any Audience... and Get Magical Results by Dave Arch

Amazing Easy to Learn Magic Tricks with Everyday Objects, DVD, by Magic Makers

Amazing Easy to Learn Magic Tricks: Money Tricks, DVD, by Magic Makers

Card Trick Magic, DVD, by Stephane Vanel

The Complete Idiots's Guide to Magic Tricks by Tom Ogden

Incredible Self-Working Card Tricks, DVD, various volumes, by Michael Maxwell

Learn Magic, DVD boxed set, starring Timothy Noonan

Learn Powerful Street Magic—Unlocking the Secrets, Volume 1, DVD, starring Jon Petz

Magic for Dummies by David Pogue

Magic: The Complete Course, book and DVD, by Joshua Jay

Presenting and Training with Magic: 53 Simple Magic Tricks You Can Use to Energize Any Audience by Ed Rose

Street Magic: Great Tricks and Close-Up Secrets Revealed by Paul Zenon

Presentation Apps

This category almost doesn't need an introduction. We list a few more apps than those you find in Chapter 7. Although grouped under one heading, there are different kinds of presentation apps: those that simply open and project a PDF file, such as a PowerPoint or Keynote deck saved as a PDF; those that open and project PowerPoint or Keynote files; and those that allow you to create a deck on your iPad. Many access your files from one or more of the most popular cloud storage services, such as Box or DropBox, and some have a proprietary online storage system that also lets other people view your presentation online.

2Screens Presentation Expert (ELP Studio), http://www.elpstudio.net/
2screens/pe/about.html, documentation manager, file viewer, web
browser, and whiteboard app

Corkulous 2 (Appigo), http://www.appigo.com/corkulous, free and pro
corkboard presentation and creation app

Doceri, http://doceri.com, presentation and whiteboard app

Haiku Deck (Giant Thinkwell), http://www.haikudeck.com/, free iPad
app to create and show slides

iPresent (Compsoft, PLC), http:// www.ipresent.com/, presentation sales
environment including enterprise cloud-based content management

Keynote (Apple, Inc.), http://www.apple.com/iwork/keynote/, iPad
presentation app

PDF Presenter (Alterme), http://www.ifomia.com/apps/presenter/index.
html, presentation app for PDF documents

Perspective (Pixxa), http://pixxa.com/perspective, presentation and
charts app

PresentationNote (Doxout), http://www.doxout.com, PowerPoint and
PDF viewer app

Prezi, http://prezi.com/, tablet presentation and slide show with cloud-
based enterprise storage

Showpad (In the Pocket), http://www.showpad.com/, presentation sales
tool incorporating cloud-based enterprise storage

SlideRocket, http://app.sliderocket.com, create presentations, import
PowerPoint and PDF files

SlideShark, http://www.slideshark.com, PowerPoint viewer app, online
viewing

Productivity Apps

In the computer world, three productivity suites (apps that create word processing, spreadsheet, and presentation files) dominate the field: MS-Office,
Apple's iWorks suite, and Open Office, the freeware version of MS-Office. In
the iPad world, although an MS-Office for iPad doesn't exist, there are many
apps that let you view, edit, create, and share MS-Office files. Most of these
apps can access your existing files through a cloud server or via an iTunes sync,
or they can access them by opening the file from an e-mail message.

Documents To Go Premium Office Suite (Dataviz), http://www.dataviz.com/DTG_iphone.html, all-in-one, cloud-enabled office editing suite for Microsoft-formatted documents

GoDocs (Lightroom Apps), http://lightroomapps.com/products/godocs/, ultimate solution for Google documents

Numbers (Apple, Inc.), http://www.apple.com/apps/iwork/numbers/, spreadsheet app

Office2 HD (ByteSquared), http://www.bytesquared.com/products/office/ipad/, all-in-one cloud-enabled office editing suite for Microsoft-formatted documents

Pages (Apple, Inc.), http://www.apple.com/apps/iwork/pages/, word processing and page layout app

Quickoffice Pro HD for iPad (QuickOffice), http://www.quickoffice.com/quickoffice_pro_hd_ipad/, create, edit, and view all Microsoft Office document, spreadsheet, and presentation formats

Utility and Document Conversion Apps

When you have to edit a document on the go, these apps help you travel light. Sync the file to your iPad with iTunes or one of the popular cloud storage services and then edit on your iPad.

GoodReader (Good.iWare Ltd), https://itunes.apple.com/us/app/goodreader-for-ipad/id363448914?mt=8

iAnnotate PDF (Branchfire, Inc.), https://itunes.apple.com/us/app/iannotate-pdf/id363998953?mt=8

Note-Taking Apps

Those undisciplined scraps of paper that hold your shopping and to-do lists as well as great ideas are banished from sight with the help of note-taking apps. These apps keep your lists and thoughts in one place, and most offer cloud backup so you eliminate the risk of accidentally throwing away your notes for the next great American novel.

Evernote, http://www.evernote.com/, cross-platform (including iPad) note-taking, media collection, and assembly application

Notability (Ginger Labs), http://www.gingerlabs.com/cont/notability.php, full-featured note-taking app including provisions for handwriting, sketching, and audio recording

Notes Plus, http://notesplusapp.com/versions/version-3, note-taking app with optional handwriting recognition module

NoteTaker HD (Software Garden), http://www.notetakerhd.com/, note-taking and PDF annotation app designed for stylus input

OneNote (Microsoft Corp.), https://itunes.apple.com/us/app/microsoft -onenote/id410395246?mt=8, note-taking app from Microsoft

Paper (Fifty-three), http://www.fiftythree.com/paper, note-taking app designed for stylus and pressure-sensitive stylus input

Paperport Notes (Nuance Communications), http://www.paperport notes.com/, note-taking and PDF markup app with audio capabilities (speech-to-text notes)

Penultimate (Evernote), http://evernote.com/penultimate/, note-taking app designed for stylus input

Simplenote (Simperium), http://simplenoteapp.com/, free no-frills note-taking app

Sketching and Drawing Apps

Say goodbye to pencil sharpeners and ink-stained fingertips with these sketching and drawing apps. Each comes with an assortment of virtual pencils, pens, and brushes with a selection of colors and widths. Create design elements and images to include in your presentations.

Art Rage (Ambient Design Ltd.), http://www.artrage.com/artrage-ipad -info.html

Art Studio for iPad (Lucky Clan), http://www.iphoneclan.com

Artist's Touch for iPad (Artamata), http://www.artamata.com/index .html, simple painting app

iDraw (Indeeo), http://www.indeeo.com/idraw/, vector drawing package

Inspire Pro (Kiwi Pixel), http://kiwipixel.com/InsprePro/index.html, brush-oriented digital painting tool

Layers for iPad (J. Benjamin Gotow), http://www.layersforipad.com/, painting app with layers

Omnigraphsketcher (Omnigroup, Inc.), http://www.omnigroup.com/
    products/omnigraphsketcher-ipad/, multitouch graph sketching tool
Procreate (Savage Interactive Pty Ltd), http://procreate.si/
Zen Brush (Psoft Mobile), http://psoftmobile.net/en/zenbrush.html,
    simple ink-brush tool, designed to work with capacitive brush styli

Teleconferencing Apps

When you can't meet with your audience in person, teleconferencing apps
are the next best thing to being there. Whether your viewers have an iPad or
computer, as long as you both are using the same app, you can communicate
in real time and display your presentation while talking to your audience and
then have an active discussion.

Adobe Connect (Adobe), https://itunes.apple.com/au/app/adobe-connect
    -mobile-for-ios/id430437503?mt=8, cross-platform conferencing and
    whiteboard sharing app
Fuzebox, http://www.fuzebox.com/, cross-platform conferencing app
    that supports audio, video, and text
Google Hangout (Google), http://www.google.com/+/learnmore/
    hangouts/, cross-platform conferencing app that supports audio,
    video, and text
GotoMeeting (Citrix), http://www.gotomeeting.com/, cross-platform
    conferencing app that supports audio, video, and text
Mighty Meeting (MightyMeeting, Inc.), http://www.mightyhd.com/,
    cross-platform conferencing and whiteboard sharing app
Skype (Microsoft Corp.), http://www.skype.com/, cross-platform video
    conferencing app
Webex (Cisco), http://www.webex.com/, cross-platform conferencing app
    that supports audio, video, and text

Meeting Apps

If you're responsible for scheduling, planning an agenda, and facilitating meetings, these apps can be a time-saver and a resource for sticking to the agenda
and keeping the meeting running smoothly, leaving you free to concentrate
on content rather than structure.

eScribe for iPad (eScribe), http://www.escribecorporate.com/escribe-for
-the-ipad.php

Meeting Pad (Sekala Software), http://www.sekala-software.com/

Meeting+ for iPad (App Potential), http://apppotential.com/

Collaboration Apps

Working on a team can often mean sending a document from one team member to the next and then incorporating everyone's ideas. Collaboration apps let you work on a document or whiteboard simultaneously. Everyone can view the same document at once and see comments and changes in real time. Correction tape and photocopiers become things of the past.

AirSketch (Qrayon, LLC), https://itunes.apple.com/us/app/air-sketch/
id376617790?mt=8, project PDF documents (such as exported Power-
Point or Keynote decks) to a computer on the same local network;
then annotate them in real time

Collusion (Collusion, Inc.), https://collusionapp.com/, make notes in real
time with other users anywhere in the world

Conference Pad (Regular Rate & Rhythm), http://www.regularrateand
rhythm.com/apps/conference-pad/, control a presentation on up to 15
iPads, iPhones, and iPod Touches from your device, simultaneously
and wirelessly over Bluetooth or Wi-Fi

Murally (Mural.ly), https://beta.mural.ly/, whiteboards on steroids for
visual collaboration

Share Board (SID 5p. z.o.o.), http://www.sid-on.com/en/business/, up to
four users connect simultaneously via Bluetooth or local Wi-Fi to
create, innovate, draw, share pictures, play games, or just have fun

Smoothboard Air (Smoothboard Tech), http://www.smoothboard.net/,
collaborative interactive whiteboard software for iPads and Android
tablets that revolutionizes interaction in the classroom

Stickyboard 2 (Qrayon, LLC), http://www.qrayon.com/home/sticky
board2/, giant whiteboard with a never-ending stack of sticky notes

SyncPad (Fifth Layer), http://mysyncpad.com/, transforms any iPad or
browser into the ultimate whiteboard for real-time collaboration

TapStream (B.U.G.), http://www.bug.co.jp/tapstream/en/index.html,
stream video from iPhone and iPad to iPad

Cases

While protecting your data may be the most important thing you do, protecting your iPad is a close second, if only to avoid the hassle of replacing it. Cases come in many shapes and materials. Some are a simple cover that protects the iPad screen and puts it to sleep when closed; others have a foldout keyboard or stand, solar panels to charge the battery, or pockets to hold papers or credit cards.

Bay Street Case (ACME Made), http://www.acmemade.com/product/
The-Bay-Street-Case-for-iPad,74,20.htm, folio case with zipper

BookBook (Twelve South), http://twelvesouth.com/products/bookbook
_ipad/, hardback leather case for iPad

Canvas (Switch Easy), http://www.switcheasy.com/product/CANVAS
_ThenewiPad, full case and stand with magnetic on-off

Chrome Bezel (HardCandy Cases), http://www.hardcandycases.com/
chrome-bezel-the-new-ipad-case.html, case with chrome bezel

Clamcase (Clamcase), http://clamcase.com/

DodoCase (Dodocase), http://www.dodocase.com, hardback leather case
for iPad

GelaSkins (Gelaskin), http://www.gelaskins.com/store/tablets_and_
ereaders/iPad_2nd_3rd_4th_Gen/collection/Most_Popular, patterned
cases and covers

Graduate Edition Case (Pad & Quill), http://www.padandquill.com/
cases-for-ipad/cases-for-ipad-ipad2-ipad3-ipad4/graduate-edition-case
-for-ipad-4-3-2.html, leather and wood case

Hardgraft Folios (Hardgraft), http://www.hardgraft.com/ - /category/
ipadcases, leather cases and folios

Latitude Case (M*Edge), http://www.medgestore.com/products/ipad3
-latitude.psp, nylon case

Logitech Ultrathin Keyboard Cover, http://www.logitech.com/en-us/
product/ultrathin-keyboard-cover

Nuud (Lifeproof), http://www.lifeproof.com/en/ipad/, full ruggedized
and waterproof case

Otterbox (Otterbox), http://www.otterbox.com/apple-ipad-cases/apple
-ipad-cases,default,sc.html, ruggedized iPad cases

PadBook (Piano Media), http://www.pianomedia.net/padbook/index
.php, soft case for iPad and Apple wireless keyboard

SeeSaw (Griffin), http://store.griffintechnology.com/ipad/seesaw-for-ipad
-2-3-4th-gen, stand and case for classroom iPad

ShockDrop (HardCandy Cases), http://www.hardcandycases.com/
shockdrop-ipad3-case.html, ruggedized case

SlateShield (PPC Techs), http://www.slateshield.com/, integrated case
solution including stand and handle

Slim Kickstand (Incipio), http://www.incipio.com/cases/ipad-cases/
new-ipad-cases/ipad-retina-new-ipad-slim-kickstand-folio-case.html,
vegan leather with kickstand

Solar Keyboard Folio (Logitech), http://www.logitech.com/en-us/
product/solar-keyboard-folio?crid=1325, solar-powered keyboard case

Survivor Case (Griffin), http://store.griffintechnology.com/ipad/
survivor-ipad-3

VersaVu (Targus), http://www.targus.com/us/ipad/versavu.aspx, flexible
display case

XTREME for iPad (G-Form), http://g-form.com/products/xtreme-ipad
-case/, ruggedized case and magnetic cover

ZeroChroma Folio (ZeroChroma), http://www.zerochroma.com/
product/folio

Stands and Holders

Portability is one of the advantages of the iPad, but there are times when a
stand is a helpful accessory. If you use your iPad as a teleprompter, you'll probably want it more than an arm's length away while you're speaking, and so a
floor stand (much like a microphone stand) makes sense. If you're watching a
video on your iPad with a small group, a tabletop stand lets you position the
iPad for maximum viewing. Magnetic and wall-mounted holders are great for
hanging your iPad on a whiteboard or refrigerator.

A-Frame (Griffin), http://store.griffintechnology.com/a-frame, foldable,
portable aluminum stand

BlueLounge Nest (Bluelounge), http://www.bluelounge.com/products/
nest/, inexpensive tablet stand

Bookarc (TwelveSouth), http://twelvesouth.com/products/bookarc
_ipad/, vertical stand for iPad

Compass Mobile Stand (TwelveSouth), http://twelvesouth.com/products/
compass/, easel-type stand

ElectroStand (Electrostand), http://electrostand.com/, flexible iPad stand
with charger

Floor Stand (Arkon), http://www.arkon.com/tablet-accessories/tablet-
floor-stand.html, extending tablet floor stand with quick-release
holder

FridgePad (Woodford Design), http://woodforddesign.com/products/
fridgepad, refrigerator magnet iPad mounting system

Joule Stand, http://www.elementcase.com/iPad-Accessories-a/274.htm

LuxA2 H4 (Luxa2), http://www.luxa2.com/media_detail.aspx?s=26,
hands-free stand

Magnus (Ten One Design), http://tenonedesign.com/magnus.php,
magnetically attached aluminum stand

Padfoot (Michiel Cornelissen), http://www.michielcornelissen.com/pad
foot_stand_for_ipad.html, lightweight and inexpensive viewing
stand

PadPivotNST (PadPivot), http://www.padpivot.com/, lap and desk
stand

Prizm (Hub Innovations), http://hubinnovations.com/home.html,
lightweight and sturdy multidevice stand

Rev360 (Hub Innovations), http://hubinnovations.com/home.html,
360-degree stand with hand strap

Stabile 2.0 (ThoughtOut), http://www.thoughtout.biz/products/
Stabile_2.0.html, robust, light steel-based stand

SwingHolder (Stand For Stuff), http://www.standforstuff.com/, floor
stand for iPad

VirtualCurve (VirtualCurve), http://www.virtualcurve.com/portfolio
-item/ipad-stand-design/, tall aluminum-based iPad stand

WallMount (Woodford Design), http://woodforddesign.com/products/
wallmount, simple and inexpensive wall mount

WedgePad (WedgePad), http://wedgepad.com/wedgepad-ipad-lap-stand,
soft lap stand

Extended Display Devices

Without a doubt, your iPad has a beautiful, high-resolution screen, but there are times when you want a bigger view. You can connect your iPad to a larger monitor either directly with the appropriate cable or wirelessly with AppleTV or Cube. Alternatively, you can connect your iPad to a projector, depending on the model, with a cable or wirelessly.

3M, http://solutions.3m.com/wps/portal/3M/en_US/Consumer Projectors/Home/Product/StreamingProjector/, streaming portable pico projector with built-in Roku stick

Acer K330 (Acer), http://us.acer.com/ac/en/US/content/model-features/ EY.JCN01.008, portable and mobile projector, streaming projector

AppleTV (Apple), http:// www.apple.com, HD content and Airplay remote display device

Cube (TeraDek), http://www.teradek.com/pages/cube, mobile wireless monitor for iPad

DLP Pico Projector for iPad (Aiptek), http://www.aiptek.de/index.php/ en/products/pico-projectors/mobilecinema-i50D, mobile cinema projector designed for iPad

IN1110 (Infocus), http://www.infocus.com/projectors/portable -projectors/infocus-in1110-projector-series/infocus-in1110-projector, lightweight projector with optional Wi-Fi

iProjection App (Epson), http://www.epson.com/cgi-bin/Store/jsp/ Landing/ProjectorApp.do, app for wireless Epson projector connections

Liteshow III (Infocus), http://www.infocus.com/accessories/wireless-and -networking/infocus-liteshow-iii, wireless interface for any VGA- based projector

Mobi-Show App (Casio), http://www.casioprojector.com/features/ features/mobi-show, app for wireless Casio projector connections

NP-3111X (NEC), http://www.necdisplay.com/p/multimedia-projectors/ np-m311x, 3,100-lumen portable projector

Pico PK120 (Optoma), http://www.optomausa.com/products/detail/ Pico-PK120, Pico DLP projector

PowerLite 915W WXGA 3LCD Projector (Epson), http://www.epson
.com/cgi-bin/Store/jsp/Product.do?sku=V11H388020, midscale
projector with Wi-Fi

XJ-M245 DLP (Casio), http://www.casio.com/products/projectors/
signature_models/xj-m245/, lamp-free Wi-Fi WXGA projector

Styli

One of the iPad's key innovations was the stylus-free touch screen that needed just a fingertip, or two, to do whatever you wanted to do. Once the fat-fingers jokes died down, everyone got used to tap-typing, but as more creative apps were developed, the need for a stylus resurfaced, as artists are loathe to stop at finger painting. Choose a tip that best matches the types of work you'll be doing and keep in mind the two types of styli available when deciding which you prefer: a capacitive stylus reacts the same regardless of how hard you press on the screen, whereas a pressure-sensitive stylus behaves more like a real pencil or charcoal so your sketches have depth, shadow, and expression. Another consideration is how the stylus connects to the iPad, either via a cable or wirelessly.

Alupen Pro (Just Mobile), http://www.just-mobile.com/iphone/
alupenpro.html, stylus with pen

Bamboo Stylus (WACOM), http://www.wacom.com/products/stylus/
bamboo-stylus, full-featured stylus with clip and small rounded tip

Boxwave Stylus (Boxwave), http://www.boxwave.com/apple-ipad-2
-stylus/bwdcd/zgcz-z?gclid=CMCKsvSav7UCFQyqnQod01YALA,
inexpensive capacitive stylus with thick tip

Crayola Light Marker (Griffin), http://store.griffintechnology.com/
crayola-light-marker-for-ipad, midair crayon using image processing
on iPad

Hand stylus (Hand Design), http://handstylus.com/, stylus with clip

Jaja (HEX3), http://hex3.co/products/jaja, fine-line touch- and pressure-
sensitive stylus, wireless without Bluetooth

Jot Flip (Adonit), http://adonit.net/jot/flip/, fine-line capacitive stylus

Jot Touch (Adonit), http://adonit.net/jot/touch/, fine-line touch- and
pressure-sensitive stylus with Bluetooth

Kuel H10 (SPIGen), http://www.spigen.com/sgp-stylus-pen-kuel-h10
-series.html, ministylus

Lunatik Touch Pen (Lunatik), http://www.lunatik.com/products/
touch-pen, pen/stylus with unique switching mechanism

LYNKtec TruGlide (LYNKtec) http://www.lynktec.com/TruGlide
-microfiber-tip-stylus-s/1819.htm, stylus with unique microfiber tip

Maglus Stylus (Applydea), http://the-maglus.myshopify.com/products/
the-maglus-stylus-with-removable-tip-and-spare-tip-and-storage-
keyring, sturdy casing with unusual shape

Monteverdi Stylus Pen (Monteverdi), http://www.monteverdepens.com/
onetouch_stylusskins.html, high-quality and stylish pen and stylus
combination

Nomad Brush (Nomad Brush), http://www.nomadbrush.com/,
capacitive brush

Pogo Stylus (TenOne Design), http://tenonedesign.com/stylus.php,
inexpensive stylus with clip

PogoConnect (TenOne Design), http://tenonedesign.com/connect.php,
Bluetooth 4.0 smart pen

Sensu Brush (Sensu), http://www.sensubrush.com/, capacitive brush for
iPad

Studio Neat Cosmonaut (Studio Neat), http://www.studioneat.com/
products/cosmonaut/, thick stylus (body and tip)

Virtuoso Stylus with Pen (Kensington), http://www.kensington.com/
kensington/us/us/s/2836/stylus.aspx, capacitive stylus with pen

Sound

Audio is a key component of your presentation, and if you make frequent presentations in your office, investing in a sound system may make sense for you.
Here we've listed Airplay-compatible receivers to which you connect speakers.
If you take your show on the road, a wireless speaker system may be the better
choice.

Audio Dock Air (Audyssey), http://www.audyssey.com/products/audio
-dock-airplay, Bluetooth wireless speaker system via Airplay

Bluetooth Music Receiver (Belkin), http://www.belkin.com/us/p/
P-F8Z492, Bluetooth receiver and adapter for iPad and iPhone

Bose Soundlink (Bose), http://www.bose.com/controller?url=/shop
_online/digital_music_systems/bluetooth_speakers/soundlink
_wireless_speaker/index.jsp, Bluetooth wireless speaker system via
Airplay

Bowers & Wilkins Zeppelin Air (Bowers & Wilkins), http://www
.bowers-wilkins.com/Wireless-Music-Systems/Wireless-Music
-Systems/Zeppelin-Air/explore.html, Bluetooth wireless speaker
system via Airplay

Denon AVR-3311CI (Denon), http://usa.denon.com/us/product/pages/
productdetail.aspx?pcatid=avsolutions%28denonna%29&catid=avrecei
vers%28denonna%29&pid=avr3311ci%28denonna%29, Airplay
-compatible audio receiver

inAir 5000 (Altec-Lansing), http://international.alteclansing.com/
iceland/index.php?file=north_product_detail&iproduct_id=inair™_
5000, Bluetooth wireless speaker system via Airplay

IoDock Pro (Alesis), http://www.alesis.com/iodock, turns iPad into a
full-blown recording system

Miccus Home RTX (Miccus), http://www.miccus.com/products/
blubridge-home, high-power, long-range Bluetooth receiver

Pioneer VSX-1021-K (Pioneer), http://www.pioneerelectronics.com/
PUSA/Home/AV-Receivers/Pioneer+Receivers/VSX-1021-K, Airplay-
compatible audio receiver

Pioneer VSX-1021-K (Pioneer), http://www.pioneerelectronics.com/
PUSA/Home/AV-Receivers/Pioneer+Receivers/VSX-1021-K, Airplay-
compatible audio receiver

Stelle Audio Pillar (Stelle), http://stelleaudio.com/our-products/, high-
fidelity stereo cylinder

TableTop Virtual Music Studio (Retronyms), http://retronyms.com/,
turns iPad into a full-blown recording system

Yamaha HTR-4065 (Yamaha), http://usa.yamaha.com/products/audio
-visual/av-receivers-amps/htr/htr-4065/?mode=model, Airplay-
compatible audio receiver

Storage

Unlike hardware, which you can repurchase with relative ease, replacing or more than likely re-creating your files and data is difficult at best, impossible at worst. Storage is an important aspect of data management, and you have a couple of choices for backing up the data on your iPad: an external drive, either wireless or wired, or cloud storage. The external drive is Internet-free but runs the risk of theft or destruction and is of limited use if kept in the same location as your iPad. Cloud storage has two advantages: (1) you, or another authorized person, can access your files from another device no matter where you are, and (2) because your files are in a remote location, it's like keeping them in a fireproof and theft-proof vault; even if your iPad, computer, and flash drive go down with a sinking ship, you'll be able to access files in the cloud as soon as you replace your hardware. Even fee-based services are a small price to pay for the peace of mind they offer. Here we give you some options for both, and you might want to consider using both: an external drive to use in the event your iPad crashes and a cloud service for sharing and extreme backup restoration.

Wireless with Built-in Battery Power

AirStash (Wearable, Inc.), http://www.airstash.com/, wireless flash drive
    with built-in streaming
iUSBport (Patronica), http://www.protronica.co.uk/onlinestore/gbuo-
    catshow/iusbport.html?gclid=CJ2LwfaunbUCFdRbPAodmoQAMw,
    USB via wireless attachment interface for mobile devices

Hard Drives

G-Drive (G-Technology), http://www.g-technology.com/products/
    g-connect.cfm, wireless storage—500 GB with battery power
GoFlex Satellite (Seagate), http://www.seagate.com/external-hard-drives/
    portable-hard-drives/wireless/seagate-satellite/, wireless storage—
    500 GB with battery power
HyperDrive (Sanho), http://www.hypershop.com/SearchResults.asp?
    Cat=183, USB drive, up to 1 TB
Wireless Plus (Seagate, Inc.), http://www.seagate.com/external-hard
    -drives/portable-hard-drives/wireless/wireless-plus/?cmpid=ppc

-_-satellite-_-g-_-us-_-seagate_wireless_plus_1tb-_-e, wireless drive up to 1 TB with 10-hour battery power

Cloud Storage Services

Box, https://www.box.com/, cloud storage, free (2G) to paid from $15 a month

DropBox, http://www.dropbox.com/, cloud storage, free (2G) to paid from $9.95 a month

GDrive (Google), http://drive.google.com, cloud storage, free (5G) to paid from $2.49 a month for 25G

iCloud (Apple), http://www.apple.com/icloud, cloud storage, free (5G) to from $20 a year for 10G

Just Cloud, http://www.justcloud.com/, cloud storage from $19.95 a month

Sugarsync, http://www.sugarsync.com/offers/affiliate1/index.2.html, cloud storage from $4.95 a month

Transporter (Connected Data, Inc.), http://filetransporterstore.com/, online, but off-cloud, storage solution for private file sharing, access, and protection

Zip Cloud, http://www.zipcloud.com/, cloud storage from $4.95 a month

Cabling

There are all kinds of iPad accessories: monitors, speakers, chargers, musical instruments, and styli, and while many offer a wireless option, often you'll find a cabled option is your best bet. (Remember, a wireless option consumes more of your iPad's battery than a cabled option.) Apple manufactures and sells most of the adapters you might ever need, but there are third-party cables too.

Apple Adapters, http://store.apple.com/us/product/, 30-pin (non-Lightning) to HDMI adapter, Lightning A/V Digital adapter, Lightning to HDMI adapter, Lightning to 30-pin adapter, Lightning to micro-USB adapter

Apple Lightning 3m/10ft Sync Cable (Woodford Design), http://woodforddesign.com/products/lightning-3m-10ft-cable, Lightning to USB extra-long sync cable

MIXIT Audio Cable (Belkin), http://www.belkin.com/us/AV10127
-Belkin/p/P- AV10127;jsessionid=538F1DBE83C40AAA6571A1E279952
ED5, mini-audio cable (mini to mini) for iPad

Power

Your iPad is a fantastic presentation tool as long as the battery is charged.
You'd be well served to invest in a charger block or power stand if you're going
to be presenting all day with your iPad. If you're on the road, keep a car charger handy so you can juice up between one appointment and the next.

Apple 12W USB Power Adapter (Apple), http://store.apple.com/us/
product/MD836LL/A/apple-12w-usb-power-adapter?fnode=3c, 12-W
USB power adapter

Car Charger with Lightning to USB (Belkin), http://www.belkin.com/
us/F8J078-Belkin/p/P-F8J078;jsessionid=538F1DBE83C40AAA6571A1
E279952ED5, car charger with Lightning to USB connector

Chargeblock for iPad (Miccus), http://www.miccus.com/products/
chargeblock-for-ipad, chargeable battery for iPad with USB battery
backup

Duracell Portable Battery (Duracell), http://www.duracellpowermat
.com/wireless-battery-backup/index.html, chargeable battery pack via
USB or Duracell Powermat

HyperJuice (Sanho), http://www.hypershop.com/HyperJuice-External
-Battery-for-MacBook-iPad-iPhone-USB-s/91.htm, external battery for
up to two iPads plus a MacBook

HyperJuice Plug (Sanho), http://www.hypershop.com/HyperJuice-Plug
-15600mAh-Atmosphere-p/p15-blue.htm, high-capacity (up to 15,600
mAh) USB battery backup

iPad Power Case (FrontGate), http://www.frontgate.com/webapp/wcs/
stores/servlet/ipad-power-case/466244?redirect=y, case doubles tablet
battery life

Mini Auto Charger (Incipio), http://www.incipio.com/cases/power
-solutions/power-solutions-for-apple/ipad-power-solutions.html, car
charger with Lightning connector

Mojo Battstation Tough Dual Pro (ibattz), http://www.ibattz.com/products_power_battstation.php - prettyPhoto, chargeable high-capacity power pack (up to 8,400 mAh)

Mophie Powerstand (Mophie), http://www.mophie.com/product-p/1195_pwrstd-ipad-alm.htm, stand with built-in power dock

Power Rack for iPad (Bretford), http://apple.bretford.com/products/powerrackforipad, charging dock for up to eight iPads

PowerBlock Plus (Griffin), https://store.griffintechnology.com/powerblock-plus, ac charger block for iPad

PowerDuo (Griffin), https://store.griffintechnology.com/powerduo-for-ipad, AC and DC charging set for iPad

Powerjolt SE (Griffin), https://store.griffintechnology.com/powerjolt-se-ipad, DC car charger for iPad

Spark Tablet Case (Voltaic), http://www.voltaicsystems.com/spark.shtml?gclid=COm_hr-54rUCFShgMgodoCwA7g, solar-powered iPad tablet case

ZAGGsparq (ZAGG), http://www.zagg.com/accessories/zaggsparq.php?gclid=CKrgoYO74rUCFYk7MgodX3Iamg

Ray Anthony is one of the most innovative presentation experts in the world today. His highly acclaimed book *Talking to the Top* broke exciting new ground on how to give winning presentations to top leaders and executives. Ray has helped numerous Fortune 500 companies close "impossible" huge deals using his visionary strategies, ideas, and techniques and coached their executives on how to give Killer Speeches.

As a charismatic keynote speaker, Ray has enthralled audiences as he instructed them in how to wow people with amazing creativity and technology in their presentations. His sixth book, *Fast Forward . . . And Step on It!* is a tour de force about organizational innovation, which he has spelled out to the CIA, NASA, and numerous other leading organizations.

He is an accomplished photographer, videographer, and producer. In his prior "corporate life," he worked for two major companies, selling multimillion dollar complex computer systems in the Wall Street area to international banks. Ray has been on numerous TV and radio programs and has a BS and MA in economics.

Bob LeVitus, often referred to as "Dr. Mac," has written or cowritten over 65 popular computer books, with millions of copies in print. His titles include *OS X Mountain Lion for Dummies, iPhone for Dummies, Incredible iPad Apps for Dummies,* and *Microsoft Office 2011 for Mac for Dummies* for John Wiley & Sons; *Stupid Mac Tricks* and *Dr. Macintosh* for Addison-Wesley; and *The Little iTunes Book*, third edition, and *The Little iDVD Book*, second edition, for Peachpit Press.

Bob has also penned the popular "Dr. Mac" column for the *Houston Chronicle* for more than 15 years and has been published in pretty much every magazine that ever used the word *Mac* in its title. His achievements have been documented in major media around the world. (Yes, he was the one juggling a keyboard in *USA Today* a few years back!)

Bob is known for his expertise, trademark humorous style, and ability to translate techie jargon into usable and fun advice for regular folks. Bob is also a prolific public speaker, presenting more than 100 Macworld Expo training sessions in the United States and abroad, keynote addresses in three countries, and Macintosh training seminars in many U.S. cities.

iPresent